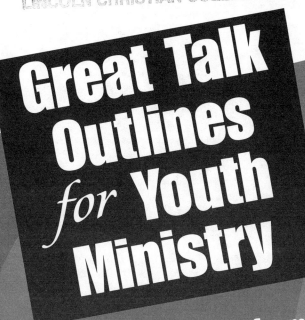

Great Talk Outlines *for* Youth Ministry

40 field-tested guides from experienced speakers

Great Talk Outlines *for* Youth Ministry

40 field-tested guides from experienced speakers

Mark Oestreicher

Youth Specialties

ZONDERVAN™

A DIVISION OF HARPERCOLLINS*PUBLISHERS*

Great Talk Outlines for Youth Ministry: 40 field-tested guides from experienced speakers

Copyright © 2001 by Youth Specialties

Youth Specialties Book, 300 S. Pierce St., El Cajon, CA 92020, are published by Zondervan Publishing House, 5300 Patterson Ave. S.E., Grand Rapids, MI 49530.

Library of Congress Cataloging-in-Publication Data
Oestreicher, Mark.
    Great talk outlines for youth ministry : 40 field-tested guides from experienced speakers / Mark Oestreicher.
      p. cm.
    Includes index.
    ISBN 0-310-23822-6 (alk. paper)
    1. Youth—Religious life. 2. Sermons—Outlines, syllabi, etc. I. Title.
BV4310 .O47 2001
251'.55 dc21

2001017559

Web site addresses listed in this book are current at the time of publication. Please contact Youth Specialties by email (YS@YouthSpecialties.com) or by postal mail (Youth Specialties, Product Department, 300 South Pierce Street, El Cajon, CA 92020) to report URLs that are not operational and to suggest alternate URLs if available.

Edited by Tamara Rice
Cover and interior design by Left Coast Design

Printed in the United States of America

04 05 06 07 /VG/ 10 9

Dedication

o my favorite speakers: Dr. Kenneth Ulmer, Mike Yaconelli, Ed Noble, Louie Giglio, John Ortberg, Doug Fields, and Brett Ray. You have moved me (not an easy thing to do!), brought me into the presence of God, altered my thinking, and shoved me toward Jesus.

Contents

Acknowledgements

hanks, of course, to the great youth speakers who contributed to this book. (See the list of contributors on page 351.) Thanks for putting up with my demanding rounds of revisions. A talk outline is often a very personal thing, but your openness to criticism and input showed amazing vulnerability and flexibility.

Thanks to the brilliant and fun product staff at Youth Specialties—for allowing me 384 deadline extensions, for your commitment to quality, and for your friendship.

Thanks to my family: my incomparable wife, Jeannie; my precious daughter, Liesl; and my adorable son, Max. You are the breath of God on my face.

The Gift of God's Sucker Punch

 just finished speaking—I'm writing this from backstage at a junior high conference—to a bunch of kids from a dozen churches. I spoke way too long tonight—you'd think that after 15 years of speaking to young teens I'd remember to keep it short. A youth pastor about halfway back fell asleep on the shoulder of a junior higher during my talk.

Not encouraging.

But in spite of my weaknesses, I saw God's Spirit moving tonight in the lives of dozens of young teens—kids who made a heart-felt commitment to get into the deep end of the pool with God. I experienced a sucker punch from God because I wasn't feeling all that prayed-up or dependent on him—but he chose to move anyway. A crying mom came up to me afterward and said she'd been praying for her daughter for years. And tonight it happened—her daughter let Jesus choose her. *That's* why I speak to kids. And it's why you do it too.

When we stand in front of a group of teenagers to speak, we have absolutely no idea how God's going to work in those kid's lives. Teenage audiences are as unpredictable as our wild and persistent God. And when you mix the two—God and teens—you've got the spiritual equivalent of a Molotov cocktail.

And speaking to teens can be harsh! They can be unresponsive and disinterested, and they don't bother with the pretense of paying attention.

But just as with the grace of God, I can't quite escape. I keep speaking to students because I keep seeing God change kids' lives. And to be used by God in this amazing and powerful way, well, you know—that's why you're reading this!

Two things I've observed

After hearing hundreds of youth workers speak to hundreds of thousands of students, I've come to some conclusions.

In churches all over the country, the youth worker is the best communicator. An overstatement? Not really. I've thought about this quite a bit. It boils down to one primary reason—we speak to the toughest audience in the world all the time. Whether you're in front of seven or 47 or 747 teenagers, you've got to be able to think on your feet, react to the group, and handle distractions. Nick, the 14-year-old in the sixth row doesn't give a rip if you've prepared for 19 hours, even if you know your talk will connect with his needs. And if Nick chooses to break wind—I guess that means he gave a rip after all—you've got to decide how to respond to all the laughter. Not too many senior pastors have to deal with these kinds of distractions.

So you learn. You adjust. You either drop-kick Nick across the room or mention that the First Seeker Church down the street has a fantastic youth ministry—or maybe you love him with a playful punch after the talk is over. And over time you develop into a quick, witty communicator with the ability to read your audience and make adjustments. And when you get your once-a-year opportunity to preach in the "big church," the congregation laughs and cries and wonders why you don't preach more often. (You probably wonder too!)

Not that all youth workers are brilliant speakers. Because another thing I've noticed is that—

Youth workers tend to put together talks with weak content, and they rely heavily on their up-front abilities and communication skills. Most of us—certainly you may be an exception—are skilled enough at winging it that we don't put much time, thought, or study into preparing our talks. That's too bad because, when we do that, we shortchange our students.

To be honest that's been the real challenge in pulling this book together—making sure these talk outlines flow smoothly, make sense, and have solid, accurate lessons to communicate. I want this resource to offer more than funny stories and clever sound bites—and it does.

Why did we publish this book?

I'm a curriculum guy at heart. I like participation-oriented discussion, active learning, small groups, drama, discovery, and handouts to interact with. It's what I studied in grad school. It's what I've taught in seminars for years. But there's no way to escape the youth talk. Sometimes a small-group exercise or an active-learning lesson isn't what's needed—a talk is.

I also know hundreds, if not thousands, of youth workers deliver youth-oriented sermons every week. In fact the church I attend has a youth church each Sunday—a teenage version of what's going on in the main auditorium.

I'm also a firm proponent of the steal, borrow, and modify principle. I can count on my hands the times I've made up a lesson from scratch instead of modifying something from another source.

But youth workers seem reluctant to do that with talks, as if it's unethical or unspiritual or just plain not as good to deliver a talk with a borrowed outline. I've heard youth workers comment, "Well, that's not his talk," as if the speaker is a low-life maggot.

How absurd! Why can't we borrow and glean from each other?

We can.

But let's get this straight: don't feel bullied into delivering these talks as they're written here. For many of you it's silly for me to tell you this at all—you'd modify and tweak these outlines even if I asked you not to.

But some of you need a little shove—permission, even—to take these skeletons and add the meat of your passion, experience, and group dynamics to them. I don't know your students. I don't know your church, your denomination, your theology, or your passion. I don't know if you're in a city church or a rural church or a non-English-speaking church. So there's no way I could pull together 40 talks that fit your group perfectly.

Modify them.

Shred them.

Use one illustration, one point, or one Scripture idea—and chuck the rest.

Or use the outline as it's written, filling in with personal illustrations.

No matter what, you can use the files on the CD-ROM to modify the outlines and add personal touches. See Using the Great Talk Outlines for Youth Ministry CD-ROM on page 12.

What you'll find in these talk outlines

The opening paragraphs and the list of materials (before **The Opening Act**) are just for you. They simply give you an overview of the talk content. (Obviously, you don't read that to the kids!)

Each talk has three sections: **The Opening Act, The Main Event,** and **The Grand Finale.** Often options are included. Choose the options that will work best for your group. You're not likely to have time or the inclination to use everything listed.

Extended information—*Personal Illustrations, Movie Clips, Object Lessons, Readings, Explanations,* and so on—is mentioned in the outline at the appropriate point, but the details are given (in shaded boxes) at the end of the sections. This helps you follow the flow of the talk more readily. When you open the electronic file, you can move the boxed text into your outline if you're going to use it; move, delete, or add subpoints; add personal illustrations, and make other changes that will make the talk perfect for you—all before you print your presentation.

Encore, the questions at the end of each outline, is for follow-up discussion after your talk. *Get It?*, the content-review questions, has middle school and high school sections. Some questions appropriate for high school students might completely confuse concrete-thinking young teens, and some questions for young teens might be met with disdain by older kids. *What If?* questions help teens process the meaning of the message and prod them to think about the implications of what they've heard. *So What?* questions help students apply the message with a concrete response. Use **Encore** questions in large- or small-group discussions following your talk. As with the outlines, pick and choose the questions that will resonate with your group. Customize the questions you want to ask or create a leader's guide for your small-group leaders by modifying the file on the CD-ROM.

About movie clip times

With the advent of DVD, it doesn't make sense to give start and stop video clip times that include the advertisements and trailers found only on videotapes. This book identifies scene times from the distribution company logo—right before the movie begins. If you're using a VCR, reset the timer to zero when you see the distribution logo, *then* fast-forward to the specified start time.

And remember, *always* view video clips before showing them to your teens. Really. Just because I think a clip makes a good point, doesn't mean *you'll* feel comfortable showing it. There's no way for me to know what will be acceptable to your supervisor and church board, your parents, or your teens. *You* have to be the judge.

Talk on!

I hope *Great Talk Outlines for Youth Ministry* is useful to you. My prayer is that this book will ultimately result in changed lives—students brought into more intense relationships with God as he molds their hearts through these talks. And I hope this book makes your job easier—so you have more time to hang with the kids!

Mark Oestreicher

Using the *Great Talk Outlines for Youth Ministry* CD-ROM

Minimum system requirements for Windows★

- Windows 98 or later
- Microsoft Word 6.0 or better
- 45 MB available hard disk space to load all graphics and outlines
- CD-ROM drive

Additional requirements for MediaShout™ EV presentation software

- 266 MHz Pentium II or equivalent
- 64 MB RAM
- 15 MB additional hard disk space
- *recommended:* 2 display cards (or single card capable of independent dual-monitor display) to run in dual-monitor mode

To install on a Windows PC

1. Close all open applications, and insert the CD in your CD-ROM drive. Click the Start button, choose Run, then type *D*:\Setup.exe in the Open field, replacing the *D* with the actual letter of your CD-ROM drive.

2. Follow the setup instructions that appear on the screen.
   Note: You'll be given the option of installing MediaShout EV (evaluation version) on your computer. If MediaShout 1.5 or later is already installed on your computer, there's no need to install MediaShout EV. Just install the GTO Media component. Then presentations included on the disk will be ready to play from MediaShout.

To open a GTO outline in Microsoft Word

- Choose the File menu, click on Open, then browse to the My Documents\GTO *Outlines* folder, then open the document you want.

A few tips when using the GTO outlines in Microsoft Word

- When you open a GTO outline in Word, you'll notice shaded boxes outlining sidebar material. To format this shaded area, click on the Format menu and scroll down to Borders and Shading, then choose the shading tab. Change or remove shading.

★Microsoft Word files and jpeg images can be accessed by a Macintosh.

- If you would like to change or format bulleted items, click on the Format menu and scroll down to Bullets and Numbering. Make the desired changes.

To run a GTO presentation in MediaShout or MediaShout EV

1. Choose the File menu, click on Open, then browse to the GTO Media folder. If you chose the defaults during the installation, you'll find this folder in C:\My Shout.

2. Open the GTO Media folder. You'll find a folder there for each talk. Open the talk folder you want (e.g., GTO_01), then double-click the Script (MediaShout presentation) file in that folder. The Script will open in the MediaShout control screen.

3. To play the Script—
   - *In single-monitor mode:* Choose the Options menu, click on Overlay Display to bring up the display overlay, then hit the Space key to display the first screen. Hit Space again to play the next screen. To end the presentation, hit Escape. If the displayed images don't fill the entire screen, you'll need to adjust the monitor's screen area. See Display & Sound: MediaShout on a Single Monitor in the Help file for details.
   - *In dual-monitor mode:* Double-click the first cue in the Script. Hit the Space key to play the next cue, and so on.

About MediaShout and ShoutPlayer

MediaShout EV is the evaluation version of MediaShout, a simple yet powerful presentation program optimized for ministry. EV allows you to open, create, edit, preview, and play a MediaShout Script (presentation file) for 30 days. After that, it's automatically disabled, and you'll need to install either the full version of MediaShout or ShoutPlayer (free) to play the Scripts.

- *MediaShout*—the full version contains all the features found in MediaShout EV, plus dozens of backgrounds, video and sound clips, and extended Bible verses and song libraries. Choose Order Info in MediaShout EV to learn more.
- *ShoutPlayer* allows you to play Scripts even if you don't have MediaShout installed on your computer. Of course, its features are limited, but if all you want to do is play an existing Script, it does the job. A free copy of ShoutPlayer is included on the CD-ROM, but you must install it to use it.

To install ShoutPlayer

1. Close all open applications, and insert the CD in your CD-ROM drive. Double-click the My Computer icon on the Windows desktop, then browse to the CD-ROM drive and open the ShoutPlayer folder.

2. Double-click on *SPSETUP.EXE* and follow the instructions that appear on the screen.

Need more assistance?

- For technical support for MediaShout™ software contact techsupport@mediashout.com or call (518) 423-4771.
- For assistance with *Great Talk Outlines for Youth Ministry* Microsoft Word documents contact YS.Products@YouthSpecialties.com or call (619) 440-2333.

Index of Themes

Index of Bible Texts

How to Let Your Conscience Be Your Guide

Contributed by **Dave Ambrose**

This outline is saved as GTO_01 on the CD-ROM.

Primary theme conscience
Themes confession, forgiveness, renewal, hope, Holy Spirit
Scripture 1 Samuel 24:1-12; Acts 24:16; 1 Timothy 4:2; Titus 1:15; 1 John 1:9
Approximate length through The Grand Finale 25 minutes

Studies are showing kids are more confused than ever about their consciences. Many have learned to ignore their consciences, but the reality is your conscience is one of the primary ways the Holy Spirit guides you—provided you listen. That little cricket in Pinocchio had a good thing going when he sang, "Always let your conscience be your guide" (though the Blue Fairy said it first!).

You'll need

- 🔊 TV and VCR

- 🔊 *Pinocchio* (Walt Disney Productions, 1940)

- 🔊 A deck of playing cards for each group of five to 10 students

- 🔊 A personal story about a time you had a clear conscience

- 🔊 Scissors and a piece of fabric large enough to provide a small swatch for each student

- 🔊 A personal story about a time you had a guilty conscience

- 🔊 A piece of Plexiglas at least two feet wide and two feet tall, a jar of peanut butter, a spoon, and some paper towels

- 🔊 A big piece of raw meat, a plate, a clothes iron, and a table or ironing board

- 🔊 *Courage under Fire*

Use what you have

Throughout this book, TV and VCR are listed whenever a movie can be shown. Of course, you can also use a video projection unit (VPU), DVD player, computer, or whatever other technical resources fit your situation.

If an activity calls for a whiteboard to list ideas or responses, you can use an overhead projector, a flip chart, or butcher paper taped to the wall.

It can get cumbersome if we list all the possible variations every time. So feel free to adapt to the technology you have available.

intro

The Opening Act

🔊 **Movie clip** *Pinocchio* (see sidebar)

🔊 **Game** *I Doubt It* (see sidebar)

🔊 Ask students to describe the conscience and how it works.

🔊 The word *conscience* comes from two words meaning "to know with"—in the sense of knowing yourself completely. And in the Bible the conscience is often referred to as a person's heart.

🔊 Then say something like—

> **I think some of you need to understand what God says about your conscience so you can sense him speaking to you more clearly! There are a few ways God speaks about our consciences in the Bible. Let's look at these verses.**

Movie clip

Pinocchio

Start 1:34:00 "Am I a real boy?"

Stop 1:36:52 Pinocchio steps into buckets and falls with a crash.

The Blue Fairy and Jiminy Cricket talk with Pinocchio about becoming a real boy—which requires that he know right from wrong. Jiminy Cricket explains the meaning of conscience to Pinocchio, and the Blue Fairy tells him, "Always let your conscience be your guide." After you've shown the clip, ask your students these questions.

- **Cute song, but how is it truthful and not truthful?**
- **What is your conscience?**
- **How does your conscience work?**
- **How often is your conscience reliable?**
- **Why don't you always do what your conscience tells you?**
- **How is Jiminy Cricket like the Holy Spirit?**

I doubt it

Yup—it's a card game! This would have gotten you booted out of most of the churches in America three dozen years ago. (Ooh!) Anyhow…divide into groups of five to 10, giving each group their own deck of cards, which should be dealt among the players till no cards remain.

The goal of the game is simply to be the first player out of cards. Players take turns discarding cards—*face down*—into a pile in the middle of their group. They can lay down one to four cards of the same face value—the two of hearts and the two of spades, for example—or they can lie by laying down one to four cards that don't match at all!

If someone in the circle doubts another player is being honest about the discarded cards, this doubter can say, "I doubt it." The cards in question must then be exposed immediately. If the person discarding is proven to be a liar, they must pick up the entire discard pile and add it to their hand. If the doubter was wrong, then that person has to pick up the discard pile. And then the game continues.

Encourage your students to play to win. In this game cheating is completely legal—provided the cheater can get away with it!

After playing the game discuss how lying about their cards affected the students' consciences, how easy or difficult it was to get away with, and how they felt while lying—don't expect them to say they felt terrible!

heart of the talk

The Main Event

1 Sometimes we have a *clear* conscience.

◁ᵖ A clear conscience means absolutely nothing to feel guilty about!

◁ᵖ **Scripture** *Acts 24:16* ("So I strive always to keep my conscience clear before God and man.") Paul was accused of stirring up the crowds, and this passage is from his defense speech.

◁ᵖ **Personal illustration** *My Clear Conscience* (see sidebar)

◁ᵖ **Object lesson** *Cutting It Close* (see sidebar)

My clear conscience

Tell a personal story about a time you were accused of something but knew you were innocent—and had a clear conscience! Contrast that with a time when you were accused of something and there was at least *some* truth to the accusation.

Cutting it close

Read—or tell in your own words—the story from 1 Samuel 24:1-12, where David cuts off a piece of King Saul's clothing in the cave. As you share the story, use scissors to cut small pieces from a cloth and hand them to students.

Wrap up the object lesson by saying something like—

David got so close he was actually able to cut off a piece of Saul's clothing—sort of a bold message for Saul and a souvenir for David!

You see, David approached Saul to take his life, but his conscience got the better of him! He was able to face Saul afterward and hold up the proof that he had spared his life. A tiny piece of fabric—just like the one you're holding—represented a conscience that was clean and clear.

2 Sometimes we have a guilty conscience.

- 🔊 A guilty conscience means a terrible feeling deep in your gut, knowing you did the wrong thing!

- 🔊 **Scripture** *1 Samuel 24:1-12* (David and King Saul in the cave)

- 🔊 **Personal illustration** *I Got Away with It.* Tell a personal story about a time when you got away with something, but the guilt ate at you so much you went back and made things right.

- 🔊 **Object lesson** *Plexiglas and Peanut Butter* (see sidebar)

Plexiglas and peanut butter

Hold up a piece of Plexiglas between you and your students, telling them it represents someone's conscience. Then use a spoon to stick a big wad of peanut butter on your side of the Plexiglas, explaining how the peanut butter represents a bad thing in the person's life. Ask if the rest of the conscience still looks pretty clear—it should, of course.

At this point smear the peanut butter around with a paper towel—it will make a wicked mess—and talk about how the bad thing in this person's life won't go away if it's ignored. It will just make a mess like the peanut butter. Ask how clear the conscience looks now and remind them that it only took one bad thing—that never got cleaned up—to create such a disaster.

3 Sometimes we have a corrupt conscience.

🔊 A corrupt conscience means a seared and polluted heart!

🔊 **Scripture** *Titus 1:15* ("But to those who are corrupted and do not believe, nothing is pure.") and *1 Timothy 4:2* ("Whose consciences have been seared as with a hot iron.") In both of these Scriptures, Paul was talking about people who are no longer bothered by the wrong things they do.

🔊 **Object lesson** *Seared Beef* (see sidebar)

Object lesson

Seared beef

This takes a bit of prep—but it will leave your kids with a *great* memory! (This is definitely something you'll want to practice beforehand!)

Use a hot iron (maybe a cheap—but working—iron from a thrift store) and fresh meat to illustrate how easy it is to become seared. First have an ironing board or table set up where all the kids can see, with a clothes iron that is hot and ready to use. With the raw meat on a plate, take your hot iron and—*carefully*—press the piece of meat like you would a piece of clothing. Your kids will think you're crazy! But show them what little effort it takes to brown—sear—the outside of the meat.

Then explain how sin—if it goes unrepented—can sear your conscience like the iron seared the meat on the outside. Your conscience will become tough and hard. It stops doing its job, and sin won't bother you anymore.

closing

The Grand Finale

🔊 **Movie clip** *Courage under Fire* (see sidebar)

🔊 Close by saying something like—

> **Would it affect the choices you make if someone were to record all your actions on videotape? Would it make it easier or more difficult for you to do the right thing?**
>
> **Choosing to do the right thing will always be difficult whether someone is watching or not. But the advantage to making good choices is that your conscience remains clear and you don't have to live with the guilt of a polluted conscience!**

Movie clip

Courage under Fire

Start 1:41:40 "I think in order to honor a soldier…"

Stop 1:46:13 "But it's a burden you're gonna have to put down, soldier."

In a movie subplot, Nat Serling (Denzel Washington) is haunted by the guilt of accidentally "lighting up a friendly" firing on one of his own tanks, killing his best buddy. His commanding officer wants to help him cover it up, but Nat's conscience ultimately wins out. In the end, he chooses to do the right thing.

One of the primary ways God communicates how he wants us to live is through our consciences. Let your kids know it will always be a struggle to choose to do the right thing, but it's the little choices we make each day that determine how our consciences will function. Those interested in following Christ have to get serious about listening to their consciences. So remind your students to always let their consciences be their guides!

discussion

Encore

| **Get It?** | **Middle School** |

- What were the three types of consciences we just heard about?

- How can we keep a clear conscience before God?

- How did you help yourself get over a guilty conscience in the past?

- What happens when you ignore your guilty conscience for a long time?

- What's a seared conscience? Why do you think Paul used that term?

- What might it mean if we don't feel guilty after doing something we know is wrong?

- Why do you think David didn't kill Saul when he had the chance? After all wasn't Saul trying to kill David?

- How far can you see on a clear day? Why? How is that related to having a clear conscience?

- What kinds of things can pollute your conscience?

Get It?   High School

- Describe the three conscience conditions we talked about in your own words.

- Talk about a time when you experienced a clear conscience.

- Talk about a time when you experienced a guilty conscience.

- What does it feel like to have a guilty conscience?

- What are some things that may help you keep a clear conscience in your personal relationships?

- What does it mean to have a seared conscience?

- How does a conscience become corrupt or seared?

- How can someone clear her conscience once it has become seared?

- What's the peanut butter in your life right now and how do you deal with it?

- When someone feels guilty for doing something that isn't wrong, it's called *false guilt*. How can we distinguish false guilt from the Holy Spirit's conviction?

What If?   The Big Picture

- Talk about a time you lied about—and got away with—something you knew would get you into trouble. Did you experience guilt? If so, how did you deal with it?

- What if you thought you got away with something and then you suddenly got caught—what would you do to solve the problem?

- If you could change one thing in your past that led to a guilty conscience, what would it be and why?

- Why would non-Christians experience a guilty conscience? Explain.

So What?	It's Your Life

What would be the easiest way to keep a clear conscience? How could you start doing that today?

First John 1:9 says, "If we confess our sins, he is faithful and just and will forgive us our sins and purify us from all unrighteousness." What does that mean? What does it have to do with this conscience stuff?

So who are we supposed to confess to? Talk about your answer.

How could confession help you have a closer relationship with God? What might be keeping you from confessing your sins to God today?

How might accountability help you as you struggle with your conscience? What can you do to set up accountability?

Do you think it's important to keep or maintain a clear conscience? Why or why not? What implications does this have for how you'll live this week?

Do I Look Like the Mother of the Future?

Contributed by **Steve Case**

Primary theme Christmas	
Themes servanthood, prayer, God's call	
Scripture 1 Kings 8:56-60; Luke 1:26-38, 45-55; James 2:14-17	
Approximate length through The Grand Finale 15-20 minutes	

You'll need

- TV and VCR
- *The Terminator*
- Bibles
- Pencils and paper for students

Okay, let's admit it right from the start—many of you can *never* use this talk! It's a Christmas talk, focusing on the radical call of God in Mary's life. It's built on scenes from the Arnold Schwarzenegger movie *The Terminator*—surprisingly parallel to the interactions of Gabriel and Mary. This talk is way outside the box. So consider yourself warned!

The reality is your kids have probably heard the story of the angel talking to Mary a hundred times, and the words can begin to lose their punch. Using this parallel modern clip will put a great what-would-you-do spin on this passage, which is ultimately an example of servanthood. Do we have the strength to say we're the Lord's servants no matter what the cost to ourselves? Mary did.

One more thing—this is a narrative talk. Use the *The Terminator* story to shed light on or draw attention to the Scripture story. As such, the main points of this talk aren't necessarily things you'd say out loud. They're guideposts to mark your way through the talk.

intro

The Opening Act

🔊 **Movie clip** *The Terminator* (see sidebar)

Movie clip

The Terminator

Describe two scenes and show a third from *The Terminator*. Let's emphasize that again: *Describe* the first two scenes. They both include plenty of swearing, and the first scene has a nude guy. Don't go there! Just describe them, okay?

What the light brought

A lonely deserted city street at night. The pavement is wet and a breeze is blowing the trash around. A homeless man huddles in the shadows muttering to himself. The streetlight begins to hum loudly, and short bursts of lightning shoot out from nowhere. The air seems to get brighter until, from out of a bright light, a man falls to the pavement.

He cautiously lifts himself as if he is in extreme pain. He stands and looks at his surroundings. He looks like he's never seen anything like this before.

The homeless man says, "Hey Buddy, did you just see a real bright light?"

The son of the future

Kyle Reese and Sarah Connor have hidden themselves in a parking garage to escape the terminator and the police. They find a car they can open. They crawl in and slump down in the seat to avoid the passing police car.

Reese begins to tell Sarah about the terminator. He explains that he is from her future where mankind is nearly wiped out of existence. The computers of the future have decided that people are no longer needed. There are hunter-killer robots that patrol the cities looking for survivors.

Reese says, "But there was one man who taught us to fight…to stand up for ourselves. His name was Connor. John Connor. Your son, Sarah, your unborn son."

Do I look like the mother of the future?

Start 1:01:36 "Are you cold?"

Stop 1:05:10 "I don't want it, any of it!"

Reese and Sarah are hiding out in a cave. Reese puts his arm around Sarah to keep her warm and she sees that he is bleeding. Sarah bandages the wound and asks Reese to talk to her so she doesn't get sick. He tells her about her yet unborn son and what kind of a man he is. "I would die for John Connor."

Sarah gets angry and begins wondering why she has been chosen for this "honor."

"Do I look like the mother of the future? I didn't ask for this honor, and I don't want it!"

heart of the talk

The Main Event

1 Make the connection.

🔊 Summarize *The Terminator's* final scene to make sure kids know what's going on in the story. Say something like—

Here we have a young woman who isn't married. She's minding her own business and living a fairly uneventful life. Then a strange man appears in a bright flash of light and explains that her son will grow up to save the world.

🔊 **Scripture** *Luke 1:26-38* (The angel comes to Mary) Read this passage out loud with lots of drama.

2 Compare responses.

🔊 Sarah Connor

- She's scared witless about this announcement!

- She tries to use logic, saying, "You're talking about things that aren't possible."

- She finally responds with, "Do I look like the mother of the future? I didn't ask for this honor, and I don't want it."

- Sarah doesn't believe from the beginning. And once she accepts this is going to happen, she focuses all her doubts on herself. She doesn't believe she can cope.

🔊 Mary

- Verse 29 says Mary was greatly troubled. Ask students what they think this means.

- In verse 34 Mary tries to use logic like Sarah Connor, saying, "How could this be, since I'm still a virgin?"

- Mary's final response in verse 38 is, "I am the Lord's servant."

- After a brief moment of processing, Mary immediately believes what the angel says! She doesn't ask for proof.

- **Scripture** *Luke 1:45-55* (Mary's prayer) Mary turns the promises of the angel into a beautiful prayer.

3 Personalize it.

📢 Most of us would probably respond more like Sarah Connor than like Mary.

📢 How can we turn God's promises into prayers as Mary did?

- **Scripture** *James 2:14-17* ("What good is it…if a man claims to have faith but has no deeds?") Don't just say you have faith—act on it.

- **Scripture** *1 Kings 8:56-60* (A model of faith and action-filled praying) Pray for God's presence, God's will, and the desire to obey him.

- **Scripture** *Luke 1:38* ("I'm the Lord's servant.") Give yourself entirely to God. Begin and end each day by saying, "I'm the Lord's servant."

closing

The Grand Finale

📢 **Activity** *Movie Casting* (see sidebar)

📢 **Activity** *Update* (see sidebar)

📢 Wrap up by pointing out that God doesn't promise to fix all our problems for us, but he does promise to walk through them with us.

Activity

Movie casting

Have your group imagine they're the casting directors for a modern telling of the story of Jesus' birth. You want your students thinking about the personality and characteristics of the two central characters. Ask who they would cast in the roles of Mary and the angel. As your students make casting suggestions, push them for explanations of their nominations.

Activity

Update

Give students pencils, paper, and Bibles. Ask them to write an updated version of Mary's prayer from Luke 1:46–55. Remind them to include the angel's promises as part of the prayer. Then have students write a second prayer, one reflecting their own lives and desire to be God's servant.

discussion

Encore

Get It?	**Middle School**

- Summarize what happened to Sarah Connor. Describe her response to Reese.
- Summarize what happened to Mary. Describe her response to the angel.
- How are the two situations similar?
- How are the responses of Mary and Sarah different?

Get It?	**High School**

- What would it take for you to believe someone who said he was from the future?
- What would it take for you to believe someone who told you he was an angel—a messenger sent by God?
- Mary and Sarah's first responses were similar. What was similar about them? How was Mary's final response different from Sarah's?
- What bad things could have happened to Mary as a result of being pregnant and unwed?
- What does Mary's response tell you about her?

What If?	**The Big Picture**

- How might you have responded if you were Sarah Connor?
- How might you have responded if you were Mary?
- Do you believe in angels? Why or why not?
- Have you ever encountered an angel? What does one look like? What does one smell like?
- If an angel appeared in your school, what are the chances he could find a servant? (No, this doesn't mean *Could he find a virgin?* It means *Could he find someone who's unselfish?*)
- Do angels show up in our regular daily lives—or just for special events and special people? Talk about that.
- What might have happened if Mary had responded like Sarah Connor? Did Mary have the option of responding in a different way to her situation? Why or why not?

So What?	It's Your Life

In the Bible God chose a variety of people to be his servants, not just pure or holy individuals. Why would God work this way?

Most of the Bible's heroes weren't so hot on the idea of being God's servants when they got the job. If being the Lord's servant meant getting kicked out of school and alienating your friends and family, would you want the job? Why or why not?

If God sent an angel to ask you to be his servant, would you feel like you have a choice? Why or why not?

What are the reasons God would want *you* to be his servant? What are the reasons he wouldn't? Talk about that.

What if you were to start and end every day with the prayer, "I'm your servant, Lord." What difference would it make in your life this week?

What would that prayer mean if you truly put it into action?

Leave the Swine Behind

Contributed by **Billy Phenix**

Primary theme temptation	
Themes forgiveness, judgment, wandering from God, God our Father	
Scripture Matthew 26:41; Luke 15:8-24	
Approximate length through The Grand Finale 30-35 minutes	

The story of the Prodigal Son has so many great lessons and themes in it, but certainly one of the primary themes is how we have a tendency to run away from the protection of God our Father. We chase popularity and money and power and all kinds of stuff hoping to find something better. And eventually we realize the new stuff stinks, and we long to go back home to Dad. This talk unpacks the stuff luring students away from God's protection. It shows how pleasure fades to misery and what happens when we return to our Father. And of course it reveals our Father's amazing forgiveness and how we can keep from running away again!

This outline is saved as GTO_03 on the CD-ROM.

You'll need

- A personal story about a time you were lost
- A few student volunteers to tell about times they were lost
- TV and VCR
- *Runaway Bride*
- A personal story about a lost pet—can be a pretend story, if necessary
- A personal story about getting scammed
- A "lost" object for a staged search — anything you could pretend to miss will do
- A personal story about something you lost then found again
- A favorite worship song to sing as a group
- Several adult volunteers to offer hugs
- Note cards, envelopes, and pencils for students

intro

The Opening Act

📢 **Personal illustration** *I'm Lost* (see sidebar)

📢 **Movie clip** *Runaway Bride* (see sidebar)

📢 Transition by saying something like—

> **We're like this with God sometimes—we're not sure if we want to draw close to him or to the other stuff in our lives. Jesus tells a great story many of you know about a guy who did the same thing. He left home for reasons he himself probably wasn't sure of and got lost in a major way.**

📢 **Scripture** *Luke 15:11-24* (The Prodigal Son)

📢 Transition by saying something like—

> **You and I act like that Prodigal Son all the time, so we can probably learn a few things by looking at his story more closely.**

Personal illustration

I'm lost

Tell a personal story from your childhood of a time you were lured away and got lost from your parents. You might not have been lured away by a person—maybe your eyes saw a toy or something that distracted you. After your story you might want to have a few student volunteers share stories from times they wandered away as children and got lost from their parents.

Movie clip

Runaway Bride

Start 1:34:00 ("All rise, please.")

Stop 1:36:52 (Reporters swarm around Ike as the FedEx truck speeds out of sight.)

Maggie (Julia Roberts) is a serial runaway bride—repeatedly leaving her beaus standing alone at the altar. This time she's found the right guy in Ike (Richard Gere) and actually makes it down the aisle…just before running away again.

Point out how excited the groom looked as his beloved bride was coming to him but how hurt and upset he looked as she ran away. Also ask your students to take note of how unsure the bride looked as she left—wondering in the back of her mind why she was leaving her groom.

heart of the talk

The Main Event

1 God tells us, "Don't be a sucker!"

🔊 We're often like the son in the Prodigal story. We're suckers for experiences that seem—at first look—way more interesting.

🔊 We foolishly believe that the grass is greener on the other side of the fence.

🔊 Ask what kinds of things tend to lure people their age away from God.

🔊 **Personal illustration** *Fluffy is Missing!* (see sidebar)

🔊 The son got everything he ran away to get—a life full of pleasure, no responsibility, and freedom from his father. We can imagine he had fun for a while, but things changed.

Personal illustration

Fluffy is missing!

Tell a personal story about your special pet. (It can be made up. Just start with, "Pretend I have a little pet…") This could be a pet you have now or a childhood pet who ran away from home because she thought she saw something better—more space, a chance to run, the mailman, whatever. Make the story overly dramatic and ham it up. Fast-forward the story to find that your pet—in the heat of the moment—chased herself right into being lost. Mention how lost and afraid and lonely your pet must have felt once she realized her situation. End by drawing the parallel to the Prodigal Son and to our own lives.

---

2 After we've run away, we eventually realize, "This stinks!"

🔊 After the son squandered away his money, he had to take a job feeding pigs. He was jealous of what the pigs were eating!

🔊 Ask what stunk about his situation. The pigs, no food, no shelter, no love, no family—just to name a few things.

🔊 **Personal illustration** *Scammed!* (see sidebar)

🔊 **Scripture** *Matthew 26:41* ("Watch and pray so that you will not fall into temptation.") Avoiding temptation takes effort!

🔊 God doesn't promise us the easiest path in life, but he guarantees it will be the best path, by far.

Personal illustration

Scammed!

Ask if students have ever ordered anything from the Internet, a catalog, or TV that turned out to be less than they expected. Or if they ever agreed to a deal that didn't pay off as expected. Then give an example or two from your life—it might be a timeshare pitch you sat through to get a free trip, only to find out the free trip was completely useless due to restrictions. It might be something you bought on e-Bay or maybe a special TV deal when you were a kid.

It would really drive home your point here if you had something physical to show—your *Sounds of the '70s* cassettes, or your funky swing-correcting golf club—anything visual will add to this illustration. Tell how you felt when you realized you'd been scammed. Then connect this illustration to how the Prodigal Son was scammed into thinking life would be better away from his father. He ended up with something completely less than he'd expected.

3   When we return, our father runs to us yelling, "Welcome home!"

📢 The Prodigal was hoping to work as a servant to pay back what he'd lost. But the father runs to him with open arms and welcomes him back as a son, not a servant.

📢 **Acting out** *The Hunt* (see sidebar)

📢 **Personal illustration** *I Found It!* Follow up with an illustration of a time you lost something valuable and then found it. Emphasize the great feeling you had when you finally found it.

📢 Ask what would have happened if the son had been too scared to come home. After fielding a few responses, remind them that we are sometimes the same way with God. We forget how much God loves us and wants us to come back to him when we stray.

📢 **Scripture** *Luke 15:8-10* ("I tell you, there is rejoicing in the presence of the angels of God over one sinner who repents.") There's actually a party in heaven every time one person comes or comes *back* to God.

📢 You can never run so far from God that he doesn't say, "Welcome home!" when you return. In fact, God runs to us with open arms, ready to forgive!

The hunt

Before your students arrive, hide something that belongs to you in a place where it's sure to be found—anything that will sound important to the kids will do. A set of keys, wallet, checkbook, or wedding ring—if you dare—all work well.

Then sometime before you begin your talk—but when most of the students are already in the room—interrupt whatever is going on to announce you have lost something valuable and need help looking for it. Use your best dramatic skills to get the students into finding it! Once they have, heap thanks on the person who found the item and take note of everyone's feelings.

Reveal it was all a set-up, then go back and dissect what happened—how everyone felt before the item was lost and once it was found (especially the person who found it). Point out how great it must have felt for the father in the parable when his son was "found" again! In the same way God is always pleased when we come back to him.

closing

The Grand Finale

◀») **Reflection** *Coming Home* (see sidebar)

◀») **Activity** *Dear God* (see sidebar)

◀») To emphasize God's forgiveness, close by inviting all of your adult leaders to the front to represent God's loving arms. Throughout the length of a worship song, invite your kids to come and get a forgiving hug in response to their sins.

Coming home

Give students a minute or two of silence to pray and identify the temptations that tend to sucker them away from God. Give them time to pray about what they need to do to "leave the swine" and come home to the Father. Depending on the maturity and vulnerability of your group, consider asking if a couple students want to share what they're thinking.

Dear God

Pass out blank note cards and envelopes to students and invite them to write a note to God. Like a letter home from camp, this note should express their desire to come back to God and thank him for welcoming them back with open arms. Your kids might think you're a bit weird, but it would be fun to address the envelopes to God—addressed to heaven—and actually mail them as an act of commitment. Don't put a return address on them, and the post office will of course throw them away.

discussion
Encore

Get It? — Middle School

- Why did the Prodigal Son leave home?

- Running from God doesn't mean you actually run away from home. What does it mean?

- How do you think the son felt when he was leaving home?

- How do you think he felt when he was working in the pigpen? How about when he was on his way back home? And when his father ran to him?

- How does the father's reaction to the son returning home reflect God's feelings about us?

- Does God expect us to live perfect lives? What does he want us to do when we mess up?

Get It? — High School

- What do you think made the Prodigal Son leave home?

- What lie did the son believe about his new life in the distant land?

- The father freely gave his son his inheritance. This allowed the son to wander far away from home. How is this like the freedom God gives us?

- Obviously, it wasn't the father's fault the son ended up in the pigpen. Why do some people blame God for their circumstances?

- The Prodigal Son went home because he believed his father would take him in as a servant—but obviously his father had much more to offer. How do the son's worries about going home compare to the way we feel about asking God for forgiveness?

- Jesus tells this story to show us how God the Father feels about forgiveness. What do we learn about God from the story?

- What does the story tell us about how God wants us to respond to sin in our lives?

What If? | The Big Picture

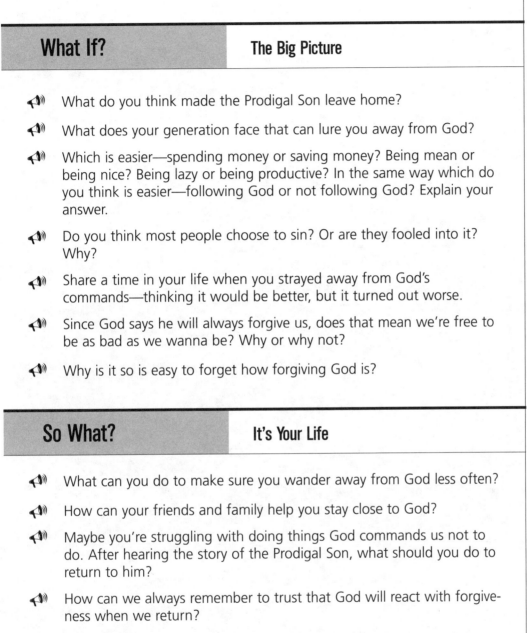

What do you think made the Prodigal Son leave home?

What does your generation face that can lure you away from God?

Which is easier—spending money or saving money? Being mean or being nice? Being lazy or being productive? In the same way which do you think is easier—following God or not following God? Explain your answer.

Do you think most people choose to sin? Or are they fooled into it? Why?

Share a time in your life when you strayed away from God's commands—thinking it would be better, but it turned out worse.

Since God says he will always forgive us, does that mean we're free to be as bad as we wanna be? Why or why not?

Why is it so is easy to forget how forgiving God is?

So What? | It's Your Life

What can you do to make sure you wander away from God less often?

How can your friends and family help you stay close to God?

Maybe you're struggling with doing things God commands us not to do. After hearing the story of the Prodigal Son, what should you do to return to him?

How can we always remember to trust that God will react with forgiveness when we return?

If you were to place yourself as the Prodigal Son in this story, where would you be right now—

- Exercising the freedom to leave?
- Checking out the party options?
- Feeding the swine?
- Thinking about returning home?
- Finding your way home?
- Resting in the arms of the father?

What can you do today to remain in the arms of our heavenly Father?

Being a Christian Isn't All It's Cracked Up to Be

Contributed by **Tim Conder**

Primary theme discipleship	
Themes evangelism, spiritual growth, myths about Christianity	
Scripture John 10:10; 21:15-17; Romans 3:21-23; 2 Corinthians 5:7; 11:24-27; 12:9; Philippians 4:13; Colossians 2:16-23	
Approximate length through The Grand Finale 25-30 minutes	

You'll need

- 📢 A personal story about a relationship that wasn't all you thought it would be
- 📢 Three or four cheap toys from a dollar store
- 📢 Leaders or students to play with each toy (optional)
- 📢 TV and VCR
- 📢 A video clip of athletic bloopers and blunders (optional)
- 📢 *Monty Python and the Holy Grail*
- 📢 A personal story about physically saving another person from harm
- 📢 A leader or student to be the voice of God

This talk is based on Colossians 2:16–23 and is a great starting point for discipleship retreats, new-believer classes, or kids who are skeptical of—or frustrated about—the Christian life. It begins with a humorous stab at disappointment—particularly our disappointments with the Christian life. But it moves from these perceived disappointments to critique common misunderstandings of the Christian life, which often prevent growth and result in disappointment.

The talk concludes with a more realistic and challenging portrait of Christian discipleship—imitating the life of Christ. Admittedly, this talk has some big words in it and is probably more suited to high school students than junior highers. But putting words into common experience—even if the words are new to students—can be an experience that allows the lights to come on.

intro
The Opening Act

🔊 **Personal illustration** *Not What I Thought* (see sidebar)

🔊 **Object lesson** *Overadvertised Product* (see sidebar)

🔊 Transition with something like—

> **If we're honest, many of us have experienced disappointment with our Christian lives, too. Some of you remain skeptical about Christianity because you've seen the disappointment of others. We're often disappointed with or skeptical about the Christian life because we don't know what the Christian life is all about! Let's look at three common misunderstandings about Christianity that often produce great disappointment.**

Personal illustration

Not what I thought

Tell a personal story about a friendship or romantic relationship you went to great extremes to start—because of the other person's image or because you had something to gain—only to be extremely disappointed once the relationship began. An alternate version of this would be a story about a vacation or journey that humorously fell short of expectations.

Object lesson

Overadvertised product

Show the students a series of cheap toys, explaining how thrilled a little child might be by the concept of each toy. Then tell how disappointed the child would be in the reality and limitations of each toy. (A toy helicopter that doesn't fly, for example.)

You could make this more fun by choosing a few students to act like excited young children being given these toys. (Allow the students to rehearse ahead of time.) As these students begin to play with the toys, they can dramatize their frustration.

heart of the talk

The Main Event

1   The first misunderstanding is that the Christian life is based on moralism.

📢 Explain moralism by saying something like—

> **Moralism is basing your Christian life on your ability to win God's attention and favor by being morally good or even perfect. In other words, moralism says, "Look, God, I'm a good person! So you have to like me and consider me a good Christian." The problem with this is we can't do it. It doesn't work. We're always failing.**

📢 If our Christian lives were based on moral perfection, then none of us could be in good standing with God. This doesn't mean that moral choices are insignificant, but it does mean our morality can't be the foundation of our faith.

📢 **Illustration** *Bowling and Baseball* (see sidebar)

📢 **Scripture** *Romans 3:21-23* ("For all have sinned and fall short of the glory of God.")

📢 God knows none of us can be perfect, and his plan for us is based on this reality. But this doesn't mean our moral choices aren't important—just that the Christian life isn't founded or dependent on our morality.

📢 **Explanation** *Jesus and Peter* (optional, see sidebar)

Illustration

Bowling and baseball

Describe how hard it is to be perfect in bowling. Only the best pros accomplish perfection once in a while. Most of us could never do it even if we practiced all the time. Yet bowling can still be fun.

Perfection in baseball is even harder—in fact it's impossible. The greatest hitters—we're talkin' Hall of Fame hitters—failed about six out of 10 times at bat.

Our Christian lives are like this. We're constantly failing. If we expect perfection we'll always be disappointed.

This illustration can be expanded humorously by showing a short video clip from one of the many bloopers and blunders tapes showing professional athletes making heinous mistakes at their games.

Explanation

Jesus and Peter

In John 21:15-17 Jesus and Peter have their classic discussion about Peter's commitment to Christ. Keep in mind it was only a few days earlier Peter had denied knowing Jesus three times. And now Jesus gives Peter three opportunities to say how much he loves Jesus. Tell the story of Jesus' forgiveness of Peter despite Peter's great failure and Jesus' great plans for Peter despite his failure.

2 The second misunderstanding is that the Christian life is based on mysticism.

📢 Explain mysticism by saying something like—

> **Mysticism is an expectation that the Christian life is filled with a series of mystical experiences—dramatic miracles, voices from God, and other obvious signs of intervention by God. A common additional element of mysticism is the expectation that our lives in Christ will be accompanied by wonderful feelings—constant excitement about Christianity, continual confidence about God's will, and an unceasing sense of peace and surety about our faith. In other words mysticism says, "The only way I know I'm a Christian is if I have constant good feelings about God."**

📢 **Acting out** *The Voice of God* (see sidebar)

📢 **Explanation** *All about Paul* (see sidebar)

📢 **Scripture** *2 Corinthians 5:7* ("We live by faith, not by sight.")

📢 There's nothing wrong with mystical experiences—in fact they're wonderful. We just can't allow them to become the foundation or summary of our Christianity.

The voice of God

Have an adult leader—prepped ahead of time—stand outside the room and interrupt your talk at this point as the loud, booming voice of God. Have "God" use a microphone, if possible, to add grandiosity to this interruption. The purpose of the voice is to dispel this misunderstanding of mysticism. Note the mode of the interruption—God speaking in a grand voice—demonstrates the inappropriateness of this expectation. "God" can offer any or all of the following points—

- "I don't often choose to speak with an audible voice to my followers. I only spoke to my own son with a voice that could be heard three times."

- "The lives of my followers recorded in the Scriptures were filled with doubt, hardships, and indecision."

- "I have called you to live by faith. Living faithfully doesn't guarantee feeling good and peaceful all the time. It certainly doesn't guarantee living with surety and free from pain."

This illustration can be shortened or lengthened to suit your purposes. The whole second point of the talk can be done as a conversation between you and God. Or this can be just a brief interruption to affirm that the expectations of mysticism are ill-founded.

All about Paul

Describe the highlights of Paul's life—

- Being jailed and flogged repeatedly
- Enduring a mysterious pain or thorn in his side
- Being shipwrecked and stranded
- Thinking God was leading him to Spain, but never getting there
- Facing constant disappointment and even attacks from the churches he planted and taught

Even Paul's one mystical experience—the Damascus Road—yielded pain and blindness. You may want to read Paul's famous list of hardships from 2 Corinthians 11:24-27.

3 The third and final misunderstanding is that the Christian life is based on some form of martyrdom.

- Martyrdom in this context means an expectation that we have to seek painful experiences to be a true disciple or that God wants to create painful circumstances for us.

- Following Christ—as already seen—can be challenging enough. But we don't need to seek pain or believe God wishes us harm.

- In other words martyrdom says, "The more pain and suffering I experience because of my faith, the better Christian I'll be."

- **Movie clip** *Monty Python and the Holy Grail* (see sidebar)

- **Personal illustration** *Safe from Harm* (see sidebar)

- **Scripture** *John 10:10* ("I have come that they may have life, and have it to the full.")

- In John 10 Jesus teaches us he is the Good Shepherd. In a dangerous world filled with wolves and other threats, a good shepherd works for the best of the sheep—protecting them, knowing what they need, and guiding them away from dangers.

Movie clip

Monty Python and the Holy Grail

Start 13:50 "You fight with the strength of many men, Sir Knight."

Stop 16:40 "All right, we'll call it a draw!"

The humor of this classic scene lies in the fact the Black Knight (John Cleese) continues to demand a fight from his opponent Arthur (Graham Chapman) despite his grievous wounds. This infamous scene hilariously illustrates the false expectation of martyrdom and is appropriate with most student audiences. (It does have a bit—well, more than a bit—of extremely fake blood and gore.)

Obviously, some of us live our Christian lives in the same manner as the Black Knight—foolishly seeking more pain for the cause!

Personal illustration

Safe from harm

Tell a story about how you—or someone else—has done some physical act to protect a child or family pet from a dangerous situation. If we care this much, how much more does God care for us? God doesn't want us to seek pain in a weird attempt to win his favor.

closing

The Grand Finale

🔊 Transition into your conclusion with something like—

> **The Christian life isn't all it's cracked up to be—thank goodness. The Christian life isn't based on martyrdom, which is seeking pain for God's sake. The Christian life isn't based on mysticism, which is always expecting dramatic experiences or good feelings because we follow Christ. And the Christian life isn't based on moralism, which is trying to prove our worth to God by being morally perfect. So what is the basis of Christian life?**

🔊 Our lives as disciples of Christ are based on being molded into Christ-likeness.

🔊 Jesus was the ultimate and only moralist, mystic, and martyr we need.

- As a moralist he was perfect and perfectly fulfilled the demands of God's law.
- As a mystic he knew perfectly his mission and God's will for his life.
- As a martyr he was the perfect and only necessary sacrifice.

🔊 **Illustration** *Halftime Contests* (see sidebar)

🔊 **Scripture** *2 Corinthians 12:9* ("My grace is sufficient for you.")

🔊 **Scripture** *Philippians 4:13* ("I can do everything through him who gives me strength.")

Illustration

Halftime contests

Halftime contests have become totally common—where someone tries to win a huge sum of money by throwing a football into a small target or sinking a half-court basketball shot. Ask your students to imagine being in one of these contests with an incredible choice. Say something like—

> **You can try to make the pass or sink the shot yourself. Or you can let the greatest football quarterback or basketball player in the world try for you. In our spiritual lives we have this same choice. We can try to build our spiritual lives on our own merits or we can rest on Jesus' ability.**

As you set up the hypothetical question, you can substitute actual names of athletes your students are familiar with and admire.

discussion

Encore

Get It?	Middle School

🔊 What did I mean when I said the Christian life isn't based on morals?

🔊 What is mysticism? How could mystical expectations hurt your faith in God?

🔊 What is a martyr? Why would purposefully trying to be a martyr not be what Jesus wants for us?

Get It?	High School

🔊 Many Christians try to base their faith on their moral choices. What is the typical result of making moral choices the core of our Christianity?

🔊 There are lots of different definitions and examples of mysticism in our society today—even Christian mysticism. What types of mystical expectations could potentially hurt your walk with God? Talk about the mystical expectations you've seen in the lives of Christians around you.

🔊 Talk about Christians who believe they need to be martyrs and seek out painful experiences. What is their motivation?

What If?	The Big Picture

🔊 What would make someone believe Christianity is based too much on rules? Talk about any personal experiences you've had that made you feel this way.

🔊 Because moral choices are so important, sometimes people unknowingly or purposefully place them at the forefront of Christianity. How can we respond to this misunderstanding without saying moral choices don't matter?

(continued)

(continued)

🔊 We live in a culture that has no problem believing in supernatural communication and influences. Maybe that's one reason we sometimes expect too much from praying, reading God's word, and practicing other spiritual disciplines. What should we realistically expect from our prayer lives and our spiritual disciplines? How can our disciplines help us to live by faith? Explain reasonable expectations for hearing from God and knowing his will for our lives.

🔊 Talk about your own idea of God's will. In what ways has your expectation of God's will affected your desire to pray and seek his direction?

So what?   It's Your Life

🔊 How has doing good things to earn God's approval—that's moralism—affected your life? Has moralism ever been a struggle for you? Talk about that.

🔊 Talk about what it would be like to live your Christian life free from the burden of moralism—the fear that your relationship with Christ is only as good as your moral choices. What would it take to help you live in this freedom? How can we encourage others not to live under this burden or communicate it to others?

🔊 Talk about any mystical expectations you've placed on your relationship with Christ. How have these expectations affected that relationship? What have been the consequences of wrong expectations? How can you build a foundation of appropriate expectations for your spiritual life?

🔊 How can you nurture the hope and belief that Jesus deeply loves you and wants only the best for your life?

🔊 Sometimes we try to substitute the things we do for what Christ has already done for us. What does it look like to adopt the life of Christ instead? What are some specific decisions you could make to foster this goal, rather than the impulses of moralism, mysticism, and martyrdom?

Jesus the Revolutionary

Primary theme Jesus' mission	
Themes God's love, sacrifice, evangelism, missions, service	
Scripture Matthew 5:38-45; 9:9-13; 10:34-39; 2 Corinthians 5:21	
Approximate length through The Grand Finale 25-30 minutes	

Contributed by **James Prior**

F idel Castro, Che Guevarra, Samuel Adams, Joseph Stalin, Joan of Arc, Jesus, Mao Zedong…Wait, was that Jesus? Does Jesus fit along side those revolutionaries?

So often our image of Christ is shaped by our childhood memories of gentle Jesus, meek and mild, sitting in a green pasture in a long flowing robe. But to the people of Palestine in the time of Christ, he was a subversive revolutionary. Has the revolutionary message of Christ grown dim with familiarity? This message attempts to recapture the revolutionary nature of the message of Jesus.

intro

The Opening Act

🔊 Ask for definitions of a revolutionary. The dictionary defines a revolutionary as "an instigator of a political or a social revolution." Ask students whether they think this definition is a good description of Jesus.

🔊 **Illustration** *Two Images of Christ* (see sidebar)

🔊 **Scripture** *Matthew 10:34-39* ("Do not suppose that I have come to bring peace.") Ask whether this sounds like "gentle Jesus, meek and mild."

🔊 Say something like—

> **Was Jesus gentle? Yes he was. Was Jesus meek? Absolutely. Was Jesus mild? Sometimes. But was he also a subversive revolutionary who challenged the religious, political, and economic institutions of his time? Most certainly.**

Illustration

Two images of Christ

Either project the two images of Christ on a screen or print them out so your kids can see them. Point out how the images of Jesus stand in stark contrast to each other. Ask which image your students connect with more. Ask which one more accurately represents how they've always thought of Jesus.

heart of the talk

The Main Event

1 Jesus revolutionized our understanding of love.

◀)) **Explanation** *The Time of Jesus* (see sidebar)

◀)) In the midst of this hate and insurrection Jesus came with a new message—a message of love.

◀)) **Scripture** *Matthew 5:38-45* ("Love your enemies.") This new message Jesus preached was revolutionary. The centuries-old message of hate and unforgivingness was being replaced with a message of love and grace.

◀)) **Movie clip** *Gandhi* (see sidebar)

◀)) Christ knew the only way to reach deep inside people was to show them revolutionary love.

Explanation

The time of Jesus

The purpose of this illustration is to give a short description of the violent and dangerous time into which Jesus was born. The Romans—who ruled a good chunk of the known world at that time—were in control of Palestine. For hundreds of years Israel had been subject to the foreign rule of one power or another. Atrocities committed against the Jewish people during this time were gruesome. The Jewish expectation for the Messiah was that he would lead his people in glorious victory against those who had done so much injustice in the past. Jesus, however, had a different message.

Movie clip

Gandhi

Start 18:24 "Hey, look what's coming!"

Stop 19:55 "…doesn't plan his day around my dilemmas."

In this great scene Gandhi is confronted with a huge mob of people while on a march, and a Presbyterian missionary prompts him to make a profound statement about one of Christ's commands.

You can either show this clip or describe it by saying—

Gandhi was once confronted by a huge mob of people while on a march. He was with a Presbyterian missionary who asked Gandhi what he was going to do. Ghandi turned around and said, "What did Jesus say about turning the other cheek?" And the missionary said that Jesus meant it symbolically.

So Gandhi turned to him again and said, "I suspect he meant you must show courage—be willing to take a blow, several blows—to show that you will not strike back, nor will you be turned aside. And when you do that, it calls on something in human nature—something that makes his hatred decrease and his respect increase. I think Christ grasped that, and I have seen it work."

2   Jesus revolutionized our understanding of God.

🔊 Transition into this point by saying something like—

Have you ever watched the film _Jesus_ or one like it? One thing coming across clearly in these movies is the more unsavory the character, the more at ease they seem around Christ.

🔊 **Illustration** _The Prostitute in Chicago_ (see sidebar)

🔊 Why is it the church is more known for judging and condemning people than for loving and accepting those in desperate need of the gospel?

🔊 **Scripture** _Matthew 9:9-13_ ("It is not the healthy who need a doctor, but the sick.") Jesus came to revolutionize our understanding of God and deepen our understanding of the people God wants to have a relationship with.

🔊 Jesus made a new rule for the religious institution of his day—in God's kingdom there are no undesirables.

🔊 **Illustration** _The Brazilian Girl_ (see sidebar)

The prostitute in Chicago

Philip Yancey tells a tragic story of a young homeless woman who came to a Christian-based urban ministry to beg for some food. When she sat down with a counselor the homeless woman told him she had been renting out her two-year-old daughter to sick men to get money for drugs. She was so disgusted with herself but didn't know where to turn for help. He asked her if she had ever gone to the church for help and she replied, "The church…the church! Why would I ever go there? They would just make me feel worse than I already do."

From *The Jesus I Never Knew* by Philip Yancey (Zondervan, 1995).

The Brazilian girl

Throughout the streets of Rio literally hundreds of thousands of teenagers wander the streets homeless. When one teenage girl left her home in the country for the big city, her mother followed her there. Unable to locate her daughter this mother went throughout the city putting up hundreds of pictures of her daughter. The street girl's mother had written faithfully on the back of each flier, "Whatever you have done, whatever you have become, it doesn't matter. Please come home." She did.

From *God Came Near*, copyright 1986 by Max Lucado. Used by permission.

3 Jesus revolutionized our understanding of sacrifice.

- 📢 **Scripture** *2 Corinthians 5:21* ("God made him who had no sin to be sin for us.") Perhaps the most revolutionary thing Christ did was become sin so we might have a relationship with God.

- 📢 Jesus' sacrifice on the cross allows us to see the depth of God's love for us.

- 📢 Jesus also expects us to live lives of sacrifice.

- 📢 **Ilustration** *Cassie Bernall* (see sidebar)

- 📢 **Quote** *Martin Luther King* (see sidebar)

- 📢 Jesus modeled sacrifice on Calvary. In doing so he demonstrated a revolutionary understanding of sacrifice. Are we willing to follow his lead?

Illustration

Cassie Bernall

This illustration has been used a lot in the last few years, but what better story is there to tell about a high school student who was willing to sacrifice for God. A normal Christian girl who attended youth group on a regular basis had her life turned around one morning in her school library when a boy held a gun to her head and asked if she believed in God. By saying yes, Cassie was willing to sacrifice everything to be a revolutionary with Jesus.

Quote

Martin Luther King

"Christianity has always insisted that the cross we bear precedes the crown we wear. To be a Christian one must take up that cross and carry it until it leaves its mark upon us and redeems us to that more excellent way which only comes through suffering."

closing

The Grand Finale

🔊 Finish this talk by saying something like—

> **Are you ready to become a revolutionary? Someone who shares the love of God, someone who spreads the message of a compassionate and graceful God, someone who's willing to model revolutionary sacrifice like Christ. Are you ready?**

🔊 Consider challenging them to put their WWJD bands into action and really become a revolutionary with Jesus.

🔊 **Discussion** *Brainstorming* Ask your students what you—as a group—can do to become revolutionaries with Christ. Give them some time to brainstorm ideas.

🔊 **Future activity** *You Say You Want a Revolution* (see sidebar)

Future activity

You say you want a revolution

This is a great time to challenge your group with a missions trip or service project or maybe even an idea they just had during their brainstorming session. Perhaps a challenge to serve for a day—or a week—with Habitat for Humanity, to meet with teenagers in a juvenile detention center, or to spend some time in the inner city. Try to be creative about giving your students options for practicing what they just heard.

discussion

Encore

| Get It? | Middle School |

-  When you think of the word revolutionary, what person comes to mind? Why?

- What did Jesus mean when he said to turn the other cheek? Would this be a hard thing for you?

- Why does God have a special place in his heart for sinners and unrighteous people?

- What are some of the tough sacrifices people make by becoming Christians?

| Get It? | High School |

- What did Jesus mean when he said anyone who loves his father more than him wasn't worthy of him?

- Did Jesus mean to turn your cheek literally or symbolically? Why is this so hard for us to do?

- Why is it so many people view the church as a place of condemnation and judgment rather than a place of love and grace?

- What are some of the tough sacrifices you make by becoming a Christian? Is it worth it?

| What If? | The Big Picture |

- Why did Jesus attract so many people the society of his day rejected— tax collectors, prostitutes, lepers, the physically handicapped, to name a few? Do you think our church or youth group is attracting people who need Jesus? Why or why not?

- Why is the word *sacrifice* so foreign to the way we live today? What would happen if we could live the life of sacrifice and unconditional love that Jesus did?

- If the call to a revolutionary life in Jesus is a valid one, what are some of the things stopping us from becoming revolutionaries for Jesus?

So What?   It's Your Life

🔊 What are some of the things that would change in your life if you were to become a revolutionary?

🔊 What are some of the things we can do at school or at home to show the revolutionary love of God?

🔊 How can you show others what it means to have a proper understanding of the grace and forgiveness of God?

🔊 What do you need to sacrifice so you can become a true revolutionary for Jesus?

🔊 Talking about living like a revolutionary may sound well and good, but what changes are required to live a revolutionary life with Christ?

God Is Full of Surprises

Primary theme grace	
Themes conversion, God's call, Christian living, salvation, unity	
Scripture Acts 8:3; 9:1-21; Romans 12:2; Philippians 3:7-8	
Approximate length through The Grand Finale 30-40 minutes	

You'll need

-  A personal story about a time someone in authority called your name
- A personal story about a time God got your attention
- A $5 bill—or $50 bill, if resources allow

Most students wonder at one time or another how this salvation stuff works. Maybe they're wondering if they're really saved or not. This is common—especially for younger teens. Maybe you're wondering if they're saved or not! This talk jumps off the biblical case study of Paul's conversion story to take a behind-the-scenes peek at the process of conversion—not that everyone's conversion process is identical to Paul's, but we can all relate to the points of his story. The real subject of this story—this is key—isn't Paul or even conversion. It's the grace of God, the vehicle of our salvation.

Contributed by **Greg Lafferty**

This outline is saved as GTO_06 on the CD-ROM.

intro

The Opening Act

📢 **Reading** *Un-dragoning* (see sidebar)

📢 Then say something like—

> **Ever since Christ first came to earth, people have been trying to invent easy, painless, no-cost ways of getting saved. But true conversion to Christ is a deep and radical change, and change is always painful. There's a great "un-dragoning" story in the Bible that illustrates the depth of this change and what has to happen to each of us if we're to enter into an authentic relationship with Christ. This story is so important it's repeated three times in one book—Acts. Here's what happens when God tears into your life.**

Reading

Un-dragoning

"I looked up and saw the very last thing I expected: a huge lion coming slowly towards me…The lion told me I must undress first. Mind you, I don't know if he said any words out loud or not.

"I was just going to say that I couldn't undress because I hadn't any clothes on when I suddenly thought that dragons are snaky sort of things and snakes can cast their skins. Oh, of course, thought I, that's what the lion means. So I started scratching myself and my scales began coming off all over the place. And then I scratched a little deeper and, instead of just scales coming off here and there, my whole skin started peeling off beautifully, like it does after an illness, or as if I was a banana. In a minute or two I just stepped out of it. I could see it lying there beside me, looking rather nasty. It was a most lovely feeling. So I started to go down into the well for my bath.

"But just as I was going to put my foot into the water I looked down and saw that it was all hard and rough and wrinkled and scaly just as it had been before. Oh, that's all right, said I, it only means I had another smaller suit on underneath the first one, and I'll have to get out of it too. So I scratched and tore again and this under skin peeled off beautifully and out I stepped and left it lying beside the other one and went down to the well for my bathe.

"Well, exactly the same thing happened again. And I thought to myself, oh dear, how ever many skins have I got to take off? For I was longing to bathe my leg. So I scratched away for the third time and got off a third skin, just like the two others, and stepped out of it. But as soon as I looked at myself in the water I knew it had been no good.

"Then the lion said—but I don't know if it spoke—You will have to let me undress you. I was afraid of his claws, I can tell you, but I was pretty nearly desperate now. So I just lay flat down on my back to let him do it.

"The very first tear he made was so deep that I thought it had gone right into my heart. And when he began pulling the skin off, it hurt worse than anything I've ever felt. The only thing that made me able to bear it was just the pleasure of feeling the stuff peel off. You know—if you've ever picked the scab of a sore place. It hurts like billy—oh but it is such fun to see it coming away."

"I know exactly what you mean," said Edmund.

"Well, he peeled the beastly stuff right off—just as I thought I'd done it myself the other three times, only they hadn't hurt—and there it was lying on the grass: only ever so much thicker, and darker, and more knobbly looking than the others had been. And there was I as smooth and soft as a peeled switch and smaller than I had been. Then he caught hold of me—I didn't like that much for I was very tender underneath now that I'd no skin on— and threw me into the water. It smarted like anything but only for a moment. After that it became perfectly delicious and as soon as I started swimming and splashing I found that all the pain had gone from my arm. And then I saw why. I'd turned into a boy again."

From *The Voyage of the Dawn Treader* by C. S. Lewis, copyright © C.S. Lewis Pte. Ltd. 1952. Extracted by permission.

heart of the talk

The Main Event

1 God singles you out.

🔊 **Scripture** *Acts 9:1-21* (Saul on the Damascus Road)

- Paul was a dragon. He was a rabid opponent of Christ and his church.

- Acts 8:3 says Saul was destroying the church—a word used of beasts gorging on their prey.

- Acts 9:1 says Saul breathed out murderous threats—words used of the sounds made by snorting beasts.

- Acts 9:20-21 says Saul raised havoc in Jerusalem—words used of beasts mauling an enemy.

🔊 Here Jesus opposes Saul as forcefully as Saul had opposed others. He calls him out and blinds his eyes, knocking him to the ground.

🔊 There's an old saying: The gospel is bad news before it's good news. It first confronts you with your sin before it offers you grace. This is what Jesus does. He accuses Saul of persecuting him!

🔊 **Personal illustration** *Calling Your Name* (see sidebar)

🔊 Ask students if this has ever happened to them. Have they ever had the sense God was confronting them—singling them out—because they were traveling down the wrong road? Maybe he's done this through a parent, a pastor, or a friend.

🔊 Sooner or later all people need to hear the painful news that spiritually they are out of line.

🔊 **Personal illustration** *When God Called My Name* (see sidebar)

Personal illustration

Calling your name

Share a personal story or two illustrating what it's like to have your name called out by someone in authority. There are two basic categories of times this would happen. One is positive—like when you win a raffle, a contest, or a pageant. Or like when you make the school play or graduate from high school. The other is negative—like when the principal tells you to report to the office or the judge calls your name in traffic court.

Try to tell one example of each from your life—ideally from when you were a teenager. Then ask your students to imagine if God called their names…and wasn't happy.

When God called my name

Consider giving a real-life example of a time when this happened to you. When you were out of line or spiritually offtrack, and God called you on it very clearly through his Word, through the voice of another person, or through your own heart.

2   God surprises you with his grace.

🔊 **Scripture** *Acts 9:5-6* (Saul realizes Jesus is speaking to him)

🔊 Jesus is the last person in the world Saul expected to meet.

🔊 But there's a greater surprise. When God confronts a person, we expect thunder and lightning and judgment. We expect there's hell to pay for sin. But Saul didn't get that. He got simple instructions to arise and begin following Christ. He got grace.

🔊 **Object lesson** *I'll Take the Cash* (see sidebar)

🔊 Grace is one of the most shocking, surprising things in the universe. Through Christ, God offers every person free forgiveness, free member-ship in his family, a free inheritance in heaven—it's an awesome deal!

🔊 Challenge students to reflect on whether they've received God's grace. Have they been gripped by what Jesus did for them when he died for their sins? Has the idea of having hell cancelled and heaven secured transformed their hearts?

🔊 Summarize the first two points.

- Saul had a head-on collision with Christ on the Damascus Road. It was painful. At that point God began to tear into his self-pride about his Jewish heritage, his self-righteous religion, and his self-chosen vocation as a persecutor of the church.

- But he also received a grace that transformed him. Later in life Paul reflected back on this event and said all those things he once loved became rubbish in comparison to knowing Christ (Philippians 3:7-8). Grace made him a new person.

I'll take the cash

Invest some bucks to make a great point. If you're a poor volunteer with no resources, use a five-dollar bill. If you've got big-time resources, a 50-dollar bill would make a killer example here!

Abruptly stop your message, and ask if there's a visitor in the room. Walk up to the first one you see and hand them the money. No questions asked, no strings attached, it's that person's to keep. If your group has no visitors, bestow the bucks on a kid who'd least expect it from you—the one who's a discipline problem or the one who's always bugging you.

3   God surrounds you with his family.

Scripture *Acts 9:17-19* (Ananias defends Paul)

When God brings you through a real conversion, he brings you to a real community. Salvation isn't just an individualized experience. When you become a child of God you also become a brother or sister to the rest of his kids. You enter his family.

The incident between Ananias and Saul demonstrates this.

- Point out that the power of the gospel makes friends out of former enemies.

- Point out how Ananias loved Saul—he called him brother, laid hands on him, restored his sight, baptized him, fed him, and presumably brought him to the rest of the believers in Damascus as a new member of God's family.

Illustration *God's Family Right Here* (see sidebar)

Emphasize the value of diversity and community. Scripture continually reminds us to keep God's family warm and welcoming. We're to greet one another warmly, keep meeting together regularly, and love each other sincerely—through all our differences.

Illustration

God's family right here

Tactfully point out how the gospel has made a wonderfully strange family out of people in your group. There's probably more diversity represented in your ministry than in any other social circle your students move in. Maybe there's gender, ethnic, economic, social, intellectual, athletic, and artistic diversity—and there should be!

4   God sends you out to serve him.

🔊 Every person who's converted is commissioned. Whether you receive an immediate, specific calling to a certain ministry or the general calling to be a witness for Christ—every true convert should have a sense of being drawn into Christ's service.

🔊 **Scripture** *Acts 9:15* ("My chosen instrument to carry my name before the Gentiles") Saul happened to have a very specific calling.

🔊 God often takes the raw material from a person's past and makes something new from it for the future. Saul found that—

- God took his fanaticism and made him a missionary.
- God took his hard-nosed personality and made him a tough, resilient martyr.
- God took his education and made him a writer of the New Testament.

🔊 A student who's un-dragoned by Christ might find—

- God turning her anger away from people and toward the enemy Satan.
- God turning his lust into passionate love for lost people.
- God transforming her addiction into a thirst for God's truth.
- God transforming his ability or hobby—that used to be an idol—into an open door for sharing the gospel.

🔊 Point out some students may be inclined to think they're too messed up to change. It's not true. Once grace enters people's lives, it's certain to transform them.

🔊 **Ilustration** *The Eternal Junior Higher* (see sidebar)

Illustration

The eternal junior higher

Everyone knows what happens right about the time a person hits seventh grade. They morph. Their feet and ears and legs grow. They get hairy and bumpy and sweaty. Their voices squeak—especially the boys. Their coordination goes out the window. And they generally feel like freaks for a couple of years. No problem—it's just the transition from childhood to adulthood. A person just has to ride it out and laugh at himself, realizing everything will be all right eventually.

But what if someone convinced you puberty is forever? That you'd always be this awkward? Well of course genetically you'd be destined to change, but mentally you wouldn't believe it anymore. And your mind might actually stunt your growth! That's exactly how conversion works. With God's Spirit inside you, you're destined for a whole new life—but you need to believe it. Romans 12:2 says, "Be transformed by the renewing of your mind."

closing

The Grand Finale

📢 **Illustration** *Real People* (see sidebar)

📢 You might want to close by saying something like—

> **We might not meet Christ in a blinding light or hear his voice boom out our names. We might not have scales drop from our eyes or receive a call to be missionaries. But most Christians experience these same things Paul experienced—and usually more than once! We get singled out by God, surprised by grace, surrounded by God's family, and sent out to serve. They're all signs of God's love and grace in our lives!**

Illustration

Real people

All around the world real young people have been transformed by grace and are now transforming the lives of those around them.

- Rick is a former party animal from suburban Chicago who has led more than a dozen people to Christ in one year—including his family—and has just entered Bible college to train for ministry.

- Lydia is a former Communist youth worker who's now a full-time church youth worker in the Czech Republic. Her youth ministry has grown from three to 50 students over the past three years.

- Kirsten—an 18-year-old woman in Cambodia—has added more than 10 percent to the overall population of Christians in that country through children's Bible clubs that she started.

- Bobby first came to his church in Southern California on a bribe from his mom. He's now training to be a missionary at a Christian college.

discussion

Encore

Get It?	Middle School

📢 What does it mean that everyone is a dragon before they meet Christ? In what ways was Saul a dragon?

📢 What does the word *conversion* mean?

📢 What did Jesus do to un-dragon Saul? What were the steps in Saul's conversion?

Get It?   High School

🔊 What does the image of a dragon say to you about life before meeting Christ?

🔊 What is most striking to you about Saul's un-dragoning in Acts 9?

🔊 What aspects of Saul's conversion are common to every true convert?

🔊 Describe the time when you felt God's presence most powerfully. How does it compare to what Saul experienced?

What If?   The Big Picture

🔊 What if you met Jesus the way Saul did? Do you think that conversion experience would have been better than your own? Why?

🔊 Describe a time when God showed you that you were totally out of line. How did he show you?

🔊 What surprises of grace have come your way? What's the best thing about God's grace?

🔊 How has meeting Christ changed your relationships? Is being surrounded with God's family a reality for you?

🔊 Do you have a sense of mission in life? If so, describe it. What has God called you to do?

🔊 How does being a Christian change your perspective on what you want to do with your future?

So What?   It's Your Life

🔊 As you compare your conversion with Saul's, what part is most similar? What is most different?

🔊 Which of these four elements of Paul's conversion story—conviction of sin, experience of grace, membership in God's family, call to service— do you think is most forgotten or neglected in your life? Why?

🔊 If you've never experienced any of these things in your life, what should you do?

🔊 Do any of you have a sense right now that God wants to change you more deeply than you've allowed him to? What's the next step you should take?

(continued)

(continued)

🔊 What are some of the things that would change in your life if you were to become a revolutionary?

🔊 What are some of the things we can do at school or at home to show the revolutionary love of God?

🔊 How can you show others what it means to have a proper understanding of the grace and forgiveness of God?

🔊 What do you need to sacrifice so you can become a true revolutionary for Jesus?

🔊 Talking about living like a revolutionary may sound well and good, but what changes are required to live a revolutionary life with Christ?

Contributed by **Brian Mount**

Never Waste Your Pain

Primary theme pain	
Themes loss, tough times, grace, spiritual growth	
Scripture James 1:2-4	
Approximate length through The Grand Finale 25 minutes	

You'll need

- A personal story about an experience with cow manure (optional)
- A large bolt

I n the now classic movie *The Princess Bride*, Princess Buttercup confronts the Dread Pirate Roberts when she learns her true love Westley might have fallen victim to an untimely demise. What she doesn't know is that the pirate is Westley in disguise. As the pirate responds callously to her sadness, Buttercup shouts, "You mock my pain!" To which he retorts, "Life is pain, Highness. Anyone who says differently is selling something."

This classic line is often repeated as a humorous antidote to difficult situations. Life on earth involves experiencing pain, loss, or disappointment. Because of sin we can be guaranteed a fair amount of pain this side of heaven.

What is in our control however, is our response to pain. This talk takes a fresh look at James 1:2-4. James is concerned with the practical aspects of Christian conduct and these verses can help your students understand the purpose of pain. The point of the message is to empower students to view a trial as a positive, character-building experience—rather than something to be avoided at all costs.

intro

The Opening Act

◀))) **Reading** *Strange News* (see sidebar)

◀))) Say something like—

> **Wow—tough breaks! I'm sure you would agree these stories are extreme, but life can be tough sometimes. Tough. Maybe you've had someone close to you die, or your parents divorced, or you're dealing with sickness. Maybe you're in despair or your friends bailed on you. Trials are going to happen no matter what— we can't change that. However we can do something about how we approach trials. The big question is— Are you going to go through trials or grow through trials? Let's see what this guy named James has to say about the tough stuff.**

◀))) **Scripture** *James 1:2* ("Consider it pure joy, my brothers, whenever you face trials of many kinds.")

◀))) Explain the difference between the popular definition of joy, which is happiness; and the Biblical definition of joy, which is confidence—confidence that God is in complete control!

◀))) Define a trial—it's anything that causes fear or doesn't go the way we planned.

◀))) **Illustration** *In Complete Control* (see sidebar)

◀))) Transition with something like—

> **James says if we choose joy—understanding God is completely in control during our trials—we'll receive certain rewards in our lives. That's what *growing* through trials is all about. Lets look at why we should choose joy during trials.**

Strange news

Read two to three stories about bad, sensational things happening to people. Below are several strange—but absolutely true—stories. Preface the stories by reminding the students these are 100 percent true, verified occurrences.

- Biagio di Crescenzo, 23, smashed his car into a tree near Rome and was badly injured. After a motorist took him to a hospital, he was sent in an ambulance toward another hospital for further treatment, but the ambulance smashed into an oncoming car. A motorist took him to another hospital, where he was again dispatched in an ambulance for further treatment. That ambulance smashed into another car in a suburb of Rome, killing di Crescenzo.

- Truck driver James R. Shaw was on Interstate 5 near Medford, Oregon, when his brakes caught fire. He pulled into a rest area and tried to douse the flames with his fire extinguisher but was unsuccessful. He hopped back into the blazing truck and raced down the road—hoping the wind would blow out the fire—but was forced to stop after nine miles when the flames completely engulfed the truck. The burning truck blocked the highway for three hours.

- The most mysterious injury attributed to the December 1988 Los Angeles earthquake was a man admitted to a Burbank hospital after he mistook the tremor for an intruder and shot himself in the leg.

- George North of Cupertino, California, was celebrating a San Francisco 49ers victory by riding a trash bin with rollers down an exit ramp at Candlestick Park when the bin crashed into a cement retaining wall, flipping the 39-year-old fan off an upper level of the ball park. He fell 42 feet!

You could also use other weird—but less than true—stories from tabloid newspapers. Or you could get a copy of *More News of the Weird* by Chuck Shepherd (Penguin, 1990). It's a great purchase—especially for this talk.

In complete control

Trusting someone to be in complete control during a situation is like flying on a commercial airplane. You don't know how they do it, but you trust pilots enough to get you where you want to go. All the switches and lights and dials mean next to nothing to most people. But of course they tell the pilots exactly what they need to know and enable them to safely fly the plane. We don't always understand what's happening around us, but we don't have to! God does and he's in complete control.

heart of the talk

The Main Event

1 When we grow through pain, we can gain *strength*.

🔊 **Scripture** *James 1:3* ("You know that the testing of your faith develops perseverance.")

🔊 **Explanation** *A People in Need* (see sidebar)

🔊 Strength comes from repetition. Athletes know this well—a runner doesn't shy away from opportunities to run and build endurance.

🔊 When we grow through trials and choose joy, we gain strength.

🔊 **Illustration** *Gold* (see sidebar)

Explanation

A people in need

James was writing to people in need. Many of them had recently lost their homes, families, and belongings. They were very familiar with suffering. James wanted to encourage them not to waste this opportunity for growth by blaming God for what happened.

Illustration

Gold

Have you ever seen pure gold close up? At least you've seen a nice gold wedding ring, right? Gold is an amazing metal. For instance, when rings are made, gold goes into a process called refining. During this process it's heated to extremely hot temperatures until it melts—then it's poured into a ring mold. The process allows the dross—the impurities, which decrease the strength of the ring—to burn or be scraped away. When the ring is cooled, it's shiny, strong, and pure.

The point? God allows the heat of pain and trials to bring about purity in our lives through dependence on him.

2   When we grow through pain, we can gain *maturity*.

- 🔊 **Scripture** *James 1:4* ("Perseverance must finish its work so that you may be mature.")
- 🔊 Ask what it means to be mature, and allow a few students to respond.
- 🔊 You can be old and still immature. Maturity is more about character and less about age.
- 🔊 Not only do trials help build strength—which leads to perseverance—but the whole process isn't considered complete until the trial actually produces maturity. In other words, until it finishes its work.
- 🔊 **Illustration** *Cow Manure* (see sidebar)
- 🔊 Spiritual maturity can't happen apart from trials. We need trials to grow.

Illustration

Cow manure

Have you ever seen or smelled cow manure? It's gross! (It would be great if you could tell a personal story about an experience with cow manure!) The very fact we bag something that comes out of a cow and belongs in a toilet is amazing. Manure is gross. But what's manure used for? For plants and grass—manure is the best thing you can put on it! Why? It makes things grow! It's the oldest known fertilizer. Trials are like manure in our lives. Trials stink, but they have a purpose. They cause growth and maturity because we learn to trust God rather than ourselves. When that happens regularly, spiritual growth takes place.

3   When we grow through pain, we can gain *completion*.

- 🔊 **Scripture** *James 1:4* ("Complete, not lacking anything")
- 🔊 Ask your students what it means to be complete and why we should want to be complete.
- 🔊 Completion is all about God seeing his plan for us through to the end. Ultimately, we'll be totally complete with Jesus in heaven. But we can also experience semi-completeness by becoming more like Christ in our day-to-day living.
- 🔊 When we choose to grow through trials instead of being bitter and just going through them, we're actually allowing God to make us more like his son—and that's what being a Christ-follower is all about!
- 🔊 **Object lesson** *The Importance of a Bolt* (see sidebar)
- 🔊 God wants us to have all we need to be capable, confident servants. When we go through trials instead of growing through them, we actually miss out on being a complete person. We miss benefits we need later.

Object lesson

The importance of a bolt

You'll want to have a large bolt hidden close by—somewhere like your pocket—while you tell a dramatic story about it's importance. Bring it out to show the group once you mention it.

Tell a story that goes something like—

Picture yourself getting on a brand-new roller coaster—it's the world's longest, tallest, and fastest. You strap yourself into your seat, and your car begins to pull away from the loading area. Just then you notice something fall to the ground up ahead. Straining down, you see it's a big ol' bolt! It's fallen from somewhere on the roller coaster, though you can't tell exactly where. What would you think about riding this coaster now? It's incomplete. It's lacking something!

closing

The Grand Finale

🔊 It's not easy choosing to grow through trials instead of go through them. Sometimes it's downright tough. But it's not impossible.

🔊 **Reading** *Dave Dravecky* (see sidebar)

🔊 Review the three benefits of trails and pain—gaining strength, maturity, and completion. Then ask the students a rhetorical question to consider: Are you going to choose joy and grow through your trials or if kick the dirt and blame God—missing that opportunity to grow?

Dave Dravecky

Dave Dravecky pitched for a major league baseball team until it was discovered he had cancer. Dravecky ended up losing his pitching arm to the disease. His career was shattered. Here's what he had to say about suffering in his book *When You Can't Come Back*.

One night...a woman came up to me and told me how she once was down and out with a drug addiction—until someone told her about Christ, and she became a Christian and was healed of her addiction. She told me God wanted all his children to be one hundred percent healthy.

But does he? What would God's children grow up to be like if...all the bumps in the road ahead of them were made smooth? Cancer introduced me to suffering. And suffering is what strengthened my faith. Yet that woman implied I was suffering because I didn't have enough faith. She seemed to be saying, have enough faith and get the life you want. But that struck me as making God into some cosmic vending machine, where if you pushed the right button, you would get a sweet life—free of suffering.

Someone once said the difference between American Christianity and Christianity as it's practiced in the rest of the world has to do with how each views suffering. In America Christians pray for the burden of suffering to be lifted from their backs. In the rest of the world, Christians pray for stronger backs so they can bear their suffering...That's why we look away from the bag lady on the street and look to the displays in store windows. That's why we prefer going to movies instead of hospitals and nursing homes.

From *When You Can't Come Back* by Dave Dravecky (Zondervan, 1992).

discussion

Encore

| Get It? | Middle School |

🔊 How do most people view pain and trials?

🔊 What kinds of trials are normal for young teens?

🔊 How do you usually respond when tough problems come your way?

🔊 What comes to mind when you think of the word *joy*? Does your definition make sense in the context of James 1:3 where God asks us to consider our trials a joy?

🔊 Why do you think when we trust God with our trials, we're better prepared to face new hardships?

🔊 Describe a mature Christian. How does a Christian become spiritually mature?

🔊 Why do trials help us grow spiritually?

🔊 What are areas in your life where you feel incomplete? How do trials help us grow in these areas and others like patience, love, and trust?

🔊 What did Dave Dravecky—the baseball player who lost his pitching arm—mean when he said to never waste your pain?

🔊 Trials are something no one in their right mind would go after. What should be our attitude toward difficulties in our lives?

Get It? — High School

- What does it mean to consider trials joy?

- How is it possible to choose joy? How is joy more than just an emotion?

- Which one of the three rewards do you think is the most important to understand and live out? Why?

- Why do you think trials are referred to as tests in some translations?

- Why do bad things happen to good people?

- What are some characteristics of a believer who might be spiritually incomplete?

- What did Dave Dravecky—the baseball player who lost his arm—mean when he said to never waste your pain?

- What is the difference between considering it all joy—as the biblical writer James put it—and actually feeling joyful?

- What is the alternative to choosing joy in the midst of trials? What does it look like in the life of a believer?

What If? — The Big picture

- Is it humanly possible to consider trials all joy? Even the really bad stuff? Why or why not?

- If your friend were to say, "God doesn't care about the bad stuff that happens to you!" how would you respond?

- Why should you desire to be complete and not lacking anything?

- How do you know if something is a trial or just a bummer coincidence?

- Our world encourages us to pursue comfort and run from discomfort. The biblical writer James is actually telling us to embrace pain as something that can help us grow. How do you handle the difference between those two perspectives?

- Sometimes God can do the most work in our lives when we're broken. So what does it mean to be broken? Can you fully trust God and not be broken? Why or why not?

- What would happen if you began to view trials as opportunities to grow and become more like Jesus?

- What should we do with feelings of sadness and despair? How do you deal with those emotions and still choose joy?

So What?   It's Your Life

🔊 What trials have you gone through in the past year?

🔊 What trials are you going through in your life right now?

🔊 Of the three rewards—strength, maturity, and completion—which one do you most need in your life right now?

🔊 What barriers stand between you and your ability to choose joy during your trials?

🔊 Are you wasting your pain? If so, how can you make it work for you?

🔊 What can you do this week to help you remember God's desire to be involved in your life during a trial?

🔊 How would you go about explaining these revolutionary truths to someone who's going through a tough time?

🔊 Who do you know who's going through a tough time right now? What can you do to help that person grow through it instead of just go through it?

Small People Can Do Big Things

Primary theme success	
Themes wisdom, security, community, persistence, growing up, decision making	
Scripture Psalm 62; Proverbs 30:24-28; Jeremiah 29:13; Luke 12:35; Romans 2:7; Galatians 6:9; 2 Timothy 2:21; Hebrews 10:36; 1 Peter 1:13; 3:15; 5:8	
Approximate length through The Grand Finale 30-35 minutes	

You'll need

- 🔊 A personal story about a time you strayed from God and got hurt
- 🔊 A personal story about persistence—or lack thereof
- 🔊 Pencils
- 🔊 Copies of **Making the Grade**, page 90

This talk takes a different approach than most. It's a nature lesson, with animal facts and illustrations. But don't write it off as too Ranger Rick for today's sophisticated students. It's a great eye-opener to the wonder of God's creation and the wisdom of God's values. God's not into the big, the bold, and the beautiful like everyone else. He doesn't define success in the world's terms. Instead he takes simple, savvy, spiritual people and makes them successful by his standards. That's an encouraging message for students who often find themselves too small and powerless to do many significant things.

intro

The Opening Act

🔊 Ask these questions to get started.

- How would you define success? What makes someone successful?

- How about wisdom—how would you define that? What makes someone wise?

- How do people get more wisdom?

🔊 **Illustration** *The Standard of Success* (see sidebar)

🔊 Lead into the Scripture passage by saying something like—

Thankfully, the values of God's kingdom aren't quite so sizeable—or shallow. In fact God loves taking smaller, less-than-spectacular creatures and making them truly successful. In that way they appreciate their success more, and he gets all the credit. A funny little nature lesson in Proverbs 30 shows us what God values most in those he wants to make successful. It's a great lesson in wisdom.

🔊 **Scripture** *Proverbs 30:24-28* (Four wise animals)

Illustration

The standard of success

Spend a few minutes talking about the world's standards of success using these facts and illustrations.

- Have you ever heard of the BHOS—the Big Head of Success? It's real. Most successful people have one. Literally. We're not talking about puffed-up egos or swelled pride here—we're talkin' about extra large noggins on their shoulders. Studies have shown most business leaders, politicians, and celebrities have at least slightly larger than average heads.

- Tall and big seem to be seen as better, don't they? Most company presidents are over six feet tall. Most models are taller than average too. And most sports teams are looking for size.

- This value of being bigger—and better and more beautiful—can even leak into the church. For years many youth ministries operated on the idea that if you could get the pretty cheerleader and the captain of the football team to come, you would be able to draw everyone else.

heart of the talk

The Main Event

1 Wise people invest a lot of energy in preparation and make decisions with the future in mind.

Illustration *Harvester Ants* (see sidebar)

The Bible puts a high value on preparation.

- Luke 12:35 calls us to "be dressed ready for service."
- 2 Timothy 2:21 tells us to be "prepared to do any good work."
- 1 Peter 1:13 challenges us to "prepare [our] minds for action."
- 1 Peter 3:15 reminds us to "always be prepared" to share our faith.

Think about Bible characters who had to prepare.

- Moses prepared for 80 years to lead Israel out of Egypt.
- Joshua prepared for 40 years to take Moses' place as leader.
- Even Jesus prepared for 30 years before he started teaching and doing miracles.

One famous preacher—Charles Spurgeon—said if he knew he had 25 years to live, he'd spend 20 of it in preparation.

Your teenage years are a time of preparation. The decisions you make today will have a huge impact on your future. What are you doing now that will positively impact your next 20 years?

Illustration

Harvester ants

The most common ant in the Middle East is the harvester ant—which doesn't just gather up picnic crumbs, but actually harvests grain off the stalk. Scientists have observed how they divide their labor.

- One group climbs up the stalk and chews off the grain.
- One group carries the fallen kernel back to the nest.
- One group husks the grain.
- One group carries the kernels underground and stacks them neatly.

If it rains the ants take all their grain out of the nest and lay it out to dry before restacking it below. And they'll travel over 200 yards to collect food—that's more than six miles in people terms—just to get ready for winter.

2   Wise people know and stay close to their source of protection.

◄») **Scripture** Reread Proverbs 30:26 (the wise coneys).

◄») The coney is what we know as a rock badger. They're smart and successful because they know the principle of protection. They live in the crags—or cracks—of the rocks where predators can't get to them.

◄») **Illustration** *The Coney* (see sidebar)

◄») Do you see the wisdom of these creatures? They know their limits; they stick close to home; and they never venture far without someone watching their back.

◄») And conies know their rocks. They know where to run and where to hide.

◄») Scripture reminds us God is our rock (Psalm 62) and the Devil is the predator seeking to devour us (1 Peter 5:8). Yet so many students think they can live—

- 21 yards from the Rock

- 25 yards from their accountability partners

- 30 yards from their church

◄») And when they're in trouble they cry to God but don't find the safety and security they need because they're not in the habit of running to him every day.

◄») Overconfidence is a killer!

◄») **Personal illustration** *Away from the Rock* Tell a story from your life about a time you strayed and got hurt because of it.

Illustration

The coney

A coney spends its entire life within 20 yards of the rock pile it calls home. But even when it strays far away, it has guards backing it up. Sentinels will stand guard on the rock, watching for danger. If a sentinel sees a land predator—like a fox or coyote—it lets out long squeaks, saying, "Danger! You have some time, but get home soon!" If the guard sees a bird of prey—like a hawk—it lets out shorter, more urgent squeaks. But if it sees a weasel, the guard simply withdraws silently.

The other conies—who look back often—will see the guard has disappeared and run for their lives. That's because a weasel can go anywhere a coney can go, even under the rocks. And weasels often just kill for sport. But even when rushing to hide, the conies don't run aimlessly. They follow set patterns and trails within the rock pile to get to the safest hideouts.

3 Wise people are into team participation and know the importance of community.

◄》 **Scripture** reread *Proverbs 30:27* (The wise locusts) Small people do big things by working together. That's the lesson of the locust.

◄》 **Illustration** *Locusts* (see sidebar)

◄》 The Bible calls believers to swarm, to advance together in rank like an army. There's a sense of buzz in any Christ-following community where people are gathering and working together with a sense of mission.

◄》 We have to be careful about getting slack in our commitment to each other.

◄》 Are you self-focused or team-oriented?

Illustration

Locusts

There are basically two kinds of insects: loners and colonists. The loners are like spiders, which you always find one at a time. The colonists are like bees and ants—always together in groups. But locusts are both. In good times locusts are sluggish loners. But in bad times—like when there's a famine—locusts get very active and begin to swarm. When that happens they become a force of nature as powerful as a volcano or hurricane. They can't be stopped.

The largest swarm of locusts on record swept Africa in the early 1900s. It was one mile wide, 100 feet thick, and 50 miles long. Experts estimated it had 10 billion insects in it—which means if you could kill one million a minute, it would take you a week to get them all! The swarm ate everything in sight, landing on trees in such mass they broke off three-inch limbs just by their weight. Only another force of nature stopped them. Winds blew them out to sea. But even then they flew for 60 straight hours before dropping exhausted into the water.

4   Wise people are bold and persistent.

◁» **Scripture** reread *Proverbs 30:28* (The wise lizards)

◁» Lizards can be captured easily, yet they somehow get past the guards to the king's palace.

◁» **Illustration** *Lizards* (see sidebar)

◁» Ask the students—

- What are your spiritual goals?

- What would you like to be like, spiritually, in five or 10 years?

- How are you being persistent in pursuing God?

◁» Scripture look at these passages that show how God wants us to pursue him and pursue spiritual goals.

- "You will seek me and find me when you seek me with all your heart" (Jeremiah 29:13).

- "To those who by persistence in doing good seek glory, honor, and immortality, he will give eternal life" (Romans 2:7).

- "Let us not become weary in doing good, for at the proper time we will reap a harvest if we do not give up" (Galatians 6:9).

- "You need to persevere so that when you have done the will of God, you will receive what he has promised" (Hebrews 10:36).

◁» **Personal illustration** *My Persistence* Share a personal story of how persistence helped you succeed or how lack of it led to failure because you quit too soon.

Illustration

Lizards

A gecko is a harmless little four- or five-inch lizard that lives in warm climates. They're easy enough to catch, but they're built for climbing into places we don't want them! Their feet have a few climbing mechanisms that are interesting:

- They have claws, which unlike a cat's are spread apart even when they're relaxed.

- They have adhesive pads in the middle of their feet that stay slightly moist for added grab.

- They have scales that catch onto rough surfaces so the gecko can easily pull himself up.

- Catch them and throw them out as often as you like—they'll keep climbing back for more.

closing
The Grand Finale

📢 Review the wisdom of these four small creatures.

- The ants are wise because they prepare and make decisions with the future in mind.
- The coneys are wise because they know their safety is in the rock.
- The locusts are wise because they understand the importance of community.
- The lizards are wise because they're bold and persistent.

📢 The world values size, strength, beauty, and charisma. God values humility, character, and a passion for him.

📢 **Activity** *Slogan Time* Divide into four groups, assigning each group a principle from your talk. Give the groups five minutes to develop either a cheer or an advertisement for their principle.

📢 **Take-home item** *Making the Grade* (optional, see sidebar)

Take-home item

Making the grade

You may want to make copies of **Making the Grade** (page 90) and give them to students. Have them grade themselves—A to F—for each principle and write comments or suggestions for improvement.

discussion
Encore

Get It?	Middle School

📢 Review the four animals discussed. What key to success did each one highlight?

📢 Define each of the points—preparation, protection, participation, and persistence—in your own words.

📢 How is this picture of success different from the one most people in the world have?

Get It? — High School

🔊 How do most people in your world define success?

🔊 If you were a motivational speaker, what could you say to convince your audience that the values highlighted in this message are the real keys to success?

🔊 In your heart do you see yourself as similar to the weak creatures in this message or much stronger? Why?

What If? — The Big Picture

🔊 If you were serious about preparing yourself for your future, what would you be doing right now?

🔊 How does preparing for what God wants you to become compare to preparing for college or a career?

🔊 How would you rate yourself in the area of staying close to God as a source of protection? On a scale of zero to 100 yards, how close are you to the Rock? (Remember, 20 yards is a safe limit!)

🔊 If you were more serious about sticking closer to God, knowing your rock intimately, and running to him often—how would your days be different? What would you do more of? What would you do less of?

🔊 Are you more of a loner or a swarmer? Do you seek success individually or on a team? What can we do to develop a greater sense of team in this group?

🔊 Have you ever quit too soon? Or failed to persist in something you should have stuck with? What happened?

🔊 In what spiritual discipline do you need to show greater persistence? What are some of the benefits you can look forward to if you persist?

So What?	It's Your Life

🔊 What are the benefits of pursuing the four values we've discussed here?

🔊 Do these outweigh the benefits of the opposite values like procrastination, overconfidence, selfishness, or laziness? Why or why not? (Unpack each one individually.)

🔊 What do you find most attractive about the four values of Proverbs 30:24-28?

🔊 Which of the four—preparation, protection, participation, or persistence—do you think God's Spirit is pointing to in you? Which is the most critical area for you to address?

🔊 What are you going to do?

Report Card

Give yourself a letter grade (A-F) for each of the following qualities
and write a brief plan of action for improving where needed.

Quality	Grade	How to improve
preparation		
protection		
participation		
persistance		

✂ -

Report Card

Give yourself a letter grade (A-F) for each of the following qualities
and write a brief plan of action for improving where needed.

Quality	Grade	How to improve
preparation		
protection		
participation		
persistance		

Dogpile Jesus

Contributed by **Darrell Pearson**

Primary theme discipleship	
Themes grace, truth, love for others, weakness, being real, God's love, Jesus' humanity	
Scripture Matthew 14:22-26; 16:5-12; Mark 9:30-37; 10:13-16, 35-45; John 13	
Approximate length through The Grand Finale 25 minutes	

You'll need

- 📢 TV and VCR
- 📢 *Stand by Me* or *American Graffiti*
- 📢 A personal story about doing something crazy with friends
- 📢 A personal story about your area of weakness

T his talk helps students see the disciples as real people—with struggles, irritations, questions, and frustrations—instead of seeing them as somewhat unrealistic spiritual giants, who were always focused on godly things. Seeing the twelve—and Jesus—as real people will help students deal with their own doubts and self-disappointments when they don't follow Christ completely. They'll also know he loves them even when they're not perfect. Hopefully, it will give your students a new vision of what being a disciple of Jesus Christ looks like.

intro

The Opening Act

🔊 **Movie clip** *Stand by Me* or *American Graffiti* (see sidebar)

🔊 **Personal illustration** *That Crazy Time* (see sidebar)

🔊 Then say something like—

> **Have you ever thought about the people in the Bible that way? How about Jesus' disciples—do you think they ever did anything a bit crazy? Or were they totally focused on God 100 percent of the time? Let's take a look at the book about the disciples and several scenes from their lives.**

🔊 **Scripture** *Mark 9:30-37; 10:35-45* (see sidebar)

Movie clip

Stand by Me or *American Graffiti*

Before you begin your talk, use one of these movie clips—or another with the same theme—to show a group of friends doing something a little over the line together.

Stand by Me

Start 6:26 "I know the Back Harlow Road!"

Stop 8:12 "Too cool! Very, very cool! Yes!"

Best friends Gordie (Wil Wheaton), Chris (River Phoenix), Teddy (Corey Feldman), and Vern (Jerry O'Connell) contemplate going on an all-night hike in search of a dead teenager's body. (This scene has one swear word in it. As with all movie clips, you should preview the clip and make an appropriate decision about using it so you don't get fired!)

American Graffiti

Start 1:16:00 "Shut up! They'll hear us!"

Stop 1:20:00 The police car comes to a jarring halt.

In this nostalgic tale about a group of friends cruisin' in the '60s, Curt Henderson (Richard Dreyfuss) ties a cable to a police car as part of his initiation into a car gang called the Pharaohs.

That crazy time

Start with a personal story of a time when you were hanging out with some friends and ended up doing something with them that was a little unexpected or crazy. For example, it could be a time when you got a little wild at a restaurant and were asked to leave. Or the time you walked through a fast-food drive-thru without a car or climbed over a fence to swim in your neighbor's pool or drove to Florida on the spur of the moment—especially good if you live in Oregon! You get the idea. The story should be funny, surprising, and unexpected. Close with an emphasis on how friends occasionally do things that are surprising.

Mark 9:30-37; 10:35-45

Set the scene before reading these verses. Say something like—

> Jesus and the disciples were on the road together again—this time on the way to the final events of the Jesus story, including the crucifixion. The road was hot and dusty, and the disciples were probably tired. Then Jesus questioned the disciples about their discussion regarding who among them was the greatest. And then James and John requested to be the right-hand men at Jesus' side, which made the others angry in Mark 10:35-45.

Follow up the Scripture reading by making a few comments like this.

> The disciples were not focused on God all the time. They were often confused about life and irritated with each other. The disciples were a bunch of guys! What do guys do on camping trips? Belch, joke, and play practical jokes. They probably had a lot of fun together while they were traveling.
>
> Imagine this: late one night the disciples and Jesus are circled around a campfire while Jesus is telling another clever parable. John whispers to James, "On the count of three, let's dogpile Jesus." Then James passes it around the rest of the circle. When everyone's ready John says, *"Alpha, beta, gamma!"* And 12 disciples dogpile on Jesus—the whole group laughing—while Jesus gasps for breath at the bottom of the pile.
>
> That may seem a little weird, but hey—guys are like that! Isn't it possible the disciples were like that too?

heart of the talk

The Main Event

1 Jesus' disciples were just like us!

📢 Sure, their culture was different, but they were real people.

📢 Ask the students what struggles the disciples might have had. Did the disciples fall in love? Did they get in fights? Did they struggle with lust? Did they have racial issues?

📢 The answer to these questions is probably yes. The disciples were as real as we are.

📢 Mention or read several other stories where the disciples acted very human.

- In Matthew 14:22-26 the disciples were afraid of the storm.
- In Matthew 16:5-12 the disciples forgot to bring the bread.
- In Mark 10:13-16 the disciples tried to turn away children, but Jesus rebuked them.

2 Jesus loved his disciples even though they weren't perfect.

📢 After scolding them for their arguments over who was the best, he concluded by telling them to be servants and reminding them he came to serve them!

📢 Since the disciples let Jesus down so often—and were confused so often—you'd think Jesus would fire the whole bunch and start over at some point! But of course he doesn't—he sticks with these imperfect guys.

📢 **Scripture** *John 13* (see sidebar)

Scripture

John 13

Summarize this passage of Scripture for your students. Here the disciples are troubled, but Jesus comforts them and even washes their feet. The gospel says Jesus loved his own. Point out that whether the disciples are goofing off or in the middle of some serious confusion or doubt, Jesus still loves them. And he goes to great lengths to prove it.

3 **Jesus loves you and me, even though we're obviously human and obviously imperfect.**

📣 **Personal illustration** *My Imperfection and Jesus' Love* (see sidebar)

📣 If Jesus could love the disciples with their problems, he can love us too. And that means we can be disciples of Jesus, even though we're imperfect and flawed! Woo-hoo!

My imperfection and Jesus' love

Tell a personal story about some area of weakness in your life. This will only be effective if you show some vulnerability. Let your teens see that you're an imperfect person. (Psst! Don't worry—they already know!) Mention it's hard to believe Jesus could love a scumbag, dirtball maggot such as you! And end by sharing how you know Jesus still loves you, in spite of your imperfections and flaws.

closing

The Grand Finale

📣 If Jesus is willing to have us imperfect idiots as disciples, we should probably be able to love each other!

📣 **Scripture** reread *John 13:34* ("As I have loved you,…love one another.")

📣 **Reflection** *Just Imagine* (see sidebar)

📣 Finish with prayer. Give thanks for a God we can relate to, who loves us as we are, and who helps us love each other.

Just imagine

Ask students to close their eyes and imagine sitting by a campfire with Jesus and the disciples. Paint a mental picture of a friendly, loving Jesus and an interesting conversation. Then count to three and have them imagine dogpiling their good friend Jesus!

discussion

Encore

| Get It? | Middle School |

🔊 Was Jesus a regular guy? Or was he sort of different—like movies sometimes show him: weird eyes, serious face, unusual appearance?

🔊 Do you think Jesus was fun to be around? Why or why not?

🔊 Do you think it's accurate to think of the disciples as regular guys? Why or why not? Why don't we normally think of them that way?

🔊 What do you think it would have been like to be one of Jesus' closest friends?

🔊 Brainstorm some games you think the disciples and Jesus might have played together.

🔊 What are some stories from Scripture that show how normal the disciples were? Share those.

| Get It? | High School |

🔊 Is it wrong to think of Jesus and the disciples as having fun? Why or why not?

🔊 In what ways do you think people 2,000 years ago were like us?

🔊 In what ways were they not like us?

🔊 Was Jesus more of a friend or a leader? Explain your answer.

| What If? | The Big Picture |

🔊 What would it be like to be one of the 12 disciples?

🔊 What would Jesus enjoy about you? What about you would he struggle with?

🔊 What areas of your life would you be embarrassed to let Jesus see?

🔊 Why is it so difficult to accept that Jesus can love us unconditionally?

🔊 How might you live differently if you believed—every moment of every day—that Jesus loves you even though you're imperfect?

So What?   It's Your Life

🔊 Does understanding the humanity of Jesus and the disciples make any difference in your desire to be a disciple of Jesus? Explain your answer.

🔊 Would you be willing to dogpile Jesus? Why or why not?

🔊 How can you improve the way you relate to Jesus? How does that reflect your desire to be yourself around him?

🔊 How will this understanding change the way you pray?

🔊 How will this understanding change the way you worship?

🔊 How will you treat others in your youth group differently, knowing Jesus is okay with them being so imperfect? What actions—we're talking specific steps—can you take this week to live differently?

"God and..." or Just "God"?

Primary theme lordship	
Themes idolatry, priorities, satisfaction	
Scripture Psalm 103:1-5; Luke 10:38-42; John 15:1-8	
Approximate length through The Grand Finale 20-25 minutes	

Face it, there's not a believer on the face of the earth—yeah, that includes you!—who doesn't struggle with placing other things or people before God. This talk's power comes from its vivid description of the idols we cling to and the way our life gets better when we get rid of them. Although this talk is geared for a churched or Christian audience, you can modify it by challenging students to make Jesus their Savior—as well as Lord.

You'll need

- ◀))) A few things for show and tell that offer you comfort (optional)
- ◀))) Four or five student volunteers to act out John 15:1-8 (optional)
- ◀))) A pitcher of water and several clear glasses
- ◀))) A personal story from your teen years about satisfaction
- ◀))) TV and VCR
- ◀))) *For Love of the Game*
- ◀))) *Just the Way You Are* by Max Lucado (Crossway Books, 1999, originally published as *Children of the King*)
- ◀))) A scanner, PowerPoint, and a video projection unit or a color copier, transparencies, and overhead projector—or Kinko's to project illustrations from *Just the Way You Are*
- ◀))) Bananas and pens (optional)
- ◀))) Pencils and paper (optional)
- ◀))) A trash can (optional)

Contributed by Kara Powell

This outline is saved as GTO_10 on the CD-ROM.

intro

The Opening Act

🔊 Describe—or better yet bring—a few things you look to for comfort when life is difficult. This could be your favorite cookies, your TV remote, a shopping bag from your favorite store—anything that makes you secure and comforted.

🔊 Ask students to share things they do to make themselves feel better when they've had a tough day.

🔊 **Discussion** *Desert Island* Ask students to name three things they would want to keep with them if they were stuck on a desert island for a year. You might want them to gather in pairs or small groups to share their answers.

🔊 Drive home the main point of the talk and transition with something like—

> **Let's be honest. Each one of us has things or people we look to when life is difficult—or maybe even when life is great or just okay. There's nothing inherently bad in most of these things, but they can become problems if we start looking to them before we look to God—or instead of looking to God. It's almost like we make them the *and*s we add to God. We need God *and* our best friend, God *and* our computer games, God *and* popularity at school. The Bible gives us a pretty good idea how important it is to get rid of these *and*s by showing us the benefits when we do.**

🔊 **Scripture** *John 15:1-8* ("I am the vine; you are the branches.")

🔊 **Acting out** *Mixed Fruit* (see sidebar)

🔊 Transition by explaining three things happen when we make sure nothing comes before God.

Acting out

Mixed fruit

You might want to have some students act out what Jesus says in John 15:1-8 by having one act as the vine, one the gardener, one the fruitful branch, and one the unfruitful branch. You might want to toss an apple into the mix to make the fruitful branch even more so!

heart of the talk
The Main Event

1   When we focus on God, we're fruitful.

- 🔊 **Scripture** reread *John 15:1-4* ("No branch can bear fruit by itself.")

- 🔊 The verb *remain* means more than just "believe"—although it means that too. What it means is to be "united."

- 🔊 Just like any other relationship, being united with God can only happen if we spend time with him instead of the *and*s—other things and other people. That doesn't mean all we do all day is read the Bible and pray, but it does mean we make sure we get time with him every day.

- 🔊 **Illustration** *Martin Luther's Prayer* (see sidebar)

- 🔊 **Object lesson** *Water Pitcher* (see sidebar)

Illustration

Martin Luther's prayer

When we get busy it's tempting to skip our time with God and spend time with other things or people. Instead we should take our example from Martin Luther—Protestant reformer of the 1500s—who used to spend one hour a day with God in prayer. But on busy days when he had a long list of things to do, he spent three hours a day with God in prayer! He knew no other *and* could bring him the strength he needed.

Object lesson

Water pitcher

Grab a clear water pitcher and a few clear glasses—plastic or glass. Designate the water pitcher as God and pick the name of a student for one of the glasses. Explain that, unless the person is united with God and being filled by him—yep, pour some water from the pitcher into the glass—she will have nothing to give to the other glasses, which represents other students.

2   When we focus on God, we're satisfied.

🔊 **Scripture** *Psalm 103:1-5* ("Who satisfies your desires with good things.")

🔊 There are tons of things we look to for satisfaction instead of God.

friends	popularity
cars	alcohol
physical appearance	sports
drugs	sex
romantic relationships	academics

🔊 The problem with these things is that since they don't satisfy, we're always looking for more. We need more friends, more sex, more clothes, better grades—in short we become addicted to all those *and*s we add to God. But we still never get our fix.

🔊 **Personal illustration** *The Fix Goes Away* (see sidebar)

🔊 And even if we do get the *and* we hope for, the good feelings are only temporary.

🔊 **Movie clip** *For Love of the Game* (see sidebar)

Personal illustration

The fix goes away

Think back to when you were a teen and identify some of the things you looked to for satisfaction. Share about one or two of these with your students, being as honest as you can about the reasons you looked to those things and how they eventually made you feel.

Movie clip

For Love of the Game

Start 1:59:15 "Strike two!"

Stop 2:05:29 Billy sobs into his hands as the scene fades.

Baseball player Billy Chapel (Kevin Costner) has just pitched the perfect game. But after the cameras and fans have disappeared, he realizes that what should've been the high point of his career has left him surprisingly miserable.

3 When we focus on God, we please him.

◀)) **Scripture** reread *John 15:7-8* ("This is to my Father's glory, that you bear much fruit.")

◀)) We often forget there's one thing that pleases God more than anything else—spending time with him. No other *and* means as much to God.

◀)) **Scripture** *Luke 10:38-42* (Mary sits at Jesus' feet) Jesus himself reinforces this point by saying Mary chooses what is better in spending time with him.

◀)) **Illustration** *Dating Times Two* (see sidebar)

◀)) **Illustration** *Just the Way You Are* (see sidebar)

Illustration

Dating times two

Ask students to imagine what it would be like to have two serious dating relationships at the same time. Describe a scene like you've seen in movies and on TV of meeting, hiding behind a menu, slipping away from the table, hurriedly talking with the other, and perhaps finally being caught by both. You'd let down both people you were dating and end up pretty miserable. The same is true with having allegiance to God and other things. God isn't very pleased. And actually, neither are you.

Illustration

Just the Way You Are

This short children's book vividly contrasts the difference between a girl who wanted to spend time with the King and some teens who were so busy getting ready for his visit they ignored him when he came. If possible, make color overheads or PowerPoint slides of some or all of the book's pictures. So when you take six to eight minutes to read the entire book aloud, every student in the room can see it in full color.

closing

The Grand Finale

🔊 Give students some time of personal reflection and meditation to think about and confess to God some of the ands they look to instead of him. To make that process come to life, use one of the following reflection activities.

Reflection *Fruit Offering* (optional, see sidebar)

Reflection *Trash It* (optional, see sidebar)

Reflection

Fruit offering

Distribute bananas and pens to each student, asking them to write—yes, on the banana—something they tend to look to instead of God. You might want to give a few examples such as e-mail, gossip, TV, food, or computer games. As students are ready ask them to place the bananas in a stack in the front of the room as a sign of turning those ands over to God and a symbol of their desire to be more fruitful.

Reflection

Trash it

This is the nonfruit option—for those groups of teens who might roll their eyes at the idea of writing on bananas. Have the students write their *ands* on small pieces of paper. After a time of quiet prayer, have them come to the front of the room, rip them up, and toss them into a wastebasket.

discussion

Encore

Get It?	Middle School

- So does God want you to get rid of your friends, clothes, and anything else important to you? Why or why not?

- Describe the fruit we were we talking about.

- It's possible to get addicted to good things. Do you agree with that statement? Why or why not?

- What do you see as the difference between Mary and Martha? If you had been in the room when Jesus said those things to them, what would you have been thinking or feeling?

Get It?	High School

- What is the difference between believing in God and remaining in him?

- Do you think it's true you and others you know get addicted to things and still end up dissatisfied? Talk about that.

- What does it means to please God? Given our sin, is it ever possible to please him 100 percent?

What If?	The Big Picture

- What are some of the *ands* you see people who don't know God rely on? How are these different—if at all—from what Christians tend to rely on instead of God?

- If I were to ask your closest friends to name some of the things you rely on, what would they say? Would they be right?

- Is it realistic for you to spend more time with God when your life gets busier? Why or why not?

- Why is it tough to rely on God alone? Think in terms of qualities of God and qualities about yourself.

- Can you think of a time recently when you got what you had hoped for but still felt dissatisfied? Talk about that.

So What?	It's Your Life

🔊 Name one to three people or things you look to before—or instead of—God.

🔊 What would you lose if you attributed less importance to that *and*?

🔊 What would you gain?

🔊 How would your relationship with God be different if he was the first person or thing you looked to for comfort and wholeness?

The God of Losers

Contributed by **James Prior**

Primary theme self-image	
Themes God's love, evangelism, accepting others	
Scripture Proverbs 11:4; Mark 1:40-42; 1 Corinthians 1:27; Colossians 4:14; 2 Timothy 4:11	
Approximate length through The Grand Finale 20-25 minutes	

Most youth workers would agree one of the biggest problems students face on a daily basis is self-image. Trying to be cool all the time creates huge pressure in the lives of our teenagers. One of the most beautiful messages of the gospel, however, is that God is in love with losers—those of us who are hurting, broken, and desperate. This talk reveals God's love for those of us who sometimes feel this way.

You'll need

- ◀)) TV and VCR
- ◀)) *Revenge of the Nerds* or *Stripes*
- ◀)) A personal story about a time something other than God's will seemed attractive
- ◀)) A personal story about the people, possessions, or events you are most passionate about
- ◀)) Pencils and paper for students

intro

The Opening Act

◀ᴹ **Movie clip** *Revenge of the Nerds* or *Stripes* (see sidebar)

◀ᴹ **Illustration** *The Personal Ad* (see sidebar)

◀ᴹ **Scripture** *1 Corinthians 1:27* ("But God chose the foolish things of the world to shame the wise; God chose the weak things of the world to shame the strong.")

◀ᴹ Say something like—

> **I know this may sound crazy to some of you, but the Bible tells us God has specifically chosen to love losers like you and me. Since it's a little uncool to think of yourself as a loser, I'm going to give you guys a little help in defining losers. Losers are—quite simply— people who have lost something. Their self-worth, their way, or their passion.**

Movie clip

Revenge of the Nerds or *Stripes*

Either of these clips are great for introducing the topic of self-image.

Revenge of the Nerds

Start 12:33 The whistle blows.

Stop 14:19 "Nerds, nerds, nerds!"

In this crazy frat-house comedy, the jocks' house gets burned down at a party, and they forcibly take over the freshmen dorms.

Stripes

Start 35:47 "They are fine men. Are they from my company?"

Stop 37:30 Ox (John Candy) is carried back to the barracks.

Army life isn't all it's cracked up to be for this group of new recruits. As they stumble through an obstacle course for the first time, they look like complete losers.

The personal ad

In *Love Beyond Reason* (Willow Creek/Zondervan, 1998) John Ortberg tells of a personal ad in New York magazine that read, "Strikingly beautiful Ivy League graduate. Playful, passionate, perceptive, elegant, bright, articulate, original in mind, unique in spirit. I possess a rare balance of beauty and depth, sophistication and earthiness, seriousness and love of fun. Professionally successful, perfectly capable of being self-sufficient and independent, but I won't be truly content until we find one another. Please reply with a substantial letter describing your background and who you are. Photo essential."

After reading that personal ad you may want to make up one of your own. You might begin with something like—

Strikingly average, scraped through high school, slightly dimwitted…

heart of the talk

The Main Event

1   God loves those who've lost their self-worth.

- The Pharisees in Jesus' day didn't have anything to do with people who were not "pure" like them.

- **Explanation** *Bruised and Bleeding Pharisees* (see sidebar)

- There are many people today who—like these Pharisees—don't want anything to do with people they don't approve of.

- Jesus was the complete opposite. Jesus sought out the broken, hurting, and lonely—in short, those who had lost their self-worth.

- **Scripture** *Mark 1:40-42* ("A man with leprosy came to him and begged him on his knees, "If you are willing, you can make me clean.")

- **Explanation** *The Life of a Leper* (see sidebar)

  - Notice the question he asked Jesus. He didn't ask if Jesus was able to heal him, he asked, "Jesus, are you willing to heal me?" When Jesus heard that, he was moved with compassion.

  - Jesus is willing to restore self-worth to the biggest of losers.

Explanation

Bruised and bleeding Pharisees

In Jesus' time there was a select group of Pharisees, casually known as the bruised and bleeding Pharisees. They believed it sinful to look upon people whom society regarded as losers—people like prostitutes, lepers, and tax collectors. They were called bruised and bleeding because they walked around with their heads covered. As a result they bumped into things and were always bruised and bleeding.

Explanation

The life of a leper

Help your students understand the weight of Jesus' action by explaining what a leper's life was like in Jesus' time. They were banished to leper colonies and not allowed to have any contact with their families. All their earthly possessions had to be burned, and it was against the law even to speak to them! Here was a guy who probably believed everything everyone in his culture was telling him about his condition. But somehow he knew Jesus would be able to restore him, to give him back his self-worth.

2 God loves those who've lost their way.

- The world is full of people trying to believe they've got it all together because they've got a nice car and a hot girlfriend or boyfriend.
- **Personal illustration** *The Great Temptation* (see sidebar)
- **Scripture** *Matthew 18:12* (the parable of the lost sheep)
- It's easy to lose your way and believe what the world treats as important—money, sex, good looks, popularity, pleasure—actually is important.
- God sent his son Jesus so "losers" can find the righteousness that delivers from death.
- **Illustration** *Arenius the Monk* (see sidebar)

Personal illustration

The great temptation

Tell of a time when you thought something other than the will of God for your life seemed attractive. Maybe it was a great job or a partner you knew you shouldn't date. Whatever it was, try to connect with your kids and let them see that even though you're a Christian leader you have struggles as well.

Arenius the monk

Arenius was a monk who lived in ancient times. One day he decided to go to the huge city of Alexandria. When he got there he spent hours walking though all the bazaars and markets of this great city. Someone eventually walked up to him and asked Arenius what he was doing. He responded, "I'm allowing my heart to rejoice at all the things I just don't need."

3 God even loves those who've lost their passion for him.

◄» Explain passion to your students by saying something like—

> **Passion is defined in Webster's dictionary as "the object of a strong desire." When I say I'm full of passion about something, I'm saying I feel strongly about it or I'm full of desire for it. I can be passionate about cheese or mountain biking or algebra. It's much more than just romantic passion.**

◄» **Personal illustration** *My Greatest Passion* (see sidebar)

◄» Ask the students to name one thing they're passionate about.

◄» Point out that not many of us could truly say our number one passion is for God.

◄» **Illustration** *Demas* (see sidebar)

◄» Whenever we turn away from God, our passion for him begins to melt away.

◄» The love and grace of God is so great if Demas were to ask forgiveness it would have been given to him in a nanosecond.

My greatest passion

Share a couple of your greatest passions. Be sure to include a passion that students can relate to—like a sport or a hobby. (They have a hard time relating to something like "my children" unless they happen to have children of their own.) Go on to share a time when you became so consumed with one of your passions that it absorbed nearly all your thoughts, time, and focus.

Illustration

Demas

In 2 Timothy 4:10 we read that Demas loved the world and deserted Paul. We don't know much about Demas. But we know at one time he was a faithful and diligent servant of God. When Paul was in prison for the first time, Demas was there right alongside him (Colossians 4:14). But in this letter Paul writes to Timothy that Demas has left the work of God because he loved the world. The passion Demas once had for God must have dissolved to the point where he was willing to pack it all in and walk away.

closing

The Grand Finale

📢 **Illustration** *Coming Home* (see sidebar)

📢 **Activity** *Personal Ads* (see sidebar)

📢 Conclude by saying something like—

> **Maybe you feel like that returned soldier. You think you're such a loser there's no way anyone—especially God—could love and accept you the way you are. One of the greatest messages in the Bible is that God loves you as you are—even if you've lost your self-worth, lost your way, or lost your passion for him.**

Illustration

Coming home

A soldier was on his way home from the Vietnam War. He phoned his parents from San Francisco and asked them if he could bring home a friend who had lost an arm and a leg in the war. His parents turned him down, saying it would be too much of a burden. Several days later the parents were called by the San Francisco Police and told their son had just jumped off a building and committed suicide. When they went to identify the body they were shocked to discover their son lay on the stretcher with only one arm and one leg.

From *Hot Illustrations for Youth Talks* edited by Wayne Rice (Youth Specialties, 1994).

Activity

Personal ads

Consider having students write out personal ads, drawing from the ideas discussed in the first point. Have them include true statements about themselves, but add a comment or two about how they're accepted by God. Ask for volunteers willing to share their ads with the group.

discussion

Encore

Get It?	Middle School

- What does it mean to be a person with worth or value? Where does this value come from?

- What would the perfect life look like for you? What things would you need to live this perfect life? How is this life different from—or the same as—the life you think God wants you to live?

- What are you passionate about? How do your passions pull you away from a close walk with God or draw you near?

Get It?	High School

- Why has God chosen the weak and foolish?

- How big an issue do you think lack of self-worth is today? Rank it on a scale of one (little issue) to 10 (BIG issue). Why do you think so many of us are plagued with this issue?

- What's pulling your focus away from the life God wants you to lead?

- There's a fine line between enjoying something and allowing it to consume you. Share some ways we can keep a balance between our passions for the things we love to do and our passion for God.

What If?	The Big Picture

- In magazines and TV shows we're often told what we need to be successful. If you had the choice of being rich, famous, beautiful, or happy, which one would you choose? Why?

- What difference does it make in the way you view yourself if you believe God loves you and accepts you the way you are? What difference does it make in the way you live your life?

- Jesus said he didn't come for the healthy; he came for the sick. What does this mean in your life?

- Some people say inviting Jesus into your life is admitting we need a crutch to hold ourselves up. Do you agree or disagree with them? Why or why not?

◀»   Having no self-worth is another way of saying you're useless and not special in the eyes of God. What are some things you can do to remind yourself how special you are to God?

◀»   What can you do to gain perspective on what's truly important in life? How can you continue to think and act this way?

◀»   What can you do this week to renew your passion for God?

◀»   It's nice to hear God loves those of us who think we're losers. But how does this impact your life?

God Can't Fail

Primary theme hope	
Themes self-image, failure, injustice, pain, trusting God, God's promises, God's character, God's will	
Scripture Job 42:2; Psalm 33:11; 34:18; 139:14; Proverbs 21:30; Isaiah 65:24; Jeremiah 29:11; John 14:27; 16:33; Romans 8:1-2, 18; 1 Corinthians 10:13; 2 Corinthians 1:3-4; 1 John 2:17; Revelation 21:1	
Approximate length through The Grand Finale 30-40 minutes	

You'll need

- A personal story about the awkwardness of your teen years

- A personal story about experiencing intense emotional or physical pain

A majority of students think God is pretty good at most stuff but he's dropped the ball in a few areas. They might not be willing to admit this, but they think it—even if they've never verbalized it to themselves. This talk names those thoughts head on and unpacks them with the truth about God—it's impossible for God to fail.

Contributed by **Doug Fields**

This outline is saved as GTO_12 on the CD-ROM.

intro

The Opening Act

📣 When things go wrong, we love to blame God.

📣 **Illustration** *Insurance Policies* (see sidebar)

📣 **Illustration** *Why Me?* (see sidebar)

📣 The reality is it's impossible for God to fail, regardless of how we feel.

Illustration

Insurance policies

All insurance contracts—as well as contracts for facility rentals and other things—have paragraphs about unexpected and uncontrolled catastrophes. Earthquakes, ice storms, floods, volcanic eruptions—these aren't referred to as acts of nature in these contracts. They're called acts of God, as if God made them happen.

Illustration

Why me?

Just like those insurance contracts, people blame God all the time when bad stuff happens in their lives. Share examples like these with your students.

- It's like the guy who gets drunk, steals his dad's car, crashes it into a lake, then asks, "Why me, God?"

- Or the girl who cheats on a test, gets caught, fails the class, and asks, "Why, God? Why have you left me?"

heart of the talk

The Main Event

1   The feelings cause the doubt.

◀⁾ Sometimes I feel like God has failed because of the way I'm designed.

- Do you ever feel like God blew it when he made you?

- **Personal illustration** *How God Messed Up* (see sidebar)

- It's normal to think about this stuff and to wonder what God was thinking.

◀⁾ Sometimes I feel like God has failed because of my pain.

- When we're going through times of pain, it's easy to blame God—or at least wonder why God isn't taking the pain away.

- **Personal illustration** *Personal Pain* (see sidebar)

- Here's some reality—If you haven't experienced some real pain in your life yet, you will.

◀⁾ Sometimes I feel like God has failed because the world is messed up.

- We live in a messed-up world, and that can make us feel like God either doesn't care or doesn't have enough power to fix things.

- People are idiots and good people get hurt in the crossfire of stupidity.

gossip	racism
hatred	stealing
drug and alcohol abuse	sexual abuse
put-downs	careless words
road rage	betrayal
unfaithfulness	cheating
lying	violence

◀⁾ The question we ask because of these feelings is, "Where is God when I need him?" Believing that God fails leads to a loss of hope.

◀⁾ This is very dangerous, because—

- When we don't have hope, we get easily discouraged.

- When we are easily discouraged, we get the life sucked out of us.

- When the life is sucked out of us, we'll try anything to find some hope.

◀⁾ This is the heart of God—

- **Scripture** *Jeremiah 29:11* ("For I know the plans I have for you…to give you hope and a future.")

Personal illustration

How God messed up

Every teen feels like their body is imperfect at one time or another—and many adults too! Share from your own experience a funny story about how you viewed yourself as a teen. Don't go for a heavy-duty serious story here—try to keep it light.

Personal illustration

Personal pain

Share a story from your own life about a time of intense emotional or physical pain, and how it made you ask questions about God's involvement. Don't offer easy answers here, like you knew God was in control. If you don't have a story you can share, consider asking another adult in the church to share a brief testimony along these lines. Again, ask this person not to wrap it up neatly—the point is the pain, not the resolution.

2 The truth is God can't fail.

🔊 God has created everyone as an original masterpiece.

- **Scripture** *Psalm 139:14* ("I am fearfully and wonderfully made.")

🔊 God comforts his children, and today's pain is only temporary.

- **Scripture** *2 Corinthians 1:3-4* ("God…comforts us in all our troubles.")
- This doesn't mean pain isn't real! Pain can be very intense.
- **Scripture** *Romans 8:18* ("Our present sufferings are not worth comparing with the glory that will be revealed.")

🔊 God has promised to create a new heaven and earth. If you read the whole Bible, you'll find out how the story ends—God wins!

- **Scripture** *Revelation 21:1* ("Then I saw a new heaven and a new earth, for the first heaven and the first earth had passed away.")
- **Scripture** *1 John 2:17* ("The world and its desires pass away…the man who does the will of God lives forever.")
- What's the will of God? That you would be reconciled with him, so you can live forever!

3   Take actions that lead to hope.

🔊 Open yourself to new beliefs.

- This is tough! We think we know what's best for us.
- **Scripture** *Proverbs 21:30* ("There is no wisdom, no insight, no plan that can succeed against the Lord.")
- **Illustration** *Santa* (see sidebar)

🔊 Learn about God's promises and believe in them.

- **Discussion** *God's Promises* (optional, see sidebar)

🔊 Live your life based on God's promises.

- **Discussion** *A Different Life* (optional, see sidebar)
- Three things you can base your decisions on—your emotions, what other people say or the situation you're in, or God's promises

🔊 Trust your future to God's promises.

- I don't understand evil, but I trust God for his goodness.
- I don't understand atoms, but I trust God to hold everything together.
- I don't understand life, but I trust God that he rules it.
- I don't understand why I've been blessed with this body, but I trust God that he knows what he's doing.
- **Scripture** *Job 42:2* ("I know that you can do all things; no plan of yours can be thwarted.")
- **Scripture** *Psalm 33:11* ("But the plans of the Lord stand firm forever, the purposes of his heart through all generations.")

Illustration

Santa

Ask how many of your group still believe in Santa Claus. If any raise their hands, you might want to say, "Okay, let's acknowledge the people who need attention." Then move on by acknowledging that none of them really still believe in Santa and that change in belief has changed their actions at Christmastime. The same is true with other beliefs—when we open ourselves up to how God wants to change our beliefs, our actions will also change as a result.

Discussion

God's promises

If you use small groups in your ministry, this would be a great subject for small group learning and discussion. Give students a list of passages containing God's promises and have them look them up and write out the promises. Here are some to get you started.

Psalm 34:18	John 16:33
Isaiah 65:24	Romans 8:1-2
John 14:27	1 Corinthians 10:13

Talk about whether believing these promises in your head and your heart would change the way you live your life—and how.

You don't have to break for small groups at this point in the talk—you can wait until you're finished, then come back to this point for small group time.

Discussion

A different life

If you don't plan on using the small group discussion exercise described above, spend a couple minutes asking students to reflect on how their lives would be different if they believe these promises of God.

- The Lord is close to the brokenhearted and saves those who are crushed in spirit (Psalm 34:18).

- Before they call I will answer; while they are still speaking I will hear (Isaiah 65:24).

- Peace I leave with you; my peace I give you (John 14:27).

- In this world you will have trouble. But take heart! I have overcome the world (John 16:33).

- There is now no condemnation for those who are in Christ Jesus (Romans 8:1-2).

- He will not let you be tempted beyond what you can bear (1 Corinthians 10:13).

closing

The Grand Finale

🔊 Review the main points—how we feel God has failed, God's inability to fail, and the challenge to take actions that lead to hope.

🔊 Wrap up by saying something like—

You can count on two things: people will fail you and God never will.

discussion

Encore

Get It?	Middle School

🔊 What's the difference between wishing for something and the hope we talked about today?

🔊 What leads us to think God has failed?

🔊 Why is it impossible for God to fail?

🔊 How can you have more hope in your life?

🔊 What does it mean to live by God's promises?

Get It?	High School

🔊 What's the difference between the hope in these two sentences?

- "I hope I pass my math test."
- "My hope in life is built on Jesus."

🔊 Why is it difficult to believe God's in control when we see bad stuff happen in the world? What kind of bad stuff makes you feel that way? Talk about that.

🔊 What does a loss of hope look like in the lives of high school students?

🔊 How can you have more hope?

What If?	The Big Picture

🔊 Since life is full of pain, hearing "Hey, live life based on God's promises!" might come across as shallow. Why is that? How can we encourage someone in pain with God's promises?

🔊 Name a promise from God. How could you live as if you believe this promise is true? Would anything change in your daily life? What?

🔊 We all like to feel in control of our future. What would it look like for you to trust God for your future?

🔊 What difference does it make in everyday life to know God can't fail?

🔊 What do you think about God's plan for a new heaven and earth?

So What?   It's Your Life

🔊 Which of the areas of doubt—questioning God because of your own design, questioning God because of your own pain, or questioning God because of the evil in the world—do you struggle with the most? These aren't simple to deal with! What can you do this week to take one step toward God? Will you do it?

🔊 What attitudes or actions should you reevaluate this week to be open to new beliefs?

🔊 Do you usually make decisions based on your emotions, what other people say, your circumstances, or God's promises? What would you be risking to make decisions based on God's promises? How can you take the risk?

🔊 How would your life be different this week if you had more hope? What will you do to get more hope?

X Marks Your Spot

Contributed by **Kara Powell**

Primary theme spiritual gifts	
Themes community, service, leadership	
Scripture Genesis 11:4; 12:2; 1 Corinthians 12:4-28; Ephesians 4:11-13	
Approximate length through The Grand Finale 25-35 minutes	

You'll need

- A personal story about searching for something you lost
- A large X made from paper or wood
- A personal story about the ministry of a volunteer staff person
- TV and VCR
- *Mr. Holland's Opus*
- A list of spiritual gifts and how they can be used in your church (optional)

What keeps your students from using their spiritual gifts and talents in your youth ministry and your church? Are they lazy, unmotivated, or only committed to doing those easy jobs they can finish quickly? Unfortunately too few students realize being God's chosen isn't only a privilege, it's a responsibility. God has a unique place—an X—marked for every one of his followers.

This talk counters three of the main deceptions that keep your students from using their gifts. It also helps them find their X with three truths that emerge from Paul's teachings to the Corinthian church.

It will be your job in the weeks that follow to design some accessible and creative service opportunities to help your students not only become hearers of the Word, but doers.

intro

The Opening Act

🔊 **Personal illustration** *My Hunt* Share a story about a time when you were desperately trying to find something—your keys, your wallet, your children.

🔊 **Activity** *Treasure Hunt* (see sidebar)

🔊 Ask students to share about an expensive or meaningful thing they've lost recently, and everything they've done to try to find it— knowing students, they won't have to think too far back to remember something they've lost.

🔊 Then transition by explaining—

> **Today we're going to check out a real treasure. Just like on pirate treasure maps, it's marked with an X. That X is the X marking your place in God's kingdom. The way God has called you and uniquely made you means no one can stand on that X but you. By the end of this session, you'll know three truths about your X that will help you overcome anything that keeps you from finding your place.**

🔊 **Object lesson** *The X* (see sidebar)

🔊 **Scripture** *1 Corinthians 12:4-28* ("There are different kinds of gifts, but the same Spirit.") The talk is built on this passage, so begin by reading it—all of it.

Activity

Treasure hunt

Design a treasure hunt in your youth room or on the church campus. Divide students into teams and give them the same sets of clues—arranged in different orders so groups don't merely follow each other around—with a treasure at the end.

Object lesson

The X

Visual reinforcement of concepts—especially somewhat tricky concepts—is a good idea. You might want to make an X out of paper or wood and continue to point to it throughout the talk, maybe even standing on it at times as a reminder of the unique place that you—and every other believer—have in this world.

heart of the talk

The Main Event

1   X Truth 1: God calls you to serve

🔊 Lots of times we're prevented from serving by what I call an X deception—the feel-good X.

🔊 **Explanation** *The Feel-Good X* (see sidebar)

🔊 Not only does God call us his beloved children, but he's given us some responsibility along with that—it's to serve him.

🔊 **Scripture** *1 Corinthians 12:5* ("There are different kinds of service, but the same Lord.")

🔊 **Illustration** *A Tale of Two Chapters* (see sidebar)

🔊 **Illustration** *Find Your Own Calcutta* (see sidebar)

Explanation

The Feel-Good X

A feel-good person is willing to serve, but only if it's not inconvenient and the person gets a lot of affirmation for it. After all the pastor is the one paid to do ministry, right? Everyone else can hang out and have a good time while the pastor—and the rest of the adults in the church—do all the work.

Illustration

A tale of two chapters

In two chapters in Genesis, we get a vivid contrast of the difference between people who are self-centered and those who are selfless. We tend to be like the people of the Tower of Babel in Genesis 11:4 who want to make a great name for themselves. They were self-centered and godless. We should be like Abraham in Genesis 12:2 who becomes great but only because God makes him great. He was God-centered and selfless.

Illustration

Find your own Calcutta

Mother Teresa was a Catholic nun who served the poor and dying in India by establishing homes and hospitals where they could come to die with some dignity. She told people who asked to work with her in Calcutta to find their own Calcutta. Ask—

- **Where is your Calcutta?**
- **Where in your place of service?**
- **Are you willing to serve regardless of affirmation from others?**
- **Are you willing to serve regardless of inconvenience to you?**

2   X Truth 2: Others need the gifts you have.

🔊 Lots of times we're prevented from using our gifts because of another X deception—Little X Syndrome. We feel that we can't do much—and that what we *can* do, we don't do as well as others.

🔊 **Scripture** Reread *1 Corinthians 12:7* ("Now to each one the manifestation of the Spirit is given for the common good."). We're all ministers, not just the pastor. We're all ministers because we all have gifts to use. Here are some of the gifts listed in Paul's letters.

wisdom	prophecy	administration
knowledge	discernment	leadership
faith	tongues	teaching
healing powers	interpretation	miracles

🔊 Saying you don't have these or any other gifts isn't humility. It's a theological slap in God's face.

🔊 Wrap up this point by saying something like—

> **God is in the process of developing your gifts. If you look at Corinthians, Paul knows the church is relatively young and needs time to mature. He doesn't designate specific leaders within the community, but he gives them vision for what they—by God's grace—will become.**

3   X Truth 3: Leaders help us find our Xs, but they don't stand in our spots for us.

🔊 Leaders are important because they ultimately equip others to find their Xs and do great jobs once they get there.

🔊 **Personal illustration** *Look Who's in the Spotlight Now* Give an example of someone in your group who does a better job than you at something. As a leader your job is to make sure that person keeps doing a good job, not to steal the job away.

🔊 Some leaders have an X deception called the Big X—they think they're needed by everyone, they have to do all the ministry, and they're the only ones who can do it right.

🔊 **Scripture** reread *1 Corinthians 12:28* ("And in the church God has appointed first of all apostles, second prophets, third teachers…")

🔊 **Scripture** *Ephesians 4:11-13* ("It was he who gave some to be apostles, some to be prophets…")

🔊 When leaders help us develop our gifts, they become conductors who bring out the amazing individual skill of each individual player.

- **Movie clip** *Mr. Holland's Opus* (see sidebar)

Movie clip

Mr. Holland's Opus

Start 2:06:30 The auditorium erupts with applause as Mr. Holland enters.

Stop 2:16:14 Mr. Holland receives a standing ovation after the last notes of the song.

Break out those tissues—this powerful scene comes toward the end of the movie as teacher Glenn Holland (Richard Dreyfuss) is honored at a surprise celebration. Surrounded by students and families he has touched, he's asked to conduct a specially assembled orchestra—composed of former students—in the symphony he's worked on most of his life. As one former student remarks, "We're your symphony. We're the melodies and the notes of your opus, and we are the music of your life."

closing

The Grand Finale

- 📣 **Discussion** *What Next?* Brainstorm service opportunities with your students that they can be involved in the near future.

- 📣 **Take-home item** *Use It or Lose It* Distribute a list of spiritual gifts and a few ideas of how each gift can be used in your church or ministry in the next few months.

- 📣 **Activity** *Every Little Thing Counts* (see sidebar)

Activity

Every little thing counts

Give each student one or more puzzle pieces from a fairly simple 50-piece puzzle, and have them complete the puzzle as an example of what can come together when everyone contributes what they have. If you have a large group, you may want to get several smaller puzzles and divide the students into teams.

discussion

Encore

Get It?	**Middle School**

- 📣 Are you supposed to stand on an actual X somewhere? Explain what an X is.

- 📣 Why would someone not want to serve?

- 📣 Who's the minister at your church? Reread *1 Corinthians 12:7*. What would Paul say about your answer?

- 📣 What were you thinking during the movie clip from *Mr. Holland's Opus?*

Get It? — High School

- Which of the following do you struggle with most? Can you give an example of when you've acted like that?

    Feel-Good X : you serve only if it's convenient

    Little-X Syndrome: you feel that don't have any gifts

    The Big X : you think you're needed by everyone

- What is a leader's role within a group of Christians?

- What does a leader give up when empowering others to do the work of ministry?

What If? — The Big Picture

- What do you do if you don't like the gifts you have or if it seems like everyone else has better ones?

- Maybe you've heard the expression, "Students are the church of tomorrow." Given what you've heard today, how might you rephrase the statement so it's more accurate? (Hint: think about the last word in the phrase.)

- If someone you know thinks he has a gift or talent but it's pretty clear to you—and most everyone else—that he doesn't, what might you say or do?

- If we were all using our gifts to serve, how would our youth ministry be different?

- How might your understanding of your gifts influence your future—your choice of career, spouse, ministry?

So What? — It's Your Life

- If Mother Teresa were to walk in this room and ask you where your Calcutta is, what would you say?

- What might some of your spiritual gifts might be? If you don't know, how can you find out?

- What might your own X look like? What might God want you to do, say, or be like when you're standing there?

- What might you give up—or lose—by serving others as God has uniquely called you?

- What might you gain by standing on your X?

The Freedom God Offers

Contributed by **James Prior**

Primary theme freedom
Themes bondage, death, grace, evangelism, Christian living, wandering from God, God's love
Scripture Luke 15:11-32; John 10:10; 1 Corinthians 15:54-57; 2 Corinthians 3:17
Approximate length through The Grand Finale 25-30 minutes

s the gospel of Christ a message of burden or freedom? This is a pretty good question to ask your teenagers, and you might be surprised by their responses. By using the parable of the Prodigal Son, we can explain how Christ came to bring us freedom. So many of our kids live in bondage and fear without understanding the true freedom Christ died to bring.

You'll need

- TV and VCR
- *Amistad*
- A stereo
- "My Own Prison" on the album *My Own Prison* by Creed (Wind Up, 1997)
- A personal story about a time you felt like running from God
- A personal story about a near-death experience (optional)

intro

The Opening Act

- 🔊 **Movie clip** *Amistad* or *Braveheart* (see sidebar)

- 🔊 Ask your students what person or image comes to mind when they think about freedom.

- 🔊 **Scripture** *2 Corinthians 3:17* ("Now the Lord is the Spirit, and where the Spirit of the Lord is, there is freedom.")

- 🔊 **Illustration** *The Theological Brad Pitt* (see sidebar)

- 🔊 **Scripture** *Luke 15:11-32* (The Prodigal Son)

- 🔊 Say something like—

> **When this guy left home he was surprised to face three things:**
>
> **1. A life of burden and bondage**
> **2. The reality of death**
> **3. How lousy a life of sin is**
>
> **Jesus offers us freedom from those three things!**

Movie clip

Amistad

Start 1:33:48 "Give us free."

Stop 1:35:11 Cutaway to prison cell.

Cinqué (Djimon Hounsou) was kidnapped from his homeland in Africa and held captive on the slave ship Amistad. When he and the other slaves onboard could no longer stand the inhumanity and suffering, they revolted. This fact-based movie chronicles their trial on American soil. In this scene Cinqué can no longer stand the frustration and the injustice of it all, so in his broken English he demands freedom.

Start 2:12:00 "There is an article in here written by…"

Stop 2:13:45 "He will try and try against all odds…to get home."

Near the climax of the movie, John Adams (Anthony Hopkins) stands before the Supreme Court and gives a passionate and insightful monologue about slavery and the meaning of true freedom.

The theological Brad Pitt

In a Rolling Stone interview Brad Pitt gave his thought on Christianity. "I would call religion oppression," he said, "because it stifles any kind of personal, individual freedom."

Continuing on the subject, Pitt attempted a description of how he views the parable of the Prodigal Son. "This," he explained, "is a story which says if you go out and try to find your own voice and find what works for you and what makes sense for you, then you are going to be destroyed and you will be humbled and you will not be alive again until you come home to the father's ways."

heart of the talk

The Main Event

1 God's freedom delivers us from bondage.

- 📢 Ask if the students have ever felt like they were in prison. As though they were trapped and couldn't get out.
  - The life the world tells us will make us free is always the life that leads us into prison.
  - **Song** *"My Own Prison"* (see sidebar)
- 📢 The prodigal son quickly found out a life of wine, women, and parties isn't what he thought it would be. Within the space of a short time, he went from the comfort and security of his father's house to eating pig food.
- 📢 **Personal illustration** *Running from God* Tell of a time when you ran from God and his plans for your life. Be as transparent as possible. Let your kids see you have dealt—and still deal with—many of the issues they face.
- 📢 Ask if anyone is running from God right now. Is anyone running from the life of freedom God longs to give?
- 📢 **Scripture** *Luke 15:17* ("When he came to his senses…")
- 📢 Running from God always leads us to a worse place than we came from.
- 📢 God wants to take you from that place and bring you into a place of freedom.

"My Own Prison"

In 1999 the popular band Creed won the prestigious Band of the Year title from Rolling Stone on the heels of their first hit, *My Own Prison*. Either play this song (or show the video or read the lyrics). "My Own Prison" describes what it's like to feel caught up in bondage.

After listening to the song, share a time when you felt you were in prison or bondage of some sort and God rescued you.

2   God's freedom delivers us from death.

📢 The fear of death is one of the strongest fears people face.

- **Personal illustration** *My Near Death Experience* (see sidebar)

📢 Verse 17 says the Prodigal Son was starving to death. His sin led him close to death, and it scared him.

📢 **Scripture** *1 Corinthians 15:54-57* ("Death has been swallowed up in victory.")

- Jesus died so we don't have to live in the shadow of death. Sure, most of us will still die physically at some point—but that's only temporary!

📢 **Illustration** *Columbus's Monument* (see sidebar)

My near death experience

Tell of a time when you came close to death or were genuinely afraid of dying—if you have been in that position. Tell how you felt and what you were thinking at the time. Otherwise, ask some of your students to share their own near-death experiences.

Columbus's monument

For centuries the motto on Spain's coat of arms was *ne plus ultra*. This is Latin for "there is no more beyond." The Spaniards believed all that could be discovered in the world had been discovered. That is, until a guy named Columbus sailed off and found the Americas. A statue has been erected in his honor. It's a lion eating the first word of Spain's motto so all that's left to read is "more beyond." This is what Christ has done for us. Through his death and resurrection there is now "more beyond" for all who believe.

3   God's freedom gives us fullness of life.

◀)) Get your students thinking by saying something like—

Why can we see colors? There are plenty of people—and animals—getting through life just fine colorblind. Why does food taste so good? Again, there are a lot of people who can get through life without ever tasting food. I think the answer to these questions is God wants us to enjoy life.

◀)) **Scripture** *John 10:10* ("I have come that they may have life, and have it to the full.")

◀)) Jesus came so we can have fullness of life.

◀)) Was the Prodigal Son experiencing fullness of life? No way!

◀)) **Illustration** *The Greatest Source of Pleasure* (see sidebar)

◀)) God wants for us to find our greatest source of pleasure and meaning and purpose in life from him.

Illustration

The greatest source of pleasure

A poll was taken in 1989 asking people what they consider the greatest source of pleasure in their lives. Of those polled, 63 percent said their families and only eight percent said their religious involvement, followed by a mere six percent who said their work.

closing

The Grand Finale

◀)) **Illustration** *Bought to be Freed* (see sidebar)

◀)) Finish by saying something like this—

This is exactly what Christ has done for all of us. He has bought us to set us free. Why do we want to live in bondage any more? Why do we want to live with the fear of death? And why do we keep thinking fullness of life is found any place other than in a relationship with God? He has bought us to set us free.

Illustration

Bought to be freed

A young Englishman went to find gold in California in the 1800s. He did indeed become very wealthy, and on the way home back to England he happened to pass by a slave auction in Louisiana. Bidding began for a young African girl, and the young man ended up spending nearly all his fortune buying her. He immediately drove his carriage to a place where he purchased papers that legally set the young girl free. All she could do was look at him and repeat over and over again, "You bought me to set me free. You bought me to set me free."

From *Hot Illustrations for Youth Talks* edited by Wayne Rice (Youth Specialties, 1994)

discussion

Encore

Get It?	Middle School

- When you hear the word *freedom*, what person or image comes to your mind?

- What are some of the things middle schoolers can be in bondage to?

- Share the time you came closest to death. How did you feel and what did you think? What if this were to happen today?

- What things do you most enjoy doing? Do you think God is pleased with you when you're doing those things?

Get It?	High School

- Comment on Brad Pitt's observation about the parable of the Prodigal Son. What do you think about his comment?

- There are many things high schoolers can be in bondage to. What are some of them?

- God wants us to experience fullness of life. Why do you think God made us with the ability to experience pleasure?

What If?   The Big Picture

- Most people don't think of the word *freedom* when they think of God. What has to happen for people to see that true freedom exists in a relationship with Jesus?

- Why do so many Christians think being a Christian is more about rules than being free? Do you ever think this?

- Saying God wants us to be free sounds nice and sweet, but what difference does it make to understand the freedom he has for us? How would your walk with him change?

So What?   It's Your Life

- What are some of the things we can do to stop living in bondage and begin living in freedom?

- Death is a painful reality for many of us. How can we gain a proper perspective of death and see it as the beginning, not the end?

- What would it take for us to see God wants us to enjoy life? How can we remove the obstacles that tell us being a believer is boring and for losers?

- What are some things you can do this week to live freely as God offers?

It's Morphing Time!

Primary theme transformation	
Themes prayer, spiritual disciplines, Bible study, judging others, spiritual growth	
Scripture Romans 8:29; 2 Corinthians 3:18; Galatians 3:1-5	
Approximate length through The Grand Finale 20-25 minutes	

Contributed by **Mark Riddle**

This outline is saved as GTO_15 on the CD-ROM.

T his talk takes a look at spiritual disciplines or spiritual habits—Bible study, prayer, Scripture memorization, worship. Most kids view disciplines negatively as something that has to be done—like taking gross medicine—or as a way to earn brownie points with God. "If I read my Bible then God will like me. If I don't, God will be mad at me and not love me as much."

These ideas come from a distorted view of God or poor teaching and lead to a faith based in works—which is surprisingly common among teenagers. Spiritual disciplines are more about transformation than information. This talk can be tailored to different kinds of students regardless of their exposure to Christianity. You could use it with church kids or kids who are visiting. It's also effective with student leaders.

You'll need

- 🔊 Kai's Power Goo morphing software program or a similar one
- 🔊 Computer
- 🔊 Pictures of your teens
- 🔊 Three or four student volunteers to act in charades
- 🔊 TV and VCR
- 🔊 *Aladdin*
- 🔊 A personal story about trying to change someone or something
- 🔊 Marathon runner to explain training
- 🔊 Copies of **Habits Help** (pages 147-148) for each student
- 🔊 Pencils and paper for students (optional)

intro

The Opening Act

🔊 **Activity** *Morphin' Me* (see sidebar)

🔊 **Activity** *Morphing Charades* (see sidebar)

🔊 Ask your students what they would change about themselves—just one thing. Give examples of things they might what to change like looks, clothes, money, friends, or popularity.

🔊 Then ask what they would change about their spiritual life. Things like lying too much, not spending enough time with God, sinning too much, having too much guilt.

🔊 Then say something like—

> **Do you have a sense deep down that something is missing? That you're not all you were created to be? That God has something more in mind for you? Well, he does. God wants to morph—to transform—you into something new!**

Activity

Morphin' me

Use *Kai's Power Goo* morphing software or another program to morph kids' faces into celebrities. Have them try to be the first to guess who the celebrity is.

Activity

Morphing charades

Have volunteers act out one thing that becomes another thing—

- Caterpillar (butterfly)
- Tadpole (frog)
- Bat (vampire)
- Person (werewolf)
- Dr. Jekyll (Mr. Hyde)

Volunteers act out the premorphed clue, but the group has to guess what the post-morphed answer is.

heart of the talk

The Main Event

1 What is spiritual morphing?

- **Movie clip** *Aladdin* (see sidebar)
- Morphing is God working in us—changing us from the inside out—to be more like Jesus.
- **Scripture** *2 Corinthians 3:18* ("And we… are being transformed into his likeness")
- **Object lesson** *Transformer Toys* (see sidebar)
- God wants to transform you into something new. That's good news because for most of us—if we're honest—there are grimy parts that we want to get rid of.

Movie clip

Aladdin

Start 35:00 "Why, you hairy little thief!"

Stop 39:30 Neon applause sign flashes over the genie.

In the most memorable scene from Disney's animated comedy *Aladdin*, the genie (Robin Williams) explains his powers to Aladdin through a spectacular song and dance number—during which he morphs into dozens of objects and characters.

Object lesson

Transformer toys

Remind your students of the transformer toys they used to have as kids—or if you want to use this as an object lesson, hold one up. Remind them how this little thing may have started out—for example—as a tiger, but after twisting a few parts it became a flying superhero with a built-in bazooka.

2   Most people want to change; few know how.

- ◀) **Personal illustration** *I Wanna Change!* (see sidebar)

- ◀) **Quote** *Søren Kierkegaard* "Now with God's help I will become myself."

- ◀) We're pretty lousy at changing ourselves. We can't choose to morph.

- ◀) **Scripture** *Galatians 3:1-5* ("After beginning with the Spirit, are you now trying to attain your goal by human effort?") Paul calls the Galatian church "fools." That's pretty strong language. He says they're idiots to think they can change themselves with their own efforts.

- ◀) God wants you to trust him to change you more than he wants you to try to fix yourself.

- ◀) When you trust him to change you, he will! But when you try to fix yourself, the change won't last.

Personal illustration

I wanna change!

Tell a funny personal story of a time you tried to change someone or something. Use a story from childhood or your teen years if possible.

One youth worker told how, when he was young, he tried to change his brother into a cow. He would put a long rope around his little brother's neck and drag him around the house yelling, "C'mon, cow!"

3   So how does this morphing thing work?

📢   Most often God brings about spiritual change through positive spiritual habits.

📢   Brainstorm spiritual habits (disciplines)—

prayer	service	confession	study
Bible reading	meditation	mentoring	simplicity
solitude	submission	Ffasting	worship

📢   Ask your students to name other spiritual habits they can think of.

📢   What habits aren't—

- Spiritual habits aren't a way to earn brownie points with God.

- Spiritual habits aren't a ticket to heaven.

- Spiritual habits aren't boring and painful—or at least they don't have to be.

📢   What habits are—

- Spiritual habits create an atmosphere for God to change us.

- **Illustration** *Greenhouse* (see sidebar)

- Spiritual habits are like training.

- **Illustration** *Marathons* (see sidebar)

📢   **Scripture** *Romans 8:29* ("Conformed to the likeness of his Son")

📢   We can't morph ourselves, but we can choose to be disciplined about spending time with God—giving him the opportunity to morph us.

Illustration

Greenhouse

Explain—or ask students to explain—the purpose of a greenhouse. Of course the purpose is to control as many plant-growing variables as possible—light, temperature, humidity, water—to create a perfect environment for growth. Spiritual habits are a greenhouse for us—they create an environment for spiritual growth.

Illustration

Marathons

Remind students that, if they're going to succeed at anything, they have to prepare and train for it. Ask what preparation they would need if they were going to run in a marathon. Have a marathon runner give a short word about her preparation routine.

Afterward make the connection (that should already be obvious)—spiritual habits act as preparation for the morphing work God wants to do in our lives.

closing

The Grand Finale

📢 Say something like—

> **God loves you as you are—you don't need to change to "get his love working." Stop trying to win God's approval by doing things for him. Instead God wants you to fix your attention on getting to know him. Take some time this week to begin developing spiritual habits or to find a spiritual mentor. It's morphing time!**

📢 **Take-home item** *Habits Help* Hand out copies of **Habits Help** (pages 147-148). It suggests a bunch of different spiritual habits students might want to try.

📢 **Activity** *Time Alone with God* (see sidebar)

Activity

Time alone with God

Nothing makes the point that we need to develop habits better than giving students an opportunity to try them. Allow kids 15 to 30 minutes alone. Encourage them to spread out and sit where someone else won't be a distraction. If they've never spent time just listening to God, encourage them to try that. You might want to give them a verse to meditate on or some paper and a pen to journal some thoughts. After the time is finished, debrief with these questions.

- **Which habits did you try? How'd it go?**

- **Which verses did you read?**

- **How did you sense God working in you during your time with him?**

- **Was it hard to concentrate for that long? Why or why not?**

- **What distractions did you experience? How did you deal with them?**

- **Where would the perfect place be for you to have time alone with God this week?**

discussion

Encore

Get It?	Middle School

🔊 It's not like your face is going to morph into someone else's face! So what did I mean by morphing?

🔊 Why does God wants to morph you?

🔊 Sometimes people feel guilty for not having a devotional time with God. Why do people feel that way? Have you ever felt like that?

🔊 Think about how you've grown in your relationship with God. What have been some things that have helped you?

🔊 What is the point of spending time alone with God? Why does it matter if you do or don't?

Get It?	High School

🔊 What's spiritual morphing? How does it work?

🔊 Are people who have devotional times more spiritual than people who don't? Why do you think that? Have you ever felt that way?

🔊 Have you ever thought reading your Bible was a way to make God like you more? Do you still think that? Explain.

🔊 What are some ways God has changed you in the past year?

🔊 What does it means that God wants you to trust him to change you more than he wants you to try and fix yourself?

🔊 Would you say you—

- Trust God to change you?
- Try to change yourself?
- Try a little of both?

🔊 Explain why you trust God or why you try to change yourself.

What If?   The Big Picture

- Which spiritual habits—if any—do you practice right now? What might God be calling you to change starting today?

- What might happen if you began each day by inviting God to make you more like him? How might you change? What might you be like one year from now?

- What difference does it make to know God loves you as you are, even if you don't make spiritual habits a regular thing in your life?

- How can you make sure these habits don't become boring and empty?

So What?   It's Your Life

- What does it mean for your life if God wants to change you—to morph you into someone new, someone more like him?

- All this talk about fixing our attention on God and allowing him to change us—doesn't God want us to try to do good things? Explain.

- What is the difference between letting God change you and trying to changing yourself?

- Try a new spiritual discipline this week. Which one? Why that one? When?

Habits Help

You might look at this paper and wonder how you'll ever do it all. Well, don't sweat it—you won't! These are just ideas to help you develop spiritual habits in your life that God can use to transform you to be more like him. Find one or two that fit you—then make a plan.

Find a spiritual mentor.

Getting a spiritual mentor is a great starting point. This person helps you find balance and help you be realistic about your plan.

- Your mentor might be your youth minister, pastor, Sunday school teacher, small group leader, or another Christian adult.
- Meet with your mentor regularly.
- Have your mentor pray for you regularly.
- Create a plan with your mentor for developing spiritual disciplines.
- Have your mentor hold you accountable.

Find time to be alone with God.

It's up to you to make it happen.

- Find time each day to practice spiritual disciplines.
- Schedule time—put it in your daily planner.
- Turn the TV and music off sometimes—have a dose of silence.
- Participate in a retreat of solitude, prayer, worship, and journaling.

Pray.

Pray at scheduled times for longer periods and at unscheduled times all the time!

- Tell God how great he is.
- Confess when you haven't been so great and ways you've messed up.
- Thank God for all he's done.
- Tell God about what you would like from him.
  - Ask for help, courage, strength, power, and self-control.
  - Pray for family, friends, school, anything—even your future spouse.
  - Pray for any other needs you have.

From *Great Talk Outlines for Youth Ministry* by Mark Oestreicher. Permission to reproduce this page granted only for use in the buyer's own youth group. www.YouthSpecialties.com

Serve someone beside yourself.

If you want to learn how to love others, one of the best ways is to serve them. Spend time meditating or praying while you're doing this
service. God might use it as a great time to speak to you!

- Mow a neighbor's yard for free.
- Do the dishes at your house for a week—or a day—without being asked.
- Clean your parents' bathroom.
- Find a homeless person and give him some food.
- Baby-sit one of your youth group volunteer's kids for free.
- Pay for someone's gas at the station without them knowing it was you.

Journal.

Put your thoughts and prayers on paper!

- Write a letter to God.
- Write about what God is telling you each day.
- Write about what you're learning in the Bible or what you think about your youth worker's talk this week.
- Write about how you saw God at work in your world today.
- Draw a picture that represents what God is doing in your life.
- Write about people who've made a difference in your spiritual life. (You can even send them a copy!)

Study the Bible.

Look closer at God's letter to you.

- Get a Bible study guide that has you read Scripture—not just cute little stories—and investigate what the passages mean.
- Ask your spiritual mentor to suggest verses you could spend time studying.
- Get a Bible that's easy to use in a translation you can understand.

Get creative.

- Memorize Scripture.
- Throw a party celebrating what God has done in your life.
- Go for walks where you can listen to God.
- Go to church with your parents.
- Get involved in a Bible study or ministry with people older than you. Older people often have great spiritual wisdom!

Footloose and Fence-Free

Contributed by **Billy Phenix**

Primary theme God's commands	
Themes discipleship, obedience to God, trusting God, God's love	
Scripture Proverbs 3:1-2; John 14:23; 2 John 1:5-6	
Approximate length through The Grand Finale 25-30 minutes	

You'll need

- 🔊 TV and VCR
- 🔊 *Jumanji*
- 🔊 An instruction guide or owner's manual from something complicated to put together or operate
- 🔊 A NO TRESPASSING sign from a hardware store (optional)
- 🔊 A portion of an actual metal or wooden fence (optional)
- 🔊 Unleavened bread and grape juice or whatever elements your church uses for communion (optional)

Most teenagers hate to be told what to do. So the idea that God has commands for us to follow can chafe a bit! Most non-Christians—especially teenage non-Christians—view Christianity as a restrictive set of rules. Nothing more. Sadly many Christian teens live with a surprisingly similar mindset. This talk uses fences as a metaphor for God's rules and commands and helps students understand why God gives us directions and commandments in the Scriptures. It brings out God's desire for us to be truly joyful, safe, and intimate with him by staying near him.

The metaphor of fences as the guidelines God puts around our lives requires abstract thinking—and some young teens won't quite understand this. If you have sixth-graders, especially, you may find you have a few kids who think you're talking about literal fences. You'll have to make sure your young listeners understand what you're talking about, or this talk will do more harm than good!

intro
The Opening Act

🔊 Ask what would happen if—in the middle of a weekday—all the fences at the zoo collapsed and the animals began to run free through the city. Spend a little time making a list of all the things that might happen.

🔊 **Movie clip** *Jumanji* (see sidebar)

🔊 Then transition by saying something like—

> **Many people perceive fences as negative. Fences hold them in. They block their path. They create boundaries that limit their freedom.**
>
> **If we think of the rules God has for us as fences— we often have the same reaction. God's the cosmic killjoy putting up random fences to mess up our lives and make them boring. So we're going to take a look at why God puts those fences in our lives. We'll look at the results of ignoring the guidelines God lays out for us and climbing over the fence!**

🔊 **Movie clip** *Mighty Joe Young* (optional, see sidebar)

Movie clip

Jumanji

Start 1:06:45 People run screaming through the alley.

Stop 1:07:35 The last rhino runs off after the other animals.

In this movie about a board game gone wrong, little Peter (Bradley Pierce) must hide in a car during a terrifying stampede of wild animals.

It's a short clip, but it paints a great mental picture. Follow the clip by pointing out how much destruction happens when things run wild in our lives.

Mighty Joe Young

If you're using this talk on a retreat—or another time when you have an extended amount of time—consider showing this movie in its entirety before you speak. Just be sure you show the new *Mighty Joe Young*, not the old one! And make sure you screen it first—there may be some scenes you don't want to show. You could simply show the significant scenes and fast-forward through the rest.

This movie illustrates the points of this talk—Joe Young, the ape, represents you and me; the caretaker represents God; and the bad guys represent Satan.

After pushing his limits and causing lots of trouble, Joe finally ends up in a very lush, very large pen at the end of the movie. It even has enough room to roam—but it still has boundaries!

heart of the talk

The Main Event

1   When we run free we hurt others!

- 🔊 Ask what would happen to an elephant running loose in a big city. Get a bunch of answers before moving on.

- 🔊 God puts fences up in our lives in the form of his commands and scriptural advice. This godly instruction keeps us out of places we shouldn't be and in places that are safe!

- 🔊 It isn't because the zookeeper wants to ruin the elephant's life that he keeps the elephant from running around the city!

- 🔊 Ask students to name some of the fences God doesn't want us to hop over.

- 🔊 **Illustration** *The Trackless Train* (see sidebar)

- 🔊 **Scripture** *Proverbs 3:1-2* ("Keep my commands in your heart, for they will prolong your life many years and bring you prosperity.") Ask what the writer means by prosperity.

The trackless train

A train is unlike a car in the sense that it's forced to follow the train tracks. On one hand that might seem like a bummer and like a lack of freedom. But think of the other option! Take a speeding train off the tracks and what do you have? You have a horrible train wreck with cars piled on top of each other. The tracks are the guides that keep the train from destroying itself. God's commands are our guides—to keep us from destroying ourselves!

2   When we run free we hurt others!

- ◀))   Ask what danger the zoo-free elephant would pose to others in the city. Field a few answers.

- ◀))   In the same way when we break through God's guidelines for our lives, those around us get hurt.

- ◀))   **Object lesson** *Have You Seen the Instructions?* (see sidebar)

- ◀))   **Scripture** *2 John 1:5-6* ("I ask that we love one another…that we walk in obedience to his commands.")

Object lesson

Have you seen the instructions?

Find an instruction book or owner's manual for something a bit complicated—if you don't keep any of this stuff and can't find anything, you should be able to find something online. An owner's manual for a car, computer, cell phone, VCR, or television would work well. Show how the manufacturer took time to write down all the instructions. We're given the do's and don'ts so we won't ruin the object and so we can know how it works! God has given us his instructions in the Bible so we know how relationships work and so we won't mess them up and hurt others.

3   When we run free we run away from the one who takes cares of us!

- ◀))   Ask what the elephant's caretaker is thinking and feeling while the elephant is rampaging the city. Field a few answers—don't settle for, "He'd be sad."

- ◀))   God has given us commands so we'll remain close to him.

- ◀))   His commands are there to protect our relationship with him.

- ◀))   If we break his commands and jump the fence, we can become distant from God.

- ◀))   **Scripture** *John 14:23* ("If anyone loves me, he will obey my teaching. My Father will love him, and we will come to him and make our home with him.") Ask what it means to make our home with God. Then get a few answers before closing.

closing
The Grand Finale

- 🔊 Have students discuss why some of God's fences—get specific—are in our best interest.

- 🔊 **Reflection** *Straightening the Boundaries* (see sidebar)

- 🔊 A great way to help your students remember God's fences would be to let them physically acknowledge his boundaries.

    Activity *No Trespassing!* (optional, see sidebar)

    Activity *Reverse Fence-Hopping* (optional, see sidebar)

- 🔊 Close by saying something like—

    God has given us commands and rules for a reason. They protect us. They protect those around us. And they keep our relationship with God—our caretaker—strong. If we don't understand this, we'll probably jump the fence because we don't understand its purpose. The result is that our lives will run recklessly out of control and away from the safety of God's loving arms.

Reflection

Straightening the boundaries

Have students spend a couple minutes in silence, thinking about which of God's fences they've been jumping lately. Invite them to ask forgiveness and to pray about staying within God's boundaries.

Activity

No trespassing!

Pick up a NO TRESPASSING sign at a hardware store. After your students spend time in silent prayer, offer them the opportunity to come forward and—using a marker—sign the sign as a show of spiritual commitment. Hang the sign in the youth areas so it can be seen each week as a reminder of this commitment.

Activity

Reverse fence-hopping

This takes a bit more set-up, but could be cool—especially at a retreat or extended event. Set up an actual fence of some sort, made of metal or wood. Have the fence up in front throughout your talk—stand alongside it, point to it. Then after students have spent time in silent prayer, asking forgiveness for fence jumping, ask them to symbolize—if they want to—their commitment to God to come back over to the protected side of his fence. They can do this by coming up and climbing over the fence.

Encourage them to really envision the other side of the fence as God's side. You might even consider having communion elements on the other side, and allow students an opportunity to consecrate their reverse fence-hopping with communion.

discussion

Encore

Get It?	Middle School

🔊 What do we mean by fences? What are some of the fences God puts around our lives?

🔊 What—or who—suffers when we hop over God's commands for us? (Hint: It's the three main points we just talked about.)

🔊 When we ignore God's commands, how can we get hurt?

🔊 When we ignore God's commands, how can we hurt those around us?

🔊 When we ignore God's commands, how does it affect God?

🔊 In what way is the Bible the instruction book for our lives?

🔊 God has said if we keep his commands, we will remain close to him. Why is that so important?

Get It?   High School

- We all like freedom. Freedom is good. So what's the danger of too much freedom?

- Why does God give us the freedom to break his commands? Why didn't he just make us like those dogs with little electric collars that get shocked when they get near the fence?

- When we ignore God's commands, how can we get hurt?

- In what ways are God's commands there to protect those around us?

- How does our defiance of God hurt our relationship with him?

- What does God tell us to do when we're on the wrong side of one of his commandments?

- What are some of God's off-limit areas your friends seem to struggle with?

What If?   The Big Picture

- Okay, let's be honest—is staying on God's side of the fence that big of a deal? Talk about that.

- Share a time in your life when you went trespassing over a fence God has commanded us not to cross and either you or someone around you got hurt—physically or emotionally.

- You can hurt God by wandering away from him . How does this idea strike you? Is it fair? Does it cause a major guilt trip? Explain your thinking.

- What do people struggle with more—knowing God's commands or following them? Why do you say that?

- How would your life be different—in positive or negative ways—if you never ever crossed one of God's fences?

So What?   It's Your Life

- 📢 What are some of the ways we, as a group, can help each other stay within God's commands?

- 📢 How can we know God's commands better? What will you do this week? (Don't allow Sunday-school answers on this one—push kids to be honest.)

- 📢 Is there someone you've hurt by fence-jumping recently? What can you do to make this right?

- 📢 Which fences would you be willing to have help with? With which would you say, "I need your strength on this one—I want to jump it." What will you do this week to keep this commitment? What behavior in your life needs to change or something that will help you stay on the God-side of the fence?

- 📢 What role does prayer have in your ability to keep God's commands?

Taking Off Your Mask

Contributed by **Dave Ambrose**

Primary theme hypocrisy	
Themes honesty, being real, judging others, depending on God	
Scripture Psalms 139:1-8; Jeremiah 2:22-23; Matthew 23:25-26; Luke 12:1; 18:9-14; Ephesians 5:8-14; Hebrews 10:22	
Approximate length through The Grand Finale 35 minutes	

Eugene Peterson said many of us go through life impersonating ourselves. He was shining a flashlight on the natural tendency we all have to wear masks, to put forth an image of ourselves that isn't truthful to manipulate how people respond to us. This outline lays that idea on the table so you can talk about it with your students.

But be warned—if you want your students to remove their masks and talk honestly, you have to lead the way by doing the same.

You'll need

- A stereo
- "Faceless Man" on the album *Human Clay* by Creed (Wind Up, 1999)
- TV and VCR
- *My Best Friend's Wedding*
- A personal story about being hypocritical
- *Indiana Jones and the Last Crusade*
- A packet of yeast
- *Powder*
- One or two inexpensive masks—freaky work better than funny
- *The Truman Show*
- Pencils and paper for students
- Mask-making supplies—paper plates, construction paper, markers, string, glitter, scissors, glue, etc.

intro

The Opening Act

🔊 Ask students to describe a time in their life when they felt a certain way inside but acted differently on the outside.

🔊 **Song** *"Faceless Man"* by Creed (see sidebar)

🔊 **Movie clip** *My Best Friend's Wedding* (see sidebar)

🔊 **Scripture** *Luke 18:9-14* (see sidebar)

🔊 **Personal illustration** *I'm a Hypocrite!* Share an experience from your life when you were hypocritical.

🔊 **Scripture** *Matthew 23:25-26* ("You clean the outside of the cup and the dish, but inside they are full of greed.") God cares deeply about our "insides" and has no tolerance for hypocrisy, as evidenced by Jesus' statement to the Pharisees.

🔊 Transition by saying something like—

> **Lots of people get turned off toward Christ because they see Christians who act like hypocrites. They see Christians living one way at church and then acting differently in school or on the job. Most people don't want anything to do with this bogus religion and who can blame them? This counterfeit religion drove Jesus crazy too! Let's take a closer look at how we can avoid playing the pretend game.**

Song

"Faceless Man"

"Faceless Man" is a song about a man struggling with his identity. Consider projecting the lyrics so your kids can follow along. This song can help students think about the many times they act one way on the outside when they feeling differently on the inside.

Ask students to identify with this so-called faceless man. Ask—

- **Why do you think he describes himself as a faceless man when so much is going on inside of him?**

- **How is this like hypocrisy?**

My Best Friend's Wedding

Start 1:23:01 Julianne sees Michael sitting alone in the train station.

Stop 1:26:07 "Well, that part I knew."

Julianne Potter (Julia Roberts) has just flown to Chicago to help her best friend Michael (Dermot Mulroney) with wedding preparations. But what she really wants is to tell him she's in love with him and he's marrying the wrong person. By the time she gets the courage to tell him the truth, she's already done every despicable thing she can to break up his engagement.

Ask—

- **Why didn't Julianne tell Michael how she felt in the first place?**

- **Why do you think she put on a front?**

Luke 18:9-14

This is the parable of the Pharisee and the tax collector. Of course the tax collector understands his need for God and cries out for God to have mercy on him. The Pharisee, on the other hand, thinks he's perfect and has no awareness of his messed up and judgmental attitudes. Ask students why they think the Pharisee would be considered hypocritical. And what can we do to keep ourselves from falling into the hypocrisy trap?

heart of the talk

The Main Event

1   Be honest with yourself.

- If you're pretending to be a goody-goody Christian but you ignore the sin in your life, you need to start by telling yourself the truth about your condition.

- **Scripture** *Jeremiah 2:22-23* (see sidebar)

- **Movie clip** *Indiana Jones and the Last Crusade* (see sidebar)

- **Illustration** *Yeast* (see sidebar)

Scripture

Jeremiah 2:22-23

Read these verses from the NASB, if possible. (Several translations are available at www.gospelcom.net; click on Bible Gateway.) The simple little phrase *know what you have done* is packed with meaning. Before you explain these concepts, however, ask students what they think the biblical phrase means—what did the prophet Jeremiah want us to understand? Author Kathleen Norris says, "It's so much easier to live not knowing what we've done." In other words—it's very easy to deny who we are, even to ourselves.

Movie clip

Indiana Jones and the Last Crusade

Start 1:49:53 Indy crawls into the room where the Holy Grail is kept.

Stop 1:54:53 "You have chosen wisely."

While on yet another adventure, Indiana Jones (Harrison Ford) has to quickly pick the Holy Grail from a room full of chalices. It is the cup Jesus used at the last supper, presumed to have healing powers. There are many fancy cups in the room—which look great on the outside—but Indiana correctly chooses the plain looking cup.

Things aren't always the way they seem on the outside. Challenge students to learn to be honest with who they know themselves to be both on the inside and the outside.

Illustration

Yeast

Hold up a packet of yeast—it's in the baking section of the grocery store—and ask if someone can explain what yeast does. In case no one knows, explain yeast is an active fungus that causes bread to rise. Explain if you leave some bread dough mixed with yeast in a warm place, it will continue to expand.

Then explain that in Luke 12:1 Jesus compared hypocrisy with yeast. He said it only takes a small amount of yeast to seep into your recipe and affect the whole loaf. And it's the same, Jesus says, with our spiritual lives—hypocrisy starts when we lie to ourselves about what we're really like. And it spreads like a cancer from there.

2 Be transparent with others.

🔊 Being transparent means letting people see the real you—faults and all!

🔊 This transparency feels risky and uncomfortable. But it allows you to live in freedom and makes it easier for you to affirm your dependence on God.

🔊 **Movie clip** *Powder* (see sidebar)

🔊 **Object lesson** *Mask* (see sidebar)

🔊 **Scripture** *Ephesians 5:8-14* ("Live as children of light.") God's desire that we be honest and transparent with each other isn't only because of his obsession with honesty. It's also because he loves us and wants what's in our best interest.

Movie clip

Powder

Start 1:20:00 "Why don't we just tell 'em all to stop and they can take our picture?"

Stop 1:24:55 Powder and Lindsey kiss.

Powder (Sean Patrick Flanery) is a boy with an unusual ability to look inside a person's soul and understand the feelings within. In this clip the tables are turned when Powder must attempt to express his own feelings and emotions to Lindsey (Missy Crider) who cares deeply about him.

This illustrates the importance of being transparent. Explain to your students that the ability to share our thoughts and emotions helps build security and safety into our relationships.

Object lesson

Mask

Go to a costume shop or a large toy store and purchase an inexpensive mask or two. Slightly freaky masks—as opposed to silly masks—will make your point better. Put the mask on during the *Powder* video clip, so students are a bit surprised to see you.

Talk for a few moments about how we all wear masks on a regular basis, trying to get people to think we're different than we are. You might have to explain this metaphor a bit if you're speaking to young teens—one of them will undoubtedly think you're talking about actual Halloween masks! Ask—

• **What kind of masks do your peers wear?**

• **Why do we put on masks from time to time?**

• **What are the masks that you wear?**

3   Be honest with God.

🔊 This means admitting to God how much you need him every day, in every area of your life.

🔊 **Scripture** *Hebrews 10:22* ("Let us draw near to God with a sincere heart in full assurance of faith.") God wants you to come to him with a sincere heart. You don't have to clean up your act before coming to God. He'll take us the way we are. It's a waste of time to try to fake out God!

🔊 **Illustration** *Without Wax* (see sidebar)

🔊 **Scripture** *Psalm 139:1-8* ("O Lord, you have searched me and you know me.") Share with your students David's honesty with God in these verses.

Illustration

Without wax

The word *sincere* comes from a Latin word meaning "without wax." Long ago when potters would craft certain pottery out of clay and allow it to dry and harden in the sun, the heat would produce small cracks, barely visible with the naked eye. To still sell their creations, the craftsman would use melted wax and rub it into the cracks to make the surface appear smooth. When you bought a sincere pot you bought one without wax—no cracks and no mask to cover them up.

closing

The Grand Finale

🔊 **Movie clip** *The Truman Show* (see sidebar)

🔊 **Reflection** *Time Alone* (see sidebar)

🔊 **Activity** *Mask Making* (see sidebar)

Movie clip

The Truman Show

Start 29:25 "Looks like another beautiful day, but don't forget to buckle up out there…"

Stop 34:32 Truman runs into the market.

Truman Burbank (Jim Carrey) is just beginning to realize he's been watched his entire life. This scene follows him around town as this realization makes him increasingly more paranoid and anxious.

Ask students how it would affect their honesty and transparency if they knew they were constantly being watched.

Time alone

Have your students spend five to 30 minutes alone—depending on how much time you have and how long you think they can handle! Challenge them to lay it on the line and be completely honest with God about the stuff going on in their lives, about their need for him, about their doubts and hopes. Then invite them to write down—in the form of a letter—how they think God would respond to them.

Mask making

Make craft materials available to your students—colored paper, markers, crayons, string, scissors, glue—and ask them to design a mask that represents how they want people to perceive them. On the other side of the mask, ask them to create something representing how they really feel or are. In small groups have students share and explain their mask creations.

discussion

Encore

Get It?	Middle School

 What's hypocrisy? How would Jesus define it?

 You already know yourself, so how can you be honest with yourself? What does *be honest with yourself* mean and what does it look like?

 What's it look like when people aren't honest with themselves? How does it show up?

 What does it mean to be transparent with other people?

 How about being honest with God—what's that look like? If God knows everything already, what's the point of not being honest? In what ways do people try to be dishonest with God?

Get It?   High School

🔊 Ask a willing volunteer to describe a time when she acted hypocritically.

🔊 What would happen if we all had TV monitors on our heads showing all of our thoughts? How would that change your behavior?

🔊 Have students explain the three main phrases in their own words.
- Be honest with yourself.
- Be transparent with others.
- Be honest with God.

What If?   The Big Picture

🔊 We're all hypocritical from time to time. Why is it so tempting to act this way? What can we gain from acting hypocritically?

🔊 What advice would you give to someone who's struggling with being hypocritical?

🔊 Why do you think so many people believe they have to clean up their lives before God will accept them?

🔊 Do you think it's possible to be sincere and still be wrong? Give an example.

🔊 Why is it so difficult to allow people to see who we really are? What's the risk of being transparent with people?

🔊 Describe a time when you felt that someone judged you simply by what they saw on the outside, instead of taking the time to find out what was going on inside. How did you respond to the other person? How did you respond on the inside?

🔊 How does it affect you to know God sees inside you and knows your motives?

So What?　　　　　It's Your Life

🔊 *Character is who you are when no one is watching you.* What do you think about that statement?

🔊 How can you bring all parts of you—who you are in front of your parents, who you are at school, who you are with your friends, who you are at church, who you are when you're alone—into alignment? In other words what can you do to remove your mask and be the same person all the time?

🔊 Imagine you could give someone a truth serum to make them tell the truth about everything—what motivates them, what they really think, what they really feel. Of all the people in the world, who would you choose to give this serum to? What do you suspect you would find out?

🔊 Who would you least want to be around if you took a truth serum? Why?

🔊 Being honest with yourself is hard. What are some ways you can move toward honesty with yourself?

🔊 Is there one person or a group of people with whom you've been acting especially hypocritical lately? What can you do about it this week?

🔊 How can you have a more sincere relationship with God this week? What action steps will you take to get this change started?

Parent Impact

Contributed by **Gregg Farah**

Primary theme parents	
Themes family, obedience to parents, respect, perspective, influence	
Scripture Exodus 20:12; Ephesians 6:1; 1 Timothy 4:12	
Approximate length through The Grand Finale 30 minutes	

Some of the students in your group probably have a fantastic relationship with their parents. But many—if not most—experience some strain as they go through their teen years. And teenagers have a tendency to assume the remedy to this strain lies primarily with their parents: If they'd just do this…If they'd stop doing that. But the reality is, your students can have an enormously positive impact on their relationships with their parents by following God's commands and suggestions.

This talk makes some assumptions—the primary one being your students have parents who are at least nominally interested in their children. This is, unfortunately, not always the case. If you're aware of any extremely unhealthy family situations in your group, it would be good to debrief this talk with those students afterward. Or maybe have the whole group process what honoring and obeying your parents looks like for someone whose parents seriously mistreat them. Be cautious not to extend the damage many churches have done over the years by saying or implying a good Christian ignores an abusive situation in the name of forgiveness.

You'll need

- Five or six pairs of shoes with different functions—construction boots, house slippers, bowling shoes, tap shoes, baseball cleats, sneakers, etc.
- TV and VCR
- *National Lampoon's Vacation*
- Bag of bite-sized candy bars
- Whiteboard and markers
- A student volunteer to share about obeying his parents at a time he didn't want to
- A list of commands for Simon Says
- *The Lion King*
- Two or three students to share how they have set an example at home
- Several student volunteers to role-play parent-child relationships
- A single shoelace to send home with each student
- Copies of **Would You Rather…?** (page 176), one for each student

intro

The Opening Act

◀》 **Object lesson** *Shoes* (see sidebar)

◀》 **Movie clip** *National Lampoon's Vacation* (see sidebar)

◀》 **Discussion** *Parental Pop Quiz* (see sidebar)

◀》 Transition to the main points by saying something like—

> **It's easy to complain about parents—I used to complain about mine too. But what would happen if we put energy into strengthening our relationship with them? It's not as easy as complaining, but it's more effective. Today we're going to focus on developing a relationship with our parents, whether they're biological, step, or adoptive parents. The truth is you can have a huge impact on the quality of your relationship with your parents by following God's plan.**

Object lesson

Shoes

Ask students what the phrase *take a walk in another person's shoes* means. A simple definition is "to understand another person's perspective on life." Display an assortment of footwear.

Invite students to speculate what it might be like to be the owner of each pair of shoes. Follow up by having students share what it might be like to be a parent of a teenager today. Ask them to rate (1 to 10) how well they understand their parents.

Movie clip

National Lampoon's Vacation

Start 1:21:25 "First ones here!"

Stop 1:23:25 "Clark, what are you doing?"

After driving cross-country for two weeks, the Griswold family finally makes it to Wally World — America's favorite theme park—only to find it closed. In this scene Clark Griswold (Chevy Chase) proves himself to be a loving father—yet completely lacking in any common sense.

Most kids think their parents are a bit strange and hard to understand at least once in a while. Have kids share stories about strange things their parents have done—stories they'd be willing to tell if their parents were in the room.

After watching the scene ask students—

True or false: *I don't understand my parents.* **Support and explain your answer.**

Parental pop quiz

Have a bag of bite-sized candy handy and ask a variety of questions to see how well students know the little stuff about their parents. Toss a piece of candy to anyone who answers correctly—you'll have to take their word for it or do some research ahead of time! Use questions like—

- **What's your mother's favorite thing to do?**
- **Where does your father like to hang out?**
- **What's the first thing your mom does at work each day?**
- **What's your father's favorite ice cream flavor?**
- **What's your mom's favorite TV show?**

heart of the talk

The Main Event

1   Be honorable—honor your parents.

- Sometimes we fool ourselves into thinking we understand the world better than our parents.

- Parents have a major advantage over you—life experience.

- **Illustration** *Seven-Year-Old's Dinner* (see sidebar)

- **Scripture** *Exodus 20:12* ("Honor your father and mother.") Ask students to define what it means to honor parents. Then have them suggest ways they can do it. Write these down on a whiteboard.

- **Illustration** *Ice Cream with Lincoln* (see sidebar) Non-American speakers should substitute a commonly respected person from their own country.

- Sometimes honoring people—our parents included—feels weird because our culture puts such a high value on everyone being equal that we've lost our understanding of how to honor people.

Seven-year-old's dinner

You're baby-sitting a seven-year-old and feeding him dinner. There's a jar of cookies and candy on the kitchen counter, beside the veggies and pasta you're supposed to make for him. If you let the kid pick what he wants to eat, he'll go for the all-candy, all-cookie diet. But you—with your massive life experience—know he'll probably puke if he only eats junk. Your life experience gives you a better perspective. (So you feed him the veggies and keep the candy for yourself!) Parents have this same life-experience advantage over you—not just for dinner plans, but in most areas of life.

Ice cream with Lincoln

Sure, Abraham Lincoln—the U.S. president who ended slavery—is dead. But pretend he isn't. And pretend you're sitting down with him at an ice cream shop. He chose a double scoop of rocky road. Abe, as he tells you to call him, is telling you about how difficult it was to stand his ground when he knew it meant leading the nation into civil war.

Do you constantly pipe up and interrupt, telling your own little trivial stories? Of course not—because, after all, he's the president. You want to honor him, show him the respect he deserves, listen to his experience and perspective, and gain everything you can from this moment.

Your parents might not be Abe Lincolns, but they deserve—according to God—this same honor. And just like you'd honor Abe Lincoln at the ice cream shop to make the most of the experience, honor your parents to make the most of your experience with them. It's in your own best interest.

2   Be obedient—obey your parents.

🔊 Our culture has turned obedience into a bad word—like slavery or something. This isn't God's idea of obedience. He wants us to obey our parents because he loves us and wants what's best for us.

🔊 **Activity** *Simon Says* (see sidebar)

🔊 **Movie clip** *The Lion King* (see sidebar)

🔊 **Scripture** *Ephesians 6:1* ("Obey your parents.")

🔊 Obedience is the ultimate sign of respect, because we're communicating that we trust those instructing us, even if we don't agree. Obedience doesn't equal agreement, but it does equal respect.

🔊 **Illustration** Have a student share about a time it was tough to obey his parents but he chose to anyway.

Activity

Simon Says

Play a quick game of Simon Says to set up a group of questions on obedience. Since you need to give commands quickly, it's helpful to have a list written out ahead of time. (Or you can have someone else lead.) When you're done ask—

- **Why is it sometimes difficult to obey the instructions?**
- **What would've made it easier?**
- **Why is it sometimes difficult to obey your parents?**
- **What would make it easier?**

The Lion King

Start 18:00 "This is it. We made it."

Stop 22:25 "I thought you were very brave."

The lion cubs Simba and Nala learn a hard lesson when they deliberately disobey Simba's father and explore the elephant graveyard. The two young cubs discover for themselves why it's so important to obey their parents.

After the clip ask—

- **Why might Simba and Nala have felt it wasn't a big deal to disobey?**

- **What would have happened if the cubs hadn't been rescued?**

- **You'll definitely have times when you disagree with your parents' instructions. What should you do in those times?**

3 Be inspirational—set the example.

- There's no question that improving your relationship with your parents is tough work. But the reward can be great—you could have a major impact on your whole family.

- **Scripture** *1 Timothy 4:12* ("Don't let anyone look down on you because you're young, but set an example.")

- **Illustration** *One Degree of Change* (see sidebar)

- **Illustration** *Student Examples* (see sidebar)

One degree of change

Ask students to imagine a line starting from where you stand and extending out for 100 miles. Now have them imagine bumping the line one degree—just a tiny nudge. One foot away from you, the line would hardly be any different. But if you walked out 50 or 75 of those miles, the difference would be huge! This is the effect students can have on their families. By being an example of love and forgiveness—by obeying, honoring, and respecting their parents—the long-term effects can be huge!

a little difference   a huge difference

Illustration

Student examples

Have two or three students share briefly how they have tried to set an example in their home. You'll want to ask them ahead of time and make sure what they'll say is appropriate and applicable.

closing

The Grand Finale

🔊 Review the main points and check for understanding.

🔊 **Acting out** *What It Might Look Like* (see sidebar)

🔊 **Take-home item** *Shoelaces* (see sidebar)

🔊 **Take-home item** *Would You Rather...?* (see sidebar)

Acting out

What it might look like

Have several students come up front to play the parts of parents and teens. Role-play honoring their parents, obeying their parents, and influencing their parents. Some will want to ham it up—which you can allow to an extent—but try to get them to a point of acting out real responses. They should focus on balancing teens' desire to honor and obey with the reality of wanting their own way.

Take-home item

Shoelaces

Buy a shoelace for each student. (Remember, there are two in a set.) You can substitute pieces of string to represent shoelaces if you need to. Invite students to make a commitment to seeing conflict with their parents from their parents' perspective. Remind them of the discussion you had about walking in their parents' shoes.

Take-home item

Would You Rather...?

Give students copies of **Would You Rather...?** (page 176) and encourage students to use the questions over a meal with their parents to stimulate discussion. The questions are written for students to ask in order to understand their parents' perspective. You could also use this as a discussion tool in your group by having kids predict their parents' answers and talk out their feelings about those probable responses.

discussion

Encore

Get It?	Middle School

- What do I mean when I say "walking in your parents' shoes"?

- What's perspective? What does it have to do with understanding your parents?

- What does it mean to honor your parents? What's that look like?

- Why is it so hard to obey your parents sometimes?

- On a scale of 1 to 10, how hard is it to believe God wants what's best for you when he asks you to obey your parents? Explain your thinking. Do you think God seems a little old-fashioned in this area? How can you overcome those feelings?

- What are some ways to set an example in your home?

Get It? — High School

- How can seeing things from your parents' perspective make a difference in your relationship with them?

- What's the big deal about honoring parents? Why does that seem to be so important? What's it look like in real life?

- Why does obedience seem like such an ugly word to so many people? What does our culture's big-time value of independence have to do with this?

- How is it possible to believe God isn't a bit clueless on this obey your parents stuff? Have you seen any connection between your obedience to your parents and their level of trust in you? Explain your answer.

- How would your parents answer that question?

- Is it appropriate for a teenager to set the example in the home? Why or why not? Describe a time when you influenced your parents. Talk about that.

What If? — The Big Picture

- How do you respond if your parents aren't willing to share much about their lives? What if they don't seem to want a deep relationship with you or don't seem to have time for you?

- What if you don't respect your parents? Is it still possible to honor them? How?

- What would you tell a person who has a terrible relationship with her parents? Where should she start?

- What if someone already has a great relationship with his parents? How would this message apply to him?

- Is it ever okay to disobey your parents? When?

- Suppose a student's parents were divorced and both remarried. Should she focus on one parental relationship first? Talk about that.

- What if your parents disagree? What should you do then?

- In what area of your family life do you think you could change things a little? What difference could that one change make a year from now?

So What? It's Your Life

🔊 Which of the main points is the easiest for you to do? How will you apply that one this week?

🔊 Which of the main points is the most difficult for you? How can you try to apply it this week?

🔊 Will you need help from anyone in particular to make progress on this? Who is it? Who can pray for you? How will you ask them to pray for you in this area?

🔊 Which of the three main points, if you lived it, would make the biggest impact on your relationship with your parents over the next six months? Why?

🔊 When will you ask your parents the **Would You Rather...?** questions?

Would You Rather...?

Sit down with your parents and ask them following questions. You might be surprised by what you learn!

- ✦ Would you rather have me be friendless and home every night or have lots of friends but break curfew all the time?

- ✦ Would you rather see me graduate with high honors and be unemployed for five years or win the lottery and quit school?

- ✦ Would you rather that I have one—and only one—great friend for life or a bunch of good friends for a few years?

- ✦ Would you rather have me get arrested for driving drunk or for selling marijuana?

- ✦ Would you rather have me be intellectually brilliant and solve world problems but live in isolation or be happily ignorant but socially comfortable and well-liked?

- ✦ Would you rather that I grow up to have 20 children or no children?

- ✦ Would you rather that I be a professional athlete or a noted professor?

- ✦ Would you rather have me date someone of another race or be a racist?

- ✦ Would you rather have me grow up to struggle with homosexuality or to struggle with pride?

- ✦ Would you rather that I have faith in God but die at 20 or not have faith and live till I'm 100?

- ✦ Would you rather that I love God and live a lonely and miserable life or ignore God and live a happy and successful life?

God-Sized Love

Contributed by **Dave Ambrose**

Primary theme God's love	
Themes selflessness, kindness, friendship, grace, the gospel	
Scripture Genesis 29:16-20; Proverbs 27:6; Ecclesiastes 4:10; Romans 5:8; 8:38-39	
Approximate length through The Grand Finale 30 minutes	

Admittedly this classic talk is a youth ministry cliché—the *eros, phileo, agape* love thing. But as many times as you may have heard this growing up—or used it as a talk outline in the past—it still has great teaching value for your teenagers.

The Greek words have been pulled out because they don't add much for students, but feel free to stick them back in if you choose—*eros* for the first point, *phileo* for the second, and *agape* for the third.

This talk challenges your students to understand the different ways love can be expressed, all pointing students toward God-sized love and putting it into practice.

You'll need

- TV and VCR
- *The Brady Bunch Movie*
- A stopwatch (optional)
- *William Shakespeare's Romeo and Juliet* (1996)
- A personal story about falling in love
- Two large magnets
- Two pieces of already chewed gum—hopefully yours!—and two pieces of paper
- *Wayne's World*
- Large nails—one for each student
- Valentine's cards signed by God—in your handwriting, of course—for each student
- Two large flowers with petals that are easy to pull off
- Pencils and paper for students

intro

The Opening Act

🔊 **Movie clip** *The Brady Bunch Movie* (see sidebar)

🔊 **Activity** *Songbirds* (see sidebar)

🔊 Play one or two popular songs with lyrics about love. Have the lyrics available for students if possible. Ask your teens to describe the love being sung about.

🔊 Then transition by saying something like—

> **Love comes in many different packages, doesn't it? You might love pizza, but that sure is different than a love for a friend or the love of a lifetime. We're going to take a look at a few different ways we can experience love in our lives. Maybe some of you need to experience love in a bigger way than you've ever imagined. Maybe today you'll discover what it's like to experience a God-sized love!**

Movie clip

The Brady Bunch Movie

Start 10:41 "Okay, troops, time for school!"

Stop 12:45 Jan puts on her glasses and walks out.

This spoof of the classic 70s TV series provides a great clip of an ideal family interacting—albeit absurdly—and solving a problem together over breakfast.

Activity

Songbirds

This is one of those great youth group activities even your more jaded high school students will have fun playing. Divide equally into two to four small groups. Tell them you're going to give each group a chance to sing 10 seconds of a song with the word *love* in its lyrics. Give the groups a couple minutes to brainstorm songs, then point at a group and have them sing in unison. A team is out if they can't think of a song to sing within 10 seconds or if they repeat a song already sung by any team. (A stopwatch will make timing easier.)

heart of the talk

The Main Event

1   Romantic love—"Hey baby, I think I love you!"

- 🔊 Romantic love has to do with attraction. It's the butterflies-in-your-stomach and sweaty-palms thing.

- 🔊 The attraction isn't always physical. Sometimes it's more of an emotional thing.

- 🔊 Christians have often made this variety of love seem like a bad thing—even a sin. But physical attraction is part of how God wired us, and it's a great thing—a gift from God!

- 🔊 This love can motivate you to do wild and crazy things.

- 🔊 **Scripture** *Genesis 29:16-20* (Jacob and Rachel) Jacob was so attracted to Rachel he was willing to serve seven years to be with her and it still only seemed like a few days to him.

- 🔊 **Personal illustration** *Falling in Love* (see sidebar)

- 🔊 **Movie clip** *William Shakespeare's Romeo and Juliet* (see sidebar)

- 🔊 **Object lesson** *When Two Worlds Collide* (see sidebar)

Personal illustration

Falling in love

Tell about a time you fell in love with someone. Describe all of the incredible feelings going on inside when you first saw the person, when you finally met, when you first talked, or even when you went on your first date. Be sure to describe all the feelings your students might feel when they're attracted someone. Play it up and get a little goofy. It would be best if your story included something stupid or silly you did because of your feelings.

Movie clip

William Shakespeare's Romeo and Juliet

Start 28:50 "Did my heart love till now?"

Stop 32:39 Romeo looks up the staircase.

In this trippy, modern version of the classic tale, the star–crossed lovers played by Leonardo DiCaprio and Claire Danes first see each other through a tropical fish tank and continue their flirtation as Juliet tries to escape her mother and her less-than-exciting date.

Object lesson

When two worlds collide

Take two magnets and put them at same polar ends so they repel one another. Explain this is similar to how you tend to react to some people—you're just not compatible or attracted. Then turn one of the magnets around and show how the two are drawn together. This symbolizes the pull you feel to certain people at times—romantic love, or at least a sample of it.

2   Buddy love—"Dude! I love you, man!"

🔊 This is the love you might have for your best friend, a brother or sister, or for your teammates.

🔊 **Scripture** *Proverbs 27:6* ("Wounds from a friend can be trusted, but an enemy multiplies kisses.") Ask students what this verse means.

🔊 **Scripture** *Ecclesiastes 4:10* ("If one falls down, his friend can help him up.") Again, ask students for their interpretations of this verse.

🔊 **Illustration** *Forfeit for a Friend* (see sidebar)

🔊 **Object lesson** *A Sticky Love* (see sidebar)

🔊 **Movie clip** *Wayne's World* (see sidebar)

Illustration

Forfeit for a friend

Kay Poe and Esther Kim grew up as best friends and fierce competitors. Their sport was tae kwon do, and both were hoping to qualify for the U.S. team to the 2000 Sydney Olympics.

In the last moments of her semifinal bout, Kay seriously dislocated her kneecap. But in spite of her serious injury, she fought strongly enough to win a spot in the final qualifying match—against her friend Esther Kim. Esther recalls seeing the coach carrying her friend Kay on his back to the dressing room. The outcome of the final match was a no-brainer. All Esther had to do was show up—her injured friend didn't have a chance.

In a moment of incredible love and sacrifice Esther made a decision. She would bow out of the final match and concede victory to her injured friend. She would give up her Olympic dream so Kay could achieve hers. Telling Kay her plan, Esther said, "Please don't think I'm throwing my dreams away, because I'm not—I'm putting my dreams into you. I want you to fulfill our dreams together."

From *Hot Illustrations for Youth Talks 4*, edited by Wayne Rice (Youth Specialties, 2001).

A sticky love

Have two pieces of paper and a piece of chewed gum ready. Stick the gum between the two pieces of paper. The gum holds those two pieces of paper together just as buddy love holds two friends together.

Wayne's World

Start 18:00 Garth whistles the Star Trek theme into the night sky.

Stop 22:25 The plane flies overhead.

Wayne (Mike Meyers) and Garth (Dana Carvey)—the ultimate heavy-metal party animals—are lying on the hood of their Pinto looking up at the stars together. They don't say much of anything serious in this scene, but somehow their friendship shines through the banter.

3   God-sized love—"I love you no matter what."

- God-sized love is unconditional love. It's not *I love you because…* or *I love you if…* It's *I love you no matter what.*

- This love is rare to receive from another person, but it's what we always get from God.

- **Scripture** *Romans 8:38-39* ("For I am convinced that…[nothing]…will be able to separate us from the love of God.") Remind students—
  - There's nothing we can do to make God love us less.
  - There's nothing we can do to make God love us more.

- **Scripture** *Romans 5:8* ("But God demonstrates his own love for us in this…Christ died for us.") Spend a minute unpacking the point of this verse—God's no-strings-attached love is for us.

- We're capable of loving with this God-sized love also!

- **Illustration** *Hands of Love* (see sidebar)

- **Take-home item** *Nails* (see sidebar)

Illustration

Hands of love

A little boy was trapped inside a burning home. His mother and father went back inside to rescue him but never came out. The gathering crowd stood listening to the boy's screams but was helpless to do anything. Suddenly someone rushed through the crowd and climbed up an iron pipe that reached the upstairs bedroom where the boy was trapped. Jumping into the flaming window, he quickly reappeared with the boy and climbed down the hot pipe as the boy hung around his neck.

A couple months later a custody hearing was held to determine where the boy would be placed to live. He didn't have relatives, but many people from the town wanted to adopt him—even lawyers, doctors, and other very wealthy people. Each was given a brief chance to share why they would make a good guardian for the boy.

The judge asked if anyone else would like to say something and from the back of the room a man stood up and walked toward the front. He stood next to the boy and took his scarred hands out of his pockets. The boy recognized him as the man who had saved his life and leaped into his arms! The choice was obvious to everyone there.

When it comes to selfless love, actions speak louder than words.

Take-home item

Nails

Hand out a large nail to each student—the bigger the better. Talk to the students about the depth of God's love for each of them. He allowed his son Jesus to die in our place on the cross! Encourage students to put the nail in their bedroom where they'll see it every day and be reminded of God's unconditional love for them.

closing

The Grand Finale

🔊 Of course you should review the three kinds of love you've talked about—romantic, buddy, and God-sized.

🔊 **Object lesson** *Petals* (see sidebar)

🔊 **Take-home item** *Valentine's Cards* (optional, see sidebar)

🔊 **Activity** *God-Sized Love* (see sidebar)

Petals

Hold a flower and pull off one petal at a time—daisies work well—while saying, "He loves me. He loves me not. He loves me." Explain this is how lots of people think of God's love. But that's a sad misunderstanding of God-sized love! Take a second flower and remove the petals, this time saying, "He loves me. He loves me. He still loves me."

Valentine's cards

If it's anywhere near Valentine's Day—which would be a great time to use this talk—buy some of those cheap Valentine's cards little kids hand out to each other. It's best if they don't say "Happy Valentine's Day" on them. If you can't find these you could use any inexpensive card. Write a personal note to each student and sign God's name on the card. Remind them God's love for them is not dependent on their actions. God is absolutely crazy about them. (Have a few spares with no name on them for visitors.) Pass them out at the end of the talk.

God-sized love

Hand out paper and pencils and have students think of a way they could show God-sized love—unconditional love—to someone this week. Remind them it doesn't qualify as God-sized love if they're looking for anything in return, even appreciation! In fact it would be great if they would show unconditional love to someone who probably *won't* thank them for it.

Then encourage your whole group to brainstorm a way they can apply this together. Maybe they could rake leaves for someone or hold a free car wash—don't accept any donations. Or offer a free baby-sitting night for young parents, so they can have a cheap night out together. In the process of this discussion and planning, you can bring out the fact God-sized love usually looks like servanthood when we see it in action.

discussion

Encore

| Get It? | Middle School |

🔊 What were the three kinds of love we talked about? Give examples of each kind.

🔊 What other ways do we use the word *love* besides the ways we've talked about here? (*I love bacon. I love my dog. I love to snowboard.*)

🔊 Which of the three types of *love* is easiest for you? Why?

🔊 Which type of love is the most important to you and why?

🔊 What's the difference between loving your friend, loving your mom, and loving God?

🔊 How do you show your love to God?

🔊 Why is it so difficult to love people without expecting something in return?

🔊 Why is God-sized love so radical?

| Get It? | High School |

🔊 What are the differences between the three kinds of love we talked about?

🔊 Why do so many churches talk about romantic love only as a bad thing—especially for someone your age?

🔊 Is it possible to be in love with someone when you're 16?

🔊 Can a blind person experience romantic love? Explain your answer. (Romantic love isn't only about physical attraction based on sight.)

🔊 How can romantic love and buddy love be confusing in a relationship with a member of the opposite sex?

🔊 Which love do you think is most difficult to practice? Why?

🔊 Why is it so difficult to love people without expecting anything in return?

🔊 Why does God love us so much? Does it ever seem weird to you or hard to believe? Talk about that.

🔊 What was the last true expression of God-sized love you were a part of—either giving or receiving?

What If?   The Big Picture

🔊 What if you had the power to make someone love you? Who would it be and why?

🔊 If you had to live without any romantic love or live without any buddy love, which one would you give up? Why?

🔊 Is there crossover between loves? In other words, can romantic love become God-sized? Can buddy love become God-sized? Talk about that.

🔊 What difference would it make in your life if God didn't love us unconditionally?

🔊 What would it take for you to believe God loves you unconditionally?

🔊 What would your life be like if you tried to love God as much as he loves you this week?

🔊 What would it take for you to begin putting God-sized love into practice more often?

So What?   It's Your Life

🔊 Have you ever experienced God's love personally? Talk about the time when you experienced God's love the strongest.

🔊 What steps do you need to take to get where you can soak in God's love?

🔊 What kinds of sacrifices would you have to make in your life to love God unconditionally, not trying to get anything from him? What would it look like? Are you willing to do this? Talk about that.

🔊 What one act of totally selfless love will you commit to doing this week?

A Welcome for the Unwelcome

Contributed by **Jonny Baker**

Primary theme grace
Themes accepting others, rejection, forgiveness, God's love, Jesus' compassion
Scripture Luke 7:36-50
Approximate length through The Grand Finale 20-25 minutes

You'll need

- Several student volunteers for a role-play
- TV and VCR
- *Gattaca*
- Pencils and paper for students

This talk is simply a retelling of the story of the woman who anoints Jesus' feet. She was known in the community as unclean, as an outcast, as a sinner. Through her encounter with Jesus she found acceptance and grace.

Stories have a power of their own. The aim of this talk isn't to use her story to illustrate other points, but to let the story speak for itself.

Often the impact of Jesus' actions is somewhat lost on us because of the different culture we live in. So this will attempt to clarify the cultural issues at work in an effort to allow the true strength of the story to emerge. Make sure you're very familiar with the story. Rather than reading the whole story from the Bible and then commenting about it, you'll read a bit at a time and expand on it before moving on to the next part.

intro

The Opening Act

🔊 Say something like—

Today I'm going to retell a story from Luke's gospel where Jesus is invited to dinner with a Pharisee. The story is in three parts: the rude welcome, the shocking behavior, and the welcoming of the unwelcome.

heart of the talk

The Main Event

1   The rude welcome

🔊 **Scripture** *Luke 7:36* (see sidebar)

🔊 **Acting out** *Meal Time* (see sidebar)

🔊 **Explanation** *The Usual Welcome* (see sidebar)

🔊 In this story the Pharisee has skipped these accepted rituals of welcome. The atmosphere must have been very tense—as if you welcomed nine guests to your house and shook their hands, but just stared at the tenth and didn't say anything.

Scripture

Luke 7:36

Jesus is invited to a meal with a Pharisee. It's not just the two of them—there are many guests present. We don't know why Jesus is invited. He has obviously been around in the area. Maybe the Pharisee has been impressed? Maybe it was a meal with the local intellectuals for discussion? Perhaps—and this seems most likely from what happens—they wanted to give Jesus a bit of a theological test to see if he knew what he was talking about, to see if they could trip him up. He had a reputation for being a prophet—as the Pharisee mentions later on. (By the way, the Pharisees were the religious leaders of the time and they would have been very cynical about Jesus being a prophet.)

Meal time

Have several students role-play what happens in our culture when someone comes over for a nice meal, like a formal dinner party. This includes things like cleaning up the house, dressing appropriately, setting the table, shaking hands at the door, taking coats, having drinks, sitting down for the meal, serving guests, and—if you are the guest—bringing a gift like flowers or wine.

If you'd rather not have the students act it out, simply ask them for suggestions of what would go on when someone comes over for a nice dinner.

The usual welcome

Just as we have expected ways of behaving and welcoming people in our culture when we host them for dinner, there were a whole set of expected behaviors in Jesus' time also. If you were to be a guest for a meal then, here are some of the things you could expect.

- The meal is a banquet.

- The gateway to the house or yard would be open, making the meal open to the public. Villagers could wander in and out, stand behind guests, and listen in on the conversation.

- Dishes of food would be set in the center of the room, and couches would be placed alongside for guests to recline on.

- When the guests arrive they would be greeted with a kiss—a kiss on each cheek for an equal, a kiss on the hand for a rabbi.

- Feet were considered offensive, so sandals would be left at the door.

- Once the guests reclined, servants would go behind them and pour water over their feet. At the very least there would be water provided. To not wash a guest's feet or at least offer water for the guest to wash his own would be considered extremely rude and would imply the guest was of very inferior rank to the host.

189

2   Shocking behavior

🔊 **Scripture** *Luke 7:37-38* ("She began to wet his feet with her tears.")

🔊 **Storytelling** *Shocking Behavior* (see sidebar)

🔊 **Scripture** *Luke 7:39* ("If this man were a prophet he would know who is touching him and what kind of woman she is—that she is a sinner.")

🔊 **Storytelling** *Sinners* (see sidebar)

🔊 **Movie clip** *Gattaca* (see sidebar)

Storytelling

Shocking behavior

The woman has heard Jesus is going to be at the Pharisee's house. She is probably a prostitute. She would be well known in a small community like this one and despised by religious people. Because it's normal for villagers to come and observe the banquet, she comes in as one of the crowd. She has decided in advance to show her gratitude to Jesus because he showed her God's love and forgiveness. She wants to do this by anointing him with perfume.

But she's upset by the rudeness shown to Jesus. She can't believe they haven't even extended a kiss of welcome to him or washed his feet. She's crying and washes his feet with her tears and kisses his feet. She then dries his feet with her hair and anoints him with perfume.

All this is strange enough, but she does something shocking! She lets her hair down. Now for us that doesn't seem like a big deal, but women only let their hair down for their husbands. In the Jewish law book, the Talmud, a man had reason to divorce his wife if she let her hair down in public. The atmosphere was probably tense from the start, but now it's electric. Everyone is shocked, but her tenderness and gratitude is clear for all to see. What will Jesus do? What will the host do?

Storytelling

Sinners

Simon the Pharisee condemns the woman. Her tenderness is completely lost on him. All he sees is a sinner. That didn't just mean a person who has done something wrong. It was a label for whole categories of people who were seen as outsiders or unclean. Tax collectors, lepers, prostitutes—all sinners. Those people were in contrast, of course, with the categories of righteous people, who, of course, included the Pharisees. Every culture has those who are in and those who are out. Today's "sinners" might be homeless people, mentally ill people, prostitutes, and drug users.

The Pharisee won't accept this woman as anything other than a sinner, and he wants nothing to do with her. His assumptions are confirmed by her outrageous behavior in his house. He rudely questions Jesus' judgment for allowing her to let down her hair and touch him. The tension is mounting in the story. The camera focuses in on Jesus. What's going to happen next?

Gattaca

This film is worth watching in its entirety with your students at another time to lead into a discussion of insiders and outsiders. (Preview this movie before showing it. Some content may be objectionable for your group.)

It would be very helpful to preface this particular clip by explaining the plot of the movie. Introduce it by saying something like—

Gattaca is set in the future when there are two types of people—valids and in-valids. Valids have been selected before birth and genetically engineered to be perfect, while in-valids have the usual human frailties. Gattaca is a scientific establishment where only valids are allowed.

The main character Vincent—played by Ethan Hawke—has always dreamed of flying a rocket to space. But being an in-valid, he won't be considered and can't even get into Gattaca. So he illegally buys the identity of a valid who gives him blood and urine samples to fool the system and prove he is valid. All through the film he manages to avoid detection.

At the end of the film he finally arrives at Gattaca to realize his dream of flying to space, but the testing procedures have changed. Vincent is caught unprepared.

Start 1:37:32 Vincent steps out of line and approaches the man in the lab coat.

Stop 1:39:44 "You're gonna miss your flight, Vincent."

3 Welcoming the unwelcome

◁» If anything is guaranteed to get Jesus upset, it's judging outsiders like this. And the good news is Jesus brings God's love and forgiveness for everybody, especially the poor, weak, and judged. In classic Jesus form he responds to Simon the Pharisee by telling a story.

◁» **Scripture** *Luke 7:41-43* (The parable of two debtors)

  • Jesus tells this story to pull the rug from under Simon and his attitude toward "sinners." Somewhat begrudgingly the Pharisee has to admit love is a response to grace. He can't wiggle out of it. But Jesus doesn't stop there!

◁» **Scripture** *Luke 7:44-48* ("Her many sins have been forgiven—for she loved much.")

◁» **Storytelling** *More Shocking Behavior* (see sidebar)

◁» **Illustration** *Jesus Was a Traveler* (see sidebar)

More shocking behavior

There's already been some pretty shocking behavior in the story. But just when the tension seems to be lessening, Jesus knocks everyone's socks off—okay, they weren't wearing socks!—by making this final speech. Two things are worth bearing in mind about the culture when we picture Jesus delivering these words.

- Women were devalued in this culture. To praise a woman in an all-male gathering was radical—a profound statement of worth.

- Even if a host isn't hospitable, it was unthinkable to publicly question the host's actions. Jesus faces the woman and addresses her. He praises her actions in front of all the men. Then he makes sly comments about the Pharisee's hospitality, "I entered your house. You were responsible to extend to me the traditional forms of hospitality but you refused. This woman who you despise and consider an outsider, a sinner, magnificently compensated for your failure." Jesus mentions three expressions of hospitality: a kiss of greeting, foot washing, and anointing with oil.

The conclusion is clear. The woman who has experienced forgiveness for her many sins is overwhelmed with gratitude and love. And someone who hasn't experienced that—Simon the Pharisee—won't show the gratitude. Jesus isn't saying Simon doesn't have many sins. He just seems to be unaware of them.

In this story we encounter rudeness, pride, selfishness, self-righteousness, harsh judgment, hardheartedness, rejection, sexism, and—worst of all—the labeling of this woman as a "sinner" in the face of her repentance. Jesus assures her of forgiveness. The response of Simon and the crowd is left open in Scripture. Draw your own conclusions.

Jesus was a traveler

A group of new age travelers were camping on the outskirts of a wealthy village in the English countryside. The villagers campaigned the police to force these outsiders to move on. The key people campaigning were also members of a local church. To their amazement, the minister's sermon one Sunday was titled, "Jesus was a traveler—they nailed him too." There was soon a new campaign to get rid of the minister!

The story reached the travelers, and they began printing the slogan on T-shirts. These modern day outsiders understood something of God's acceptance because of the minister's courage.

closing

The Grand Finale

 Say something like—

> **I love this story because it breaks down our categories of who's in and who's out. Jesus came to bring good news to everyone, but especially to those who are treated poorly. It says so much about God. It says so much to those who feel on the edge, despised, rejected, and unwelcome. And it says so much to us when we start assuming we're the ones who are in and have it all together. God's love and forgiveness are for all. His welcome is for the unwelcome.**

 Activity *Script It* Have students—individually or in small groups—rewrite this story imagining it in a contemporary setting with somebody they think is an outsider in our culture. Have several read or act out their finished stories.

 Pray and ask God to bring to mind any people you judge or despise. Ask Jesus to help you see them as he sees them and to show his grace and acceptance to them.

 Future event *Come One, Come All* (see sidebar)

Future event

Come one, come all

Note that much of Jesus' ministry took place around the meal table. Consider having your group plan a party, a banquet, and invite those you wouldn't normally invite—just have fun with them—don't hit them over the head with 20-pound Bibles.

discussion

Encore

Get It?	Middle School

 List some groups of people churches might automatically call "sinners" today.

 Who are the outsiders at your school? What kinds of people are they?

 What was so radical about what Jesus did in this story?

 Can you think of anyone who—like the lady in the story—has been forgiven for a lot of sins, so now that person seems to understand God's love? Talk about that.

Get It? — High School

- Who are today's perceived sinners?

- What about today's Pharisees? Who are they?

- What was so radical about Jesus' words and actions? Can you think of other radical things Jesus did and said?

- Are you someone who has been forgiven much or a little?

- What can you learn about yourself from Jesus' parable?

What If? — The Big Picture

- What would happen if we showed people the love and acceptance Jesus displayed in this story?

- What might have happened next—after the end of this story as we've heard it?

- Put yourself in Simon's shoes. What would you do or say next?

- What would you do if you were the woman?

- Is your church attractive to "sinners"? How about your youth group? How can you make it a more welcoming group?

- What would happen in your youth group if a few people from one of those groups you mentioned earlier showed up? How would they be treated?

- Do you think we should welcome people as they are or ask them to change and then welcome them? Talk about that.

So What? — It's Your Life

- What things can we do to welcome the unwelcome in our group?

- Jesus treated women with respect and dignity. What ways can we ensure we do the same in our youth group?

- Picture the story again—put yourself in the role of the woman. Let Jesus speak to you at the end. What does he say to you? How will that affect your life this week?

Two Funerals and a Wedding

Contributed by **Tim Conder**

Primary theme discipleship	
Themes faith, Christian living, depending on God, fear, self-reliance	
Scripture Psalms 23; 90:1-6; Matthew 18:3; Mark 8:34-35; Romans 8:35-39; Ephesians 2:8-9	
Approximate length through The Grand Finale 25-30 minutes	

hrough a funeral and wedding theme, we examine what are appropriate expectations and lifestyles for Christian disciples. The talk capitalizes on the humor and common embarrassment we share by acting inappropriately in public settings and challenges students to move away from lifestyles and life expectations inappropriate for those who share in the life and hope of Christ.

The ultimate goal is to define and recommend a life of radical faith as the foundation for both the expectations and lifestyle of Christian disciples.

This talk contains a few big words. To use it with young teens you'll need to be proactive about explaining and checking for understanding.

You'll need

- A personal story about acting inappropriately in public
- TV and VCR (optional)
- *Big Daddy* or another Adam Sandler movie (optional)
- A personal story about fear
- A student or leader to be the subject of a fake interview regarding fear
- A personal story about being self-reliant
- A student or leader to be the subject of a fake interview regarding risky behavior
- A personal story from your childhood about putting faith in someone or something
- Pencils and paper for students (optional)

intro

The Opening Act

🔊 **Personal illustration** *I'm an Idiot* Tell a funny story about a time you acted inappropriately or cluelessly in a public setting.

Movie clip *Big Daddy* (optional, see sidebar)

Then begin by saying something like—

> **It's easy—and embarrassing—to act inappropriately in public. It's also easy to have priorities and actions in our lives that are totally inappropriate for people who share in the life and hope of Jesus Christ. Let's look at two common and inappropriate lifestyles for followers of Jesus, and then recommend a third lifestyle that should be our goal if we seek to follow Christ.**

Movie clip

Big Daddy

In lieu of a personal story, you might show a funny movie clip where a misinformed character acts inappropriately or foolishly in a public setting. Several Adam Sandler movies (*Happy Gilmore, The Wedding Singer, Big Daddy*) can provide humorous clips to make this point. Here's an example of a scene that works from *Big Daddy*.

Start 6:00 "That relationship's lasted a lot longer than I thought."

Stop 7:14 Applause and cutaway to the rooftop.

Adam Sandler's character Sonny Koufax—having already ruined the surprise in a surprise party for his roommate (Jon Stewart)—now ruins his roommate's attempt to propose to his girlfriend.

heart of the talk
The Main Event

1   Panic—a lifestyle of fear

- **Illustration** *Fear at a Funeral* (see sidebar)

- **Discussion** *Face the Fear* Ask students to describe their greatest fears. Follow this question by asking how their fears affect the way they live their lives.

- **Personal illustration** *Scaredy Cat* Describe a fear of your own and how this fear has shaped your actions and choices. This can be serious or humorous, depending on your group and which way you want to spin the tone of the talk.

- **Acting out** *A Person in Panic* (see sidebar)

- A lifestyle dominated by fear doesn't make sense for a disciple of Christ. When we're obsessed with and overwhelmed by fear, we lose sight of the fact we share an eternal hope in Christ.

- We're people who are called to live in hope and in the confidence of God's love and presence!

- **Scripture** *Psalm 23* ("Even though I walk through the valley of the shadow of death I will fear no evil for you are with me.")

- **Scripture** *Romans 8:35-39* ("Who shall separate us from the love of Christ?")

Illustration

Fear at a funeral

Have students imagine a large church funeral. The church is filled with flowers and mourners. An elaborate casket and photos of the deceased sit at the front of the altar, surrounded by large flower arrangements. An organ plays sad music. The sounds of muffled tears and the hush of quiet reverence fill the sanctuary. Just before the minister stands to offer some words of comfort, a 16-year-old from the back row runs up to the casket shouting, "It's horrible! It's horrible! We're all going to die too! Everyone protect themselves now!"

As crazy and inappropriate as this scene is, this is the way many of us live our lives—in panic, in a lifestyle dominated by fear.

Acting out

A person in panic

Interview a person—student or adult—planted in your audience, who pretends to be dominated by fears. This can be both illustrative and funny if this person hams up the responses and expresses a wide range of irrational fears and a paranoid lifestyle. Have her reference simple fears at first—fear of spiders and flying, for example. Then have her move on to more irrational fears—fear of poodles or sidewalks or men wearing red. Have your actor go into detail about how these fears infringe on her life. If the person can pull it off, have her end by expressing a fear of people. She can then pretend to realize the room is full of people and run screaming from the room.

2 Invincibility—a lifestyle of self-reliance

◁» **Illustration** *Self-Reliance at a Funeral* (see sidebar)

◁» **Discussion** *My Way* Ask the students to share some personal examples of being overly self-reliant or self-confident. What were some risky or crazy actions that went along with this attitude?

◁» **Personal illustration** *I Can Do It Myself* Describe a situation when you were too self-reliant. Describe how this false confidence put you at risk—again, this could be serious or funny—whatever's most appropriate for your group.

◁» **Acting out** *An Extreme Risk-Taker* (see sidebar)

◁» A lifestyle built on self-reliance and invincibility is as out of line with a disciple's lifestyle as the opposite extreme of constant fear. When we live this way, we lose sight of the fact we are God's creation and only our Creator is limitless.

◁» We're people who are called to accept our limits and live in a way that acknowledges our need for God.

◁» **Scripture** *Psalm 90:1-6* ("You sweep men away in the sleep of death; they are like the new grass of the morning.")

Illustration

Self-reliance at a funeral

Tell the students you want them to imagine another scene. It's a funeral again—a big one in a church, with flowers, quiet mourners, reverent organ music, and a gentle minister ready to speak. This time identify the deceased as an elderly person loved by all.

Just as the minister opens his mouth to speak, a 20-year-old bodybuilder rushes the altar and jumps up on the casket. He begins flexing his muscles and posing at the shocked crowd. He starts shouting, "This will never happen to me! I'm young! I'm strong! I'll never get old!"

As crazy and foolish as this second scene is, this is also an inappropriate lifestyle some of us lead. Many of us live life thinking we're invincible—nothing will ever hurt us. This is a life dominated by foolish self-reliance and false confidence.

An extreme risk-taker

If you did a set-up interview for the first point, your students will be expecting it here—but it could still be lots of fun, as well as a reinforcement of your point. Plan with someone—student or adult—ahead of time and conduct a mock interview revealing this person's extreme recklessness and extremely risky behavior. Make sure this reveals a self-reliant and invincible attitude.

You might start with extreme sport types of things, like skydiving and off-road skateboarding. But move on to absurdity, with things like getting blown out of a cannon, walking through a shooting range, and picking fights with gang members. If your acting partner can pull it off in a fun way, end the interview with the interviewee declaring a need to try jumping from a plane without a parachute—or some other absurd idea—and running from the room.

3 Pursuit of Christ—a lifestyle of radical faith and radical dependence on Christ

◁» **Illustration** *True Commitment at a Wedding* (see sidebar)

◁» A disciple of Christ isn't a fearful person who holds onto his life with a clenched fist. Instead, a disciple releases control of his life.

◁» **Scripture** *Mark 8:34-35* ("For whoever wants to save his life will lose it, but whoever loses his life for me and for the gospel will save it.")

◁» A disciple doesn't depend on personal capabilities or strength. Instead, a disciple is radically dependent on the person of Jesus Christ—dependent on God's grace, on what Jesus has done for us.

◁» **Scripture** *Ephesians 2:8-9* ("For it is by grace you have been saved…not from yourselves.")

◁» Both fear and invincibility are selfish lifestyles. A radical faith is the wonderful and appropriate alternative. Instead of being absorbed by your fears or your capabilities, in faith you should become dependent on Christ.

Illustration

True commitment at a wedding

Tell your students you now want them to imagine one last scene. Instead of a church funeral, this is a church wedding. The church is filled with bright flowers and is decorated beautifully. The congregation is happy for the couple but only mildly enthusiastic—they've seen it all before. Maybe they're skeptical since they've seen so many well-intentioned marriages fail.

The pastor mindlessly mentions the point where anyone who has objection to this marriage should speak now or forever hold their peace. With these words hanging in the air, one person speaks up loudly, yelling, "I object! I don't believe they really love each other!"

The congregation is in shock. The pastor is astounded and doesn't know what to do. But in this moment, the bride turns around and shouts back boldly, "I do love this man! We have no guarantees of long life. But I will love him as long as I live. We have no guarantees of wealth, good fortune, or even good health. But still I will love him. I don't know what to expect out of life or even marriage. But I will assure you of this—I will do everything in my power to love this man unconditionally and eternally."

This final scene helps us begin to understand the lifestyle and appropriate expectations of a follower of Christ.

closing

The Grand Finale

- 🔊 Jesus encourages us to have childlike faith.

- 🔊 **Scripture** *Matthew 18:3* ("Unless you change and become like little children")

- 🔊 Children are innocent and aren't paralyzed by fear. Children are also wise enough to know they have to depend on someone stronger than themselves. Childlike faith is a radical faith.

- 🔊 **Personal illustration** *The Faith of a Child* Tell a story from your own childhood about how you placed your faith in a loving parent or another caring adult.

- 🔊 **Discussion** *What Would You Do?* (optional, see sidebar)

What would you do?

This discussion can be very effective in driving home the three points of the talk by asking student to relate the three lifestyles to specific situations. Describe a series of scenarios. After each scenario ask the students to describe a fear response, an invincibility response, and a faith response. Some suggestions for scenarios might include—

- A girl has an opportunity to share her faith.
- A guy is asked to vandalize a building.
- A teen encounters a coach who harshly criticizes her performance at a meet.
- A friend complains about a student's efforts on school work.
- A teen has sex with whoever propositions.

Feel free to add greater detail to the scenarios. As an alternative this can be done as a reflection, passing out pens and paper and having students write responses individually.

discussion

Encore

Get It? Middle School

- Not all fear is wrong, right? What kind of fear is okay? What kind of fear doesn't make sense for those who follow Jesus?

- Describe an example of building a life around a fear.

- Describe what it looks like to live self-reliantly or as if you're invincible.

- What does it mean to have a radical faith and be dependent on God?

- Childlike faith doesn't mean acting like a kid. What does Jesus mean when he calls us to have childlike faith? What are some examples?

Get It? High School

- Describe a fear-based lifestyle.

- What are some of the consequences of continually living in fear? How is this lifestyle at odds with Christian discipleship?

- Describe an invincible, self-reliant lifestyle.

- What are some of the consequences of living as if you're invincible and being excessively self-reliant? How can this lifestyle be at odds with Christian discipleship?

- How would you explain radical faith to someone who hasn't heard of it?

What If? — The Big Picture

🔊 What's the difference between a healthy respect of dangerous situations and a lifestyle of excessive fear and panic?

🔊 Describe some appropriate and healthy fears we should maintain. With these examples describe how you can keep a sense of caution without being ruled by fear.

🔊 What's the difference between a positive and healthy self-esteem and a lifestyle of foolish self-reliance?

🔊 What is the difference between a childish faith and the childlike faith Jesus challenges us to model? Give some examples.

🔊 In the competitive and sometimes dangerous world we live in, we can still count on God. How? What's it look like in real life to depend on God?

So What? — It's Your Life

🔊 What fears do you have that paralyze you or demand too much of your attention? How do these fears affect your life and your relationship with Christ?

🔊 What would it take to minimize these fears and focus more on Christ's presence in your life?

🔊 What are some of your personal gifts and capabilities that tempt you to live self-reliantly? Are there certain situations when you're more tempted to be self-reliant? How does extreme self-reliance affect your relationship with Christ?

🔊 What would it take to decrease your self-reliance and increase your God-reliance in these situations?

🔊 What are the next steps to take that would encourage you toward more radical, childlike faith in Christ?

🔊 What would childlike faith look like for you this week? What one thing will you do to depend on God more this week?

Contributed by **Gregg Farah**

Leaving the Purple Penguin Behind

Primary theme racism	
Themes prejudice, judging others, stereotypes, accepting others, God's love	
Scripture Psalm 139:13-14; Galatians 3:28; 6:7-9; Ephesians 2:14; Philippians 3:13-14	
Approximate length through The Grand Finale 25-30 minutes	

You'll need

- whiteboard and markers (optional)
- TV and VCR
- *Schindler's List*
- A student or leader willing to share about their struggle with prejudice
- *The Shawshank Redemption*
- Several adults willing to be involved in a panel discussion about their struggles with prejudice (optional)

 'mon, admit it—you have some prejudices. At least once in a while—if not more often—you make a judgment about someone simply based on the person's race or some other defining factor. And you assume. We all do this unfortunately. And almost always those assumptions carry the weight of judgment—the idea that I am in some way better than he is. And we all know moving beyond prejudice and racism is more than striving to be politically correct—it's striving to align ourselves with the heart of God. Because God is grieved by racism.

Today's teens are an odd bunch—like we needed to tell you that! On one hand they're more multicultural and race-blind than any generation in history. But in other ways they still have deep-seated assumptions and prejudices. They're strongly opposed to racism but still prejudiced at the same time. This talk goes a step further than simply communicating God's disdain for racism. It attempts to help students erase negative stereotypes and establish a new perspective—a God perspective.

intro

The Opening Act

🔊 Have students define racism, and write their responses on a whiteboard.

🔊 **Movie clip** *Schindler's List* (see sidebar)

🔊 True or false—Every person is racist. Ask your teens to respond to the statement with their opinion.

🔊 **Scripture** *Ephesians 2:14* ("For he himself is our peace, who has made the two one and has destroyed the barrier.") Point out Jews and Gentiles hated one another, so it was a big deal that God would want those two groups to connect. In the same way God wants us to remove any barriers keeping us from developing relationships with others.

🔊 **Scripture** *Galatians 3:28* ("There is neither Jew nor Greek, slave nor free, male nor female, for you are all one in Christ Jesus.") Have students add phrases to this verse that include races, cliques, and groups in their schools. Suggest something like—There are no Goths or Skateboarders, no Asians or Caucasians, for you are all...

🔊 Transition to the main points by saying something like—

> **We're surrounded with examples of racism and prejudice every day. And if we're honest, we all struggle with thoughts of prejudice against certain people or groups of people. Today we're going to focus on erasing those negative thoughts and replacing them with healthy ones.**

Movie clip

Schindler's List

Start 1:10:00 The young girl hides under the bed.

Stop 1:12:35 The soldiers survey a stack of dead bodies.

Watch this powerful clip from Steven Spielberg's movie depicting the horrors of the holocaust. This scene takes place after a day of "cleansing the city," as Nazi soldiers search for remaining Jewish residents.

When the clip is over ask—

• **What emotions did you experience while watching the clip?**

• **While we don't usually see such extreme examples of racism as you saw in that scene, what examples are you aware of from around the world? In our country? In our community?**

heart of the talk

The Main Event

1   Erase your past memories.

- 🔊 **Illustration** *Eat Your Veggies* (see sidebar)

- 🔊 Quote Palestinian Elias Chacour: "When you look at your enemy, remember he was once a baby, created in the image and likeness of God."

- 🔊 **Scripture** *Philippians 3:13-14* ("Forget what's behind…straining toward what is ahead")

- 🔊 **Illustration** *Purple Penguin* (see sidebar)

- 🔊 **Illustration** *Testimony* (see sidebar)

Illustration

Eat your veggies

Remember when you were a kid and you had to eat vegetables you didn't like? If you could focus on the fact that broccoli looks like fun little trees, eating it wasn't that bad. And sooner or later you might even start liking broccoli. The same is true for other things in life—including people and people groups. Instead of focusing on the fact that a member of that race or group did or said something very hurtful to you once, focus on the fact the person in front of you is a special creation of God, created in his image, and loved by him—just like you! Got a negative stereotype in your mind about a person or a group? Come up with one positive quality about that person, and focus on that.

Illustration

Purple penguin

Sin happens in your mind long before it's expressed through your actions. So we need to learn how to deal with our thoughts in this area. Here's an example to share with your students. Say something like—

Do not let your mind think about a purple penguin, wearing a blue scarf and bright white high-top basketball shoes…What did you do? Probably thought about a purple penguin! Why? Because you didn't have anything else to think about.

Now think of a bright white polar bear wearing a baseball cap. Think of the polar bear and not the purple penguin. Got it? The penguin may or may not have disappeared from your mind view, but you were able to make a choice to focus on something else. It's the same way with racist thoughts—or other sinful thoughts. If a negative stereotype comes into your head, train yourself to think of something positive about that same person or group.

Illustration

Testimony

Ahead of time invite a student or adult to share how they previously struggled with negative feelings toward someone due to race or social group, and how they're now overcoming those thoughts. Emphasize progress—not perfection.

2   Evaluate your present actions.

- 🔊 True or false—God Loves Everyone. Of course your students will say the answer is true, but sometimes we don't live as if we believe it to be true.

- 🔊 **Activity** *To Tell the Truth* (see sidebar)

- 🔊 When we don't love others like God does—regardless of their social group, race, popularity, or beliefs—we place ourselves in opposition with God.

- 🔊 It's as if God says, "I totally love that person." And we say, "You're wrong, God—that person isn't worth loving."

- 🔊 **Scripture** *Psalm 139:13-14* ("I am fearfully and wonderfully made.")

- 🔊 Because God made and wired each of us, we can be confident we—and others we see—have value and worth.

- 🔊 **Illustration** *Sometimes Life Can Be Fair!* (see sidebar)

Activity

To tell the truth

To get your students to admit they sometimes struggle with prejudice, try this truth workout. Have your students physically own up to the feelings and actions they've experienced in the past.

- **Stand up if you've ever wished bad stuff on someone else.**

- **Raise your right hand if you've ever thought you were better than someone else.**

- **Wave your left hand if you've ever talked about people behind their backs.**

- **Wave both hands in the air if you've ever made assumptions about people based on the color of their skin.**

- **Jump up and down if you've ever judged others by their appearance. (Everyone ought to be jumping!)**

Illustration

Sometimes life can be fair!

On a British Airways flight from Johannesburg, a middle-aged, well-off, white South African lady found herself seated next to a black man. She called the flight attendant to complain, saying, "I can't possibly sit next to this disgusting human being. Find me another seat!" The woman shot a snooty look at the outraged black man beside her—not to mention many of the other passengers who were suddenly paying attention.

The flight attendant returned saying, "Madam, unfortunately this flight is very full. No seats remain in coach and no seats remain in business class. However we do have one seat available in first class." Before the woman had a chance to respond, the flight attendant continued, "It's quite unusual to make this kind of upgrade; however, I checked with the captain for special permission. And given the circumstances, the captain felt it was outrageous that someone should be forced to sit next to such an obnoxious person."

With that the flight attendant turned to the black man and said, "So if you'd like to get your things, Sir, I have your first-class seat ready for you." At which point the surrounding passengers broke into applause while the man walked to the front of the plane.

From *Hot Illustrations for Youth Talks 4* edited by Wayne Rice (Youth Specialties, 2001).

3 Establish your future plans.

- It's easy to believe the first two points, but how do you live them? How can you put your beliefs into action?
- **Scripture** *Galatians 6:7-9* (see sidebar)
- **Movie clip** *The Shawshank Redemption* (see sidebar)
- **Discussion** *I've Been There* Ask for a volunteer willing to share his experience with trying to overcome prejudice. Ask what was helpful in overcoming it and why.
- Coming up with ideas is easy, but putting our faith into action is what God desires.
- **Illustration** *Panel on prejudice* (optional, see sidebar)

Scripture

Galatians 6:7-9

These verses are all about reaping what you sow. If a farmer wants to grow corn, it doesn't do him any good to plant wheat. In the same way, if you want to invest in developing healthy relationships, it doesn't do you any good to prejudge people you meet. Put healthy effort into a relationship and you've got a good chance at producing a friendship.

Movie clip

The Shawshank Redemption

You can show both of these clips if time allows. Otherwise the first will make your point by itself.

Start 1:45:10 "That's the way it is. It's down there, and I'm in here."

Stop 1:47:00 "You'll have to pry it up to see."

In this scene the two main characters, Andy (Tim Robbins) and Red (Morgan Freeman) invest in developing a strong friendship, despite the many differences between them.

Start 2:13:00 Red looks for the treasure.

Stop 2:15:45 Red reads the letter.

This is the follow-up scene to show what happens when Red gets out of prison and tries to connect with Andy. After the clip ask for some ways to build a relationship with a person who is different from you.

Illustration

Panel on prejudice

Have a panel of guests—or the same individual who shared earlier—dialog with students about how they've tried to overcome their wrong feelings in this area. Include a story of failure as well as stories of success.

This discussion can easily add 15 minutes or more to this talk.

closing

The Grand Finale

🔊 Review the main points. If we want to mirror the heart of God and move beyond racism and prejudice, we need to—

- Erase past memories.
- Evaluate present actions.
- Establish future plans.

🔊 **Activity** *Application Letters* (see sidebar)

Application letters

Pass out a piece of paper, a pen, and an envelope to each student. Have students write a letter to themselves, addressing specifically how they'll tackle this area in their own lives. Suggest they list specific people they've been prejudiced toward and draft action plans for how they'll deal with each of these people. It would be good to play some quiet music while everyone writes to lessen distractions. Have students seal the letters in the envelopes and address them to themselves. Tell them you'll mail the letters to them in a month—and make sure you do!

discussion

Encore

Get It?	Middle School

- 🔊 God loves everyone—even murderers. How can that be true? Is it possible God loves some people less than others? Talk about that.

- 🔊 How can you love someone from another race, even if they won't talk to you?

- 🔊 So we're supposed to keep trying to build relationships. What if you were to try and you got laughed at or treated badly? What then?

- 🔊 Why should you erase a past memory if you've been hurt? What if you don't want to forgive? What should you do?

- 🔊 What should you do if your assumptions about another race or social group proves to be true based on your experience?

- 🔊 Why does this topic matter at all?

Get It?	High School

- 🔊 What's the biggest challenge in replacing negative thoughts with positive thoughts? If you've been hurt, how can you get past previous pain?

- 🔊 On a scale of one to 10, how easy or difficult is it to believe God actually loves everyone. Talk about that.

- 🔊 Why is it so difficult to love everyone like God does?

- 🔊 How should you respond if people of a certain race or social group treat you poorly?

- 🔊 If you're nice to people with your actions but think bad thoughts about them, what's the harm?

What If?   The Big Picture

🔊 How realistic is it for someone brought up in a racist environment to apply this message? What can people do to overcome their environment?

🔊 If someone doesn't feel loved by God, is it possible for that person to believe God loves everyone? What would you tell that person?

🔊 At what point would you advise a friend to give up loving or caring for someone who doesn't respond to the effort?

🔊 What would you tell someone who is afraid to step out in faith?

🔊 What would you tell someone who doesn't believe she has any racist thoughts or feelings?

So What?   It's Your Life

🔊 Who could you have lunch with this week in order to apply these ideas and begin to move your heart into alignment with God's?

🔊 Is there someone you need to apologize to because of something you said or did? How can you do this? When will you do this?

🔊 Are you willing to ask God to search your heart and to reveal any prejudice in your life? When will you do that?

🔊 Who are some of the people or groups you don't like because of how they look or act? What can you do about your feelings this week? What positive things can you use to replace your negative thoughts or assumptions?

🔊 How would your day be different if you saw people the way God sees them?

Jesus the Rescuer

Contributed by Jonny Baker

You'll need

- A personal story about being physically rescued from danger
- TV and VCR
- A video clip or newspaper clipping about a recent real-life rescue
- *Titanic*
- *Backdraft*
- *Speed*
- A personal story about escaping a dangerous situation
- *Batman*
- *Robin Hood, Prince of Thieves*
- A personal story about being rescued by transformation (optional)

Primary theme salvation

Themes hope, redemption, heaven, environment, Jesus' mission

Scripture Matthew 24:37-41; Romans 8:19-25; Revelation 21:1-5

Approximate length through The Grand Finale 20-25 minutes

This talk considers what Jesus came to do by showing him as a rescuer of the world. By connecting Jesus with other heroes it raises the question of what type of rescue Jesus was involved in. Did he come to help us escape from the world by getting us a ticket to heaven? Or did he come to rescue the creation itself? The goal of the talk is to show that what Jesus has done gives us hope for the future of the world as well as ourselves. It's a talk to pull the rug out from under your group and their assumptions. Get 'em thinking.

This talk outline presents, in an easy-to-understand form, a classic amillennial view of the end times—though it never actually talks about end times, keeping good form with most amillennialists. In some churches this talk could get you into lots of trouble. You might be called a liberal or a tree-hugger—oh, my!

It's possible however, to present this talk in a modified form where you soften some of the so-this-is-the-way-it-is statements. Even if you don't agree with the amillennial position, this talk makes for an intriguing discussion!

intro

The Opening Act

🔊 Get students into pairs and ask them to discuss why Jesus came into the world. What was the goal of his mission? Get some feedback and write the answers down.

🔊 **Illustration** *I Got Rescued* (see sidebar)

🔊 **Illustration** *From the Headlines* (see sidebar)

🔊 Transition by saying something like—

> **Lots of words are used to describe Jesus and what he came to do. The one we're going to look at today is rescuer. Nearly all heroes are involved in some type of rescue, and these rescues fall into two main types: rescue by escape and rescue by transformation. We'll consider which of these best describes Jesus' work.**

Illustration

I got rescued

Tell a story from your own experience of being rescued—in the physical, cliffhanger sense. (Not your spiritual rescue story.) The more dramatic the event the better—trapped in a car wreck, lost in the woods, lost in a mall. In your telling use as much drama and suspense as you can without stretching the truth.

Illustration

From the headlines

Show a video clip from the news of a current story involving a rescue. Or show a story from a current newspaper involving a rescue. It's best if this is something with a big profile—something most of your students would've heard about.

heart of the talk

The Main Event

1   Rescue by escape

🔊   Rescue by escape involves saving people from a bad or dangerous place to a place of safety. (You shouldn't show all three of these movie clips. Choose one to screen and simply describe the others.)

🔊   **Movie clip** *Titanic* (see sidebar)

🔊   **Movie clip** *Backdraft* (see sidebar)

🔊   **Movie clip** *Speed* (see sidebar)

🔊   **Personal illustration** *My Escape* Tell a story from your own experience of this type of rescue—rescue by escape.

Movie clip

Titanic

Start 2:05:24 "Jack! Will this work?"

Stop 2:06:27 "You did it!"

Jack (Leonardo DiCaprio) finds himself handcuffed to a pipe deep inside the Titanic—which is sinking fast—and the only way to escape drowning is to get the handcuffs off and get to a lifeboat. Thankfully his rescuer Rose (Kate Winslet) is handy with an ax.

Movie clip ·

Backdraft

Start 51:56 "My baby! Please, my baby's in there!"

Stop 54:12 The hero emerges from the burning room with the little boy.

Firefighters and brothers Stephen (Kurt Russell) and Brian (William Baldwin) enter a blazing building to help a small child escape the flames.

Movie clip

Speed

Start 1:24:57 "There is a camera on the bus, just over my left shoulder."

Stop 1:28:12 Distant shot of the buses driving next to each other.

Jack Traven (Keanu Reeves) has the daunting task of helping passengers escape from a city bus that will explode if the bus slows down or if the terrorist who planted the bomb sees—through his hidden camera—any passengers being rescued.

2 Rescue by transformation

- This involves changing peoples' surroundings from bad or dangerous to good or safe.

- This rescue doesn't involve physically taking people from a bad place to a good place—they end up rescued, but in the same place.

- **Movie clip** *Batman* (see sidebar)

- **Movie clip** *Robin Hood, Prince of Thieves* (see sidebar)

- **Illustration** *Flash Gordon* (see sidebar)

- **Personal illustration** *My Transforming Rescue* (optional, see sidebar)

Movie clip

Batman

You could use almost any clip from the Batman movies to illustrate this, but here's a good one.

Start 2:30 A distant shot of Gotham City, immediately following opening credits.

Stop 6:30 One of the muggers stares over the ledge as sirens blare.

Our mysterious superhero Batman (Michael Keaton) wreaks havoc on the thugs who attacked a lost and defenseless family in this opening scene from the first of the modern Batman movies. Batman rescues Gotham City by transforming it into a safe place. He does this by removing the evil from the city, as opposed to merely rescuing the innocent people from dangerous situations.

Movie clip

Robin Hood, Prince of Thieves

Describe or show this scene from Robin Hood—the version with Kevin Costner ignoring any attempt at a British accent.

Start 57:30 "You brought this misery on us, Locksley."

Stop 1:00:00 "Then, by God, we take it back!"

Robin of Locksley (Kevin Costner) has joined a band of men who've settled for a small corner of land in Sherwood Forest. But in an impassioned speech he implores them not to accept oppression and poverty. He challenges them to transform the whole land by driving out the baddies—the Sheriff of Nottingham and his men.

Illustration

Flash Gordon

Flash Gordon—of comic book and classic TV fame—is described as the "Savior of the Universe." This is because he frees people from being oppressed by the evil Ming. Once he has done this, people continue to live on in the same place, not somewhere different. He has transformed the universe into a safe place.

Personal illustration

My transforming rescue

If you have a personal story fitting this kind of rescue, tell it. Maybe someone helped you transform a wrong attitude or understanding you had about something, and it had a profound impact on your life. Or maybe something transformed a bad family situation when you were growing up. Be creative. Your explanation of a story from your own life will help to clarify what this rescue looks like in real life.

3 Jesus the rescuer

When we consider the world we live in, it's obviously in need of rescue. Ask students if they can list some of the things about our world that prove rescue is necessary. Things like—

injustice	environmental disaster	violence
greed	hatred	gossip
war	racism	

It's far from a perfect world.

Discussion *Jesus Our Superhero* (see sidebar)

Lots of Christians seem to have opted for the first view—the world is a bad place and Jesus rescues us out of it to somewhere safe (heaven).

Quote *James Watt* (see sidebar)

But there are increasing numbers of Jesus-followers who are opting for the second rescue definition. Christ has come to rescue the creation itself by transforming it so ultimately it will be freed from evil and God will live with his people in the new—or renewed—earth and heavens.

Scripture *Romans 8:19-25* ("The creation itself will be freed from its bondage to decay.") This passage seems to speak of creation being freed from evil rather than destroyed, and God's children should help bring that freedom.

Scripture *Revelation 21:1-5* ("Then I saw a new heavens and a new earth.") This might appear to support either type of rescue, but there are two words for new in Greek. The one used in this passage means "renewed" rather than "brand new." So it's a future vision of the same creation renewed.

Scripture *Matthew 24:37-41* (see sidebar)

The weight of biblical material seems to point to Jesus' rescue being by transformation.

- Christ has come to transform the world itself by driving out Satan and evil from all of life and ultimately the earth.

- Heaven will be a future heaven and earth where the whole creation will be made new, healed, restored.

- We will have a post-resurrection bodily existence, and there will be no suffering.

Jesus our superhero

This is a good place to make sure your students are processing the two different kinds of rescue and how they relate to our understanding of Jesus. Ask—

- **We all know Jesus is our rescuer, but which kind of rescue has he come to make?**

- **Is it rescue by escape—meaning he has primarily come to rescue us away from a dangerous place (earth) to somewhere safe (heaven)?**

- **Or is it rescue by transformation—meaning Jesus has come to rescue us by driving out the baddies (the devil and all types of evil) and transforming the world into a good and safe place so we can live again in peace?**

After allowing several students to respond, state that our answer to the questions should have a dramatic impact on how we view the world and our place in it.

James Watt

The view of rescue by escape suggests it doesn't matter too much what happens to creation— the important thing is getting out of it. After all, it will all be destroyed anyway, won't it? Use this infamous statement by James Watt—a Christian who was Ronald Reagan's Secretary of Interior—to illustrate the weakness of this theology. Watt—who also happened to be in charge of U. S. environmental stuff—told the House of Representatives committee concerned about the forests and rivers that he didn't worry about the destruction of the earth's resources. "Because," he said, "we don't know how many future generations can count on them before the Lord returns!"

Matthew 24:37-41

This passage speaks about the final rescue, how it all ends when Jesus returns. It says in short, "As it was in the days of Noah…so it will be at the coming of the Son of Man…Two men will be in the field; one will be taken, the other left." The question is, who's taken and who's left behind? The standard answer has been that the Christian is taken and the non-Christian is left behind, which seems to point to rescue by escape.

But another interpretation of this passage is to focus on a comparison with Noah and the flood. The flood took away those who didn't believe, who were not faithful to God. The faithful were rescued along with the creation itself. When the Son of Man—that's Jesus—comes, the same is true.

In other words this verse might mean the direct opposite of how many understand it! And if this explanation is correct, then it points to the second type of rescue—rescue by transformation.

closing
The Grand Finale

🔊 Wrap up by saying something like—

Are you ready to be a rescuer? Someone who will join Jesus in transforming the world? We don't have to wait around for the final rescue. We can begin acts of transformation now. An accusation often leveled by young people against the Christian faith is that it's irrelevant. This is tragic. If you pressed most people on what their dream is, it would be to see the world free from suffering, pain, and injustice—a creation healed. This is precisely the Christian vision of hope for the future and the kind of rescue Christ came to bring. It's time to start getting people to know and be involved in the rescue plan.

🔊 **Future Activity** *Rescue Party* (optional, see sidebar)

🔊 Even if you don't hold a rescue party, make sure you brainstorm a list of application ideas with your students. Use a poster board and title it—Joining Jesus in the Rescue. Leave it up for a few months to help students remember to apply this idea.

Future activity

Rescue party

Plan a rescue party as a group. Brainstorm different ways your students can be involved in helping Jesus transform the world.

- Environmental work or a park clean-up—the earth is ours to care for responsibly today!

- Acts of kindness—when light shines in the darkness, darkness flees!

- Racial reconciliation activities—this might include getting together with the youth group from a church of a primarily different race, having some fun together, and worshiping together.

Push your group to be creative and to think outside the box.

discussion

Encore

Get It?	Middle School

- How would you describe rescue by escape?

- How about rescue by transformation?

- Have you ever been rescued? Which kind of rescue did you experienced? Describe what happened.

- Which rescue by Jesus have you grown up believing? What does your church say?

Get It?	High School

- What does salvation through Jesus look like if it's rescue by escape?

- What does salvation through Jesus look like if it's rescue by transformation?

- How do I know which type of rescue is right if some Christians think one and some the other?

- Do you think it's possible the truth is somewhere in the middle? Or a combination of the two ideas? Why or why not?

- In what ways would rescue by transformation make Christianity more relevant for your friends?

What If?	The Big Picture

- If heaven is God's creation transformed, what things will we do in heaven? Will there be football, parties, music, and surfing in the renewed creation? Will it be one long praise sing-along in white dresses? Talk about your idea of heaven.

- If you assume rescue by escape, what are the implications for how we treat the world now?

- How about if you assume rescue by transformation? What are the implications for how you live now?

- Do most of your friends see Christianity as having a positive or negative view of the world? How about you?

- Do you have hope for the future? Why or why not?

So What?

It's Your Life

📢 If God's rescue plan is for the whole world, what can you do to get involved as a rescuer? What can you do this week?

📢 What are your gifts? How can you bring rescue to your part of creation with your gifts?

📢 Lots of people see God as a killjoy—meaning he kills our joy by making us keep rules. How can you let others know this isn't the case?

📢 How can you thank God for sending Jesus as a rescuer?

Not Just Hot Air

Contributed by **Steve Case**

Primary theme seeing God	
Themes belief, faith, trusting God	
Scripture 1 Kings 19:11-13; Psalm 29:1-4; 2 Timothy 3:16-17; Hebrews 11:1	
Approximate length through The Grand Finale 15-20 minutes	

Children need concrete ways to picture God. Most Sunday school material pictures a robe-wearing old man with long white hair. Once kids hit junior high they learn to think in more abstract terms. And they start to question their childhood perception of God. But they still wonder about seeing him.

This short talk uses a concrete object lesson but still allows young teens to think abstractly. You can lead into a discussion on faith in what we don't see.

Junior high students will respond best to this talk.

You'll need

- Pictures of God (see page 224 for ideas)
- TV and VCR
- *The Ten Commandments*
- A stereo
- "What If God Was One of Us" on the album *Relish* by Joan Osborne (Mercury, 1995)
- Flat balloons for each student
- A personal story about someone who helped you see God

intro

The Opening Act

🔊 **Discussion** *Pictures of God* (see sidebar)

🔊 **Movie clip** *The Ten Commandments* (see sidebar)

🔊 **Song** *What If God Was One of Us* (see sidebar)

Discussion

Pictures of God

Ask your students to talk about what they thought God looked like when they were small children. Find pictures of God in children's Sunday school books. Hold up a copy of the famous painting of God from the Sistine Chapel. You can find one to print out at www.christusrex.org. (You may want to trim Adam out of the picture for your talk. Adam's masculinity might end up being the focus instead of the image of God.)

Or you might use pictures of God described in *Wild Truth Journal: Pictures of God* (Mark Oestreicher, Youth Specialties, 1999). This student journal gives 50 self-portraits of God from Scripture.

Movie clip

The Ten Commandments

Start tape 2, 1:16:15 "From the burning bush, oh Lord…"

Stop 1:22:00 God's fire disappears, and Moses leaves with the tablets.

This classic clip shows Moses (Charlton Heston) receiving the Ten Commandments from God, while the Israelites are partying at the bottom mountain. It shows the cheesy, Hollywood, special-effects God. Tell your students in advance it's okay to laugh, so they don't think you're taking this clip too seriously!

Afterward ask students how accurate the portrayal of God was.

Song

"What If God Was One of Us?"

This song asks, "What if God was one of us, just a slob like one of us, just a stranger on the bus, trying to make his way home?" It angered some Christians when it was released. They thought it presented a low image of God. Make sure they understand the person asking the questions is someone who doesn't know God. Then ask students what they think of these ideas of God.

heart of the talk
The Main Event

1   How can we see God?

- 🔊 **Scripture** *1 Kings 19:11-13* (see sidebar)
- 🔊 **Object lesson** *The Balloon Experiment* (see sidebar)
- 🔊 **Discussion** *Shapely Christians* (see sidebar)

Scripture

1 Kings 19:11-13

Elijah is told he's going to see God. God doesn't appear to Elijah in a storm, earthquake, or fire. God is in the gentle breeze. We want God to appear to us in flashy special effects—like in movies. But God usually comes to us in a "still small voice," as it's described in 1 Kings 19:12 (KJV).

Object lesson

The balloon experiment

Ask students if they have ever seen air. After getting a few responses, pass out a balloon to each student. Have students blow up their balloons and tie them off. Be sure they all get tied off. A balloon rocketing around the room will basically kill the analogy you're trying to create! Explain they may not actually see the air, but, because the air is affecting the balloon, we know the air exists.

Most of us won't physically see God with our eyes until we get to heaven. But we can "see" God all over the place when we look for God's impact on the world and people.

Discussion

Shapely Christians

Ask your group can name people they think are filled with God. (Maybe you could make a joke here about being "full of it.") Explain what makes us able to see God in the way this person lives their life. Name someone in you own congregation who can walk the walk and talk the talk.

2   Where can we see God?

- 🔊 God is everywhere—and you'll see him all the time if you pay attention and know where to look.

- 🔊 We can see God in Scripture.

- 🔊 **Scripture** *2 Timothy 3:16-17* ("All Scripture is God-breathed.") Anytime we pick up the Bible we're making a connection with God.

- 🔊 **Quote** *Mike Yaconelli* (see sidebar)

- 🔊 **Discussion** *His Handiwork* (see sidebar)

- 🔊 **Scripture** *Psalm 29:1-4* ("The voice of the Lord is over the waters; the God of glory thunders…")

- 🔊 We can see God in our culture, in some music, in some movies. God inserts himself into our world. But we have to open our minds and see him to make the connection.

- 🔊 Ask your group to name popular secular bands that have released songs with spiritual themes.

- 🔊 We can see God in other believers—shaping them, like the air in a balloon.

- 🔊 **Personal illustration** *I've Seen God* Talk about a person in your own life who has greatly influenced your beliefs. Share specifically how you've seen God in this person. Then ask for student volunteers to share about a person they've seen God in.

Quote

Mike Yaconelli

Explain that even if the most devout atheist picks up the Bible and reads some of it, they might catch a glimpse of God. A guy named Mike Yaconelli said, "Give them the Truth and let the Truth do its own work."

Discussion

His handiwork

We can see God in nature. This isn't just new age, weirdo stuff. God made nature, and we can see him and learn about him in his beautiful work. Help your students to connect nature with the one who created it. Ask—

- **What do sunsets tell you about God?**

- **How about a beautiful mountain setting, with trees, a river, and wildlife—what does that tell you about God?**

- **How about the ocean—do you think you can see God there? How?**

closing
The Grand Finale

🔊 **Discussion** *Special FX* (see sidebar)

Discussion

Special FX

Tell your group they're the special effects team for *God: The Movie*, and they have an unlimited budget. How will they portray God in the movie? What special effects will they use? If your group has more than a dozen kids, you might want to break them into smaller groups for this discussion. Then have the groups present their ideas to the whole group as if pitching them to the director or producer of the film.

discussion
Encore

Get It?	Middle School

🔊 What does God look like to you?

🔊 Children often think of God as a white-haired, bearded old man in a long white robe. How would you describe God to a kindergarten Sunday school class? How would you describe God to someone your own age?

🔊 How is the way God reveals himself to us sometimes different than our expectations?

🔊 What are some ways we can see God?

🔊 What is faith? (For a biblical definition see Hebrews 11:1.)

Get It?   High School

- Pretend you are the defense lawyer in a trial to prove God doesn't exist. What evidence would you offer in defense of his existence?

- Why is it hard to take some assertions or statements on faith?

- How can someone look at you and see God?

- How can we feel the presence of God's Holy Spirit in our lives?

- Have you ever heard a song or read a passage of Scripture that made you feel like God was speaking directly to you? What was it and what happened?

- Have you ever seen a picture of God where he was anything but white? Describe what he looked like in that picture.

What If?   The Big Picture

- Why doesn't God just show up and put an end to all our questions?

- There are people on TV who claim they have daily conversations with God and he tells them all sorts of things. Do these people actually talk with God? Talk about that.

- God seems to have out loud one-on-one conversations with people in the Bible. Do you think God still communicates that way? Why or why not? Do you think God would ever talk to you this way? How would you respond if he did?

- Can a person be filled with God and not be Christian? Why or why not?

- Can a person see God if she's not a Christian? Why or why not?

So What?   It's Your Life

🔊 Pretend God came to you in a dream that seemed totally real. Pretend he asked you to do something for him. Would you do it? What would it take for you to believe it was a real visit from God?

🔊 Children can't understand abstract ideas like we do. Yet the Bible says God is beyond even our most grown-up understanding. How do you picture God now? How can you increase your understanding of who God is?

🔊 What difference would it make in your life if you made looking for God a major focus? Are you willing to try it? What would it cost you?

🔊 Maybe you have heard the phrase, *You are the only Jesus some people will see.* What understanding of Jesus do you think people would get by watching you live your life? Is this something you'd like to change? What could you do about it this week?

🔊 What can you do this week to look for God?

🔊 What can you do this week to listen to God?

Can We Disagree without Being Disagreeable?

Primary theme unity	
Themes community, conflict, the church	
Scripture 1 Corinthians 1:10-17; 3:1-4, 8-9	
Approximate length through The Grand Finale 20-30 minutes	

You'll need

🔊 A leader to stage a fight with you (optional)

🔊 A TV and VCR (optional)

🔊 A clip from a television program involving conflict (optional)

🔊 A personal story about conflict from your teen years (optional)

🔊 A personal story about how God has worked in your youth ministry recently

Most students feel united or connected to others who dress like them, listen to the same music, or like to do the same things after school. This talk invites students to consider a new kind of unity—the unity every believer has in Christ. Regardless of how your students dress, talk, or spend their free time, they're part of the same body. And as they experience their unity in Christ, they'll realize what it means to be united for him.

Contributed by **Kara Powell**

intro

The Opening Act

📣 Begin with one of these options.

- **Acting out** *Fight!* (see sidebar)

- **Video clip** *Tension on the Tube* Videotape a TV program involving conflict and show it to your group. Most TV shows do, but if you have no idea what to tape, you could try taping a few daytime talk shows.

- **Personal illustration** *My Conflict* Share a conflict you had when you were a teen. Describe in detail what you were thinking and feeling, as well as how it was resolved. If you don't have a story from that time, tell about something more recent.

📣 Transition with something like—

Let's face it. We all get into conflict—sometimes even with people in this very room. How are we supposed to handle it? Are we supposed to like everyone? Is it okay to hate people? Can we disagree without being disagreeable? The Apostle Paul gives us some pretty astounding answers to these tough questions relating to the unity we have as believers.

Acting out

Fight!

Stage a fight with one of your adult volunteers—prepare him ahead of time, of course. Have the volunteer interrupt you and continue to talk while you're talking. Ask him to stop talking several times. Then just lose it and start yelling, telling him to leave the room. Your students will probably be simultaneously intrigued and uncomfortable with the conflict. When you feel your point has been made, call the leader back in and explain it was fake.

heart of the talk

The Main Event

1 All believers are united in Christ.

🔊 **Scripture** *1 Corinthians 1:10-17* ("Perfectly united in mind and thought.")

🔊 **Explanation** *Take Me to Your Leader* (see sidebar)

🔊 The same thing holds true today. No school, gender, music style, race, ethnicity, clothing type, or free-time activity should divide us.

🔊 So does that mean we all have to act the same? Although that might be cool for a few minutes, pretty soon it would get boring. It's the diversity of believers that brings richness and great flavor to the church.

🔊 **Group Brainstorming** *Synergy* (see sidebar)

🔊 So will we always agree with every other believer? No way. But when we disagree with other Christians, we need to remember the one thing we share that unites us—our relationship with Christ.

Explanation

Take me to your leader

The believers in Corinth met at house churches, which were gatherings of 30 to 40 people who met in private homes. As a result, different house churches tended to develop special allegiances to different leaders, for instance to Paul or Apollos or Peter. Paul asks the rhetorical question in 1 Corinthians 1:13, "Is Christ divided?" The answer, of course, is no.

Group brainstorming

Synergy

Explain to your group that *synergy* is when the combination of the parts is more than the total of the parts. In other words, by putting several elements together, you come up with something much better than the individual elements in a group. Ask students for illustrations from life when this occurs. Some ideas: the right players making up a great sports team, a bunch of ingredients making a fantastic soufflé or casserole, the right colors and strokes coming together into a breathtaking painting. After you solicit some ideas, explain that we—the body of Christ—can be just the same way. That's how God designed us!

2   All believers are united for Christ.

📢 Being united for Christ means we work together to see his will being done all around us.

📢 **Scripture** *1 Corinthians 3:1-4, 8-9* ("For since there is jealousy and quarreling among you, are you not worldly?")

📢 Being God's fellow workers doesn't mean we're helping God or that he needs us. Rather, it means he is ultimately doing the work, but we each play a small part as we work together for him and his work.

📢 There are lots of things keeping us from being united for Christ and being fellow workers:

- We compare what we have to what others have, and we get jealous.
- Or we sit around, watching others work.

📢 Yet as we work together in our diversity, God uses us to reach out to others and impact them.

📢 **Illustration** *Arm in Parts* (see sidebar)

📢 **Personal illustration** *Right Here, Right Now* (see sidebar)

Illustration

Arm in parts

Illustrate the way we all need to work together by asking students to reach forward with their left arm by only using their shoulder—they won't be able to move their elbow or wrist or fingers. Then have them try it by only using their elbow, next their wrist, and finally their fingers. It's impossible to do. Finally let them use all four parts.

Explain that only when we all work together can we reach our full potential. The fingers are no more or less important than the shoulder.

Personal illustration

Right here, right now

Think about the last major way God worked in your youth ministry. Who was involved? How did he work through the diversity of gifts and people in your group? Share about that, specifying individual students and adult leaders who were involved and the impact that resulted from working together.

closing

The Grand Finale

🔊 **Reflection** *Saying Sorry* (see sidebar)

🔊 Encourage students to find another person in the room whom they normally don't talk to and spend time talking to him or her afterward. They might be surprised at how much they enjoy getting to know each other.

🔊 **Future activity** *Gettin' Together* (see sidebar)

Reflection

Saying sorry

Invite students to think about someone in the group they have judged or decided they don't like. Give them time to repent in quiet prayer and ask God to help them be united with other believers—even when they get a little annoying.

You may even want to invite students to go to someone in the room whom they have judged or decided they don't like. When they find that person, they should sincerely apologize for what they've done and ask the other person to forgive them.

Future activity

Gettin' together

Either schedule a service project or pick an upcoming activity and challenge teens to come to the activity and hang out or work with someone they normally wouldn't spend much time with. Make sure you remind them of this when they show up for the event.

discussion

Encore

Get It?	Middle School

🔊 If we're supposed to be united, are we all supposed to be the same? Why or why not?

🔊 What are some of the things that tend to unite friends? Are these good or bad things? Explain your answer.

🔊 Are cliques worse at school or at your church? How so?

🔊 Think of a time when God worked in a great way because of all the different people who were involved. Talk about that.

Get It? — High School

- 🔊 What defines the group you hang out with at church? How does "having a group" relate to the idea of unity?

- 🔊 In what ways do you compare yourself with others? How does that affect your unity in Christ? How about your unity for Christ?

- 🔊 When are you most likely to sit around and watch others do the work? What causes you to do that?

What If? — The Big Picture

- 🔊 Do you tend to spend time with people who are like you or unlike you? Is there anything wrong with your answer? Is there anything right about your answer?

- 🔊 What kinds of people are you most likely to judge or decide you dislike? How do you feel about that? How do you think God feels about that?

- 🔊 Would a new person feel more comfortable showing up at your school or your church? Talk about that.

- 🔊 Is it possible to be united with other believers, even if you don't like them? Talk about your answer.

- 🔊 What should you do if another believer makes you angry?

- 🔊 Does the talk about unity also apply to people who don't know Jesus yet? Why or why not?

So What? — It's Your Life

- 🔊 How would our youth group be different if you decided to be united, even though we're different? What would others think when they show up?

- 🔊 What keeps you from working with other Christians to reach out to people?

- 🔊 What is one way you could work with other Christians to reach out to students at school?

Sleeping with Bread

Primary theme depending on God	
Themes bondage, discipleship, security, hope, freedom, communion	
Scripture Matthew 22:37-40; John 6:35; 8:31-32; 8:34; Romans 6:17-18; 6:23; Revelation 21:1-4	
Approximate length through The Grand Finale 25-30 minutes	

Contributed by **Tim Conder**

This talk begins with a memorable metaphor of security, need, and dependence. It moves quickly to expose areas of false security and inappropriate dependence in the lives of students. The ultimate purpose is to highlight the foundation and security Christ offers us when we become joyfully dependent on him. Because of the themes and issues of security and dependence, this talk connects easily and rapidly with the heartfelt needs and concerns of students. It serves equally well in discipleship and evangelistic settings and can benefit both these goals simultaneously. This talk is also great for a communion service.

You'll need

- ◀)) A personal story about a time your trust was misplaced

- ◀)) A large loaf of unsliced bread or several loaves of fresh, warm bread and nice display tables for them (optional, see page 237 for details)

- ◀)) TV and VCR

- ◀)) *The Matrix*

- ◀)) A teddy bear or other object of childhood security

- ◀)) A personal story about a time you pursued a goal only to find it didn't matter

- ◀)) Pencils and paper for students

intro

The Opening Act

🔊 **Illustration** *Sleeping with Bread* (see sidebar)

🔊 **Discussion** *Security Check* (see sidebar)

🔊 **Personal illustration** *My Misplaced Dependence* Tell a personal story of dependence. Describe a situation where you relied on something or someone other than Christ for security and hope and were deeply disappointed.

🔊 Transition by saying something like—

> **Everyone—to differing degrees—depends on tempo-rary, insufficient, or even dangerous measures for security and meaning. Many live comfortably in the belief they're truly safe and secure. This is dangerous. Jesus said in John 6:35, "I am the Bread of Life. He who comes to me will never go hungry, and he who believes in me will never be thirsty." Jesus means he is the only real source of security. Let's consider what "bread" or meaning Jesus offers us.**

Illustration

Sleeping with bread

We live in a country untouched by war for many, many years. It's hard to imagine the destruction and despair war causes. But ask your students to try to imagine and recreate in their minds the horror and desperation Europe faced after the six years of World War II. One of the great tragedies was the number of children who were orphaned. These children were terrified by loss, hunger, and the constant fear of death. In many orphanages, children were so terrified they were not able to sleep at night.

In one orphanage the staff began to brainstorm about what they could do to help the kids sleep more securely. A wonderful experiment was suggested. They would let the children cradle a loaf of bread when they went to bed. It worked! The loaf of bread symbolized stability, protection, and at least the surety of a meal the next day. Many of the children began to sleep more regularly and more peacefully.

Discussion

Security check

Ask students to share what their peers and people in our society cling to for security. Ask if the things we clutch and cradle actually provide security. What are some of the consequences of seeking security and meaning in temporary or even dangerous measures? Help your students process the subtle effects of misplaced dependence.

heart of the talk

The Main Event

1　The bread of freedom

- 🔊 **Object lesson** *Loaf of Bread* (see sidebar)

- 🔊 Jesus is the Bread of Life because Jesus offers us true freedom.

- 🔊 The freedom Jesus offers is often not appreciated because many of us don't know what true freedom is.

- 🔊 Freedom isn't doing whatever you want to do, whenever you want to do it—a world without rules.

- 🔊 **Illustration** *Streets without Lanes and Traffic Laws* (see sidebar)

- 🔊 **Scripture** *John 8:34* ("Everyone who sins is a slave to sin.")

- 🔊 **Movie clip** *The Matrix* (see sidebar)

- 🔊 Jesus offers us freedom from the bondage, guilt, and shame of sin.

- 🔊 **Scripture** *John 8:31-32* ("You will know the truth and the truth will set you free.")

- 🔊 **Scripture** *Romans 6:17-18* ("You used to be slaves to sin…you have been set free from sin.")

- 🔊 True freedom is the freedom to do what we were created to do. We were created to know, love, worship, and be in relationship with God. This is the bread of freedom Jesus offers us.

Object lesson

Loaf of bread

Bring a large loaf of unsliced bread to hold and point to during various points of the talk. Especially with smaller groups and in smaller rooms, it can be effective to buy several warm loaves of bread from a local bakery and place them around the meeting room. The aroma of the bread will fill the room and will add a sensory affirmation to the points of the talk. Simple decorations around the bread—nice tables, tablecloths, candles—can add to the atmosphere and affirm the value of Jesus' gifts to us.

Illustration

Streets without lanes and traffic laws

Most of us imagine a world without rules as a perfect place, a place of never-ending fun. In reality this would be like driving in a huge city without traffic laws. Can you imagine a metropolitan area with no traffic lanes, stop signals, right-of-way laws, or rules of driving? Total chaos! It would take longer to travel to wherever you're going, and travel would be dangerous!

In reality, good rules, laws, and boundaries create a platform in life for greater freedom. Our world is a lot like this traffic illustration. Because of the chaos our sin has created, we aren't truly free. We live in bondage to sin and our sinful desires.

Movie clip

The Matrix

Start 25:15 Neo is led into the room to meet Morpheus

Stop 29:39 Neo selects a pill.

This scene describes the premise of this thoughtful sci-fi movie—and the very point we're making about our illusion of freedom. The scene begins with the lead character Neo (Keanu Reeves) being brought before a strange man called Morpheus (Laurence Fishburne). Morpheus explains the world isn't as it appears. The lives humans are living are all illusions. The reality is a state of horrible bondage.

The scene ends with Neo being given a choice. He can take one pill and return to his life of illusion—with no memory of their conversation—or he can take another pill and learn the truth. He takes the pill that will bring the truth.

2   The bread of hope

🔊 Jesus also offers us the bread of true hope.

🔊 Hope is life's greatest motivator. Without hope we only have despair.

🔊 As we said earlier, many of us cling to false hopes for security—things that are temporary, unlikely, or even dangerous. These false hopes ultimately lead to despair.

🔊 **Discussion** *False Hopes* (see sidebar)

🔊 **Object lesson** *A Teddy Bear* (see sidebar)

🔊 True hope is sufficient for our needs. This is the bread of hope Jesus offers us. It's knowing we'll spend an eternity in God's presence and protection.

🔊 **Scripture** *Revelation 21:1-4* ("He will wipe every tear from their eyes. There will be no more death or mourning or crying or pain.")

🔊 **Scripture** *Romans 6:23* ("The gift of God is eternal life.")

False hopes

If you didn't use the discussion option in the introduction, it works well here. Ask students to describe the false hopes they and their peers rely on. Also ask students to describe the consequences of relying on these false hopes.

A teddy bear

Bring out a teddy bear—or another childhood security item like a blanket or pacifier—to illustrate the point of false hope, comfort, and security. This illustration can be done effectively in a serious manner. Describe how important this item was to you—or whomever it belonged to—and the harsh process of realization that the item offered no real protection from the fears and dangers of our world.

This illustration can also be done in a creative, humorous manner. Have the teddy bear or stuffed animal fight and lose in battle with imagined monsters. Add lots of silly sound effects or real monsters—in the shape of volunteers who know some great professional wrestling moves! The teddy bear could even be put on trial for failure to keep you safe and secure all at times. The possibilities are endless.

3   The bread of mission

🔊   Jesus is the Bread of Life because Jesus also offers us true purpose—a mission that matters.

🔊   Sometimes our lives seem like a cruel joke. We can work very hard on tasks and for goals we find out ultimately don't matter at all.

🔊   **Personal illustration** *If I Knew Then What I Know Now* (see sidebar)

🔊   **Illustration** *The Wizard of Oz* (see sidebar)

🔊   **Discussion** *Lousy Goals* (see sidebar)

🔊   Jesus offers a mission that matters. That mission is simply to glorify God who's all-powerful, all-loving, totally perfect, and completely faithful. And the mission is to proclaim this God to a lost world with all our words and actions.

🔊   **Scripture** *Matthew 22:37-40* ("Love the Lord your God with all your heart...Love your neighbor as yourself.")

Personal illustration

If I knew then what I know now

Tell a personal if-I-knew-then-what-I-know-now story. Describe some goal you relentlessly pursued or some task you sacrificed greatly to accomplish—only to find out later the goal or task didn't matter in the grand scheme of life..

Illustration

The Wizard of Oz

No one has escaped childhood without seeing this movie, so you don't have to show a clip. Remind your kids about the story and how it offers a great metaphor. We perceive life as a grand and sometimes dangerous journey with a dramatic experience and end in mind. But so often the great wizards we pursue end up being short, fat, balding imposters. Our true mission often lies much closer to the heart.

Discussion

Lousy goals

If you haven't used a discussion option yet or if you're in a setting where you prefer to use more dialogue, ask a few students to share some illustrations of goals and purposes they have pursued, only to be later disappointed by the insignificance of these goals.

closing

The Grand Finale

📢 Remind students of the opening illustration, *Sleeping with Bread*, since the whole bread idea is built on it!

📢 Summarize how Jesus is the Bread of Life. He offers the breads of true freedom, true hope, and true purpose.

📢 Because Jesus is the Bread of Life, we can live in total dependence on Christ. Christ is the only one who can give us security!

📢 **Reflection** *Exchanging False Expectations, Hopes, and Purposes for the Bread of Life* (see sidebar)

Exchanging false expectations, hopes, and purposes for the Bread of Life

Pass out paper and pens have the students write down confessions about the things they've held onto in the pursuit of freedom, hope, and security. This will be way tough for young teens, so you'll have to help them with suggestions.

Or you can continue on in the Loaf of Bread object lesson from the first point, by having students take their sheet of confessions to one of the loaves and exchange their confessions for a piece of bread.

discussion
Encore

Get It? — Middle School

◀ When Jesus claimed to be the Bread of Life, he didn't mean he would be actual food for his followers, did he? What did he mean?

◀ Why is being able to do whatever we want to do not really freedom? What would happen if everyone did as they pleased?

◀ What's false hope? What are some examples of false hopes?

◀ Name some goals your peers pursue that aren't truly meaningful.

◀ What true gifts does Jesus offer to us?

Get It? — High School

◀ When Jesus declares he is the Bread of Life, what does he mean?

◀ Describe what fake freedom looks like in your world. What do you think about the idea that we're far less free than we imagine?

◀ What are the characteristics of false hope? Offer some specific examples.

◀ What's the focus of the hope Jesus offers?

◀ What purpose or mission does Jesus offer to us?

What If? — The Big Picture

🔊 If Jesus offers true freedom, why do so many people who examine and reject Jesus claim Christianity is restrictive or takes away our freedoms?

🔊 Have you experienced Christian faith as a source of great freedom or as a source of restrictions and loss of freedom? Why?

🔊 Does the hope Jesus offers actually matter to you and change the way you live your life? What changes in perspective or lifestyle might result if you choose to accept the hope Jesus offers?

🔊 If you chose to reject the less meaningful purposes and goals that often drive us and shape our lives, how would your life be different?

🔊 What would it look like in daily life for you to accept the mission Jesus offers? What does it mean to live out Jesus' mission in the normal, everyday parts of our lives? Can we live out Jesus' mission without moving overseas and becoming missionaries? Talk about that.

So What? — It's Your Life

🔊 What are some areas of your life in which you'd like to experience more freedom? How can you accomplish this?

🔊 What are some false hopes you would like to reject? This has gotta be more than just saying it, right? What will you do this week to move away from those false hopes and continue rejecting them?

🔊 Do you have any goals in life that don't line up with the mission Jesus gives us? How do you handle this? Will Jesus wreck your life if you loosen your grip on those goals? What step are you willing to take in this direction right now?

🔊 What would it take for you to trust Jesus more for freedom, hope, and mission?

🔊 What would being more dependent on Christ look like in your life? How can you be more dependent on Christ this week?

Contributed by **Tim Baker**

You've Got God-Mail

Primary theme God's will

Themes obedience to God, discipleship, God's call, trusting God

Scripture Exodus 3:1-7, 11-12; 12:31-36

Approximate length through The Grand Finale 25-30 minutes

hen you stand in front of your kids with a well-prepared lesson or talk, what do you see? Are you passionate about that group of nose-picking, hormonally-charged, self-conscious, impressionable teenagers changing the world with God? Do you think they have any clue God can use them this way—that God is calling them to do amazing things for him? God has huge plans for your students! And this talk will help them begin to answer the questions—

- What is God calling me to do with my life?

- How should I respond when God asks me to do something for him?

- One dollar bill—or a $5 or $10, if your budget allows

- Several student volunteers to search for the money

- Written directions to help students find the money (see page 244 for ideas)

- A personal story about a time someone tried to get your attention

- A personal story about a time God tried to get your attention

- TV and VCR

- *The Prince of Egypt*

- A personal story about a time you felt God urge you to act

- A stereo

- A favorite Christian song

- Pencils and paper for students

intro

The Opening Act

🔊 **Activity** *Listening for the Real Instructions* (see sidebar)

🔊 **Personal Illustration** *Getting My Attention* (see sidebar)

🔊 Then transition by saying something like—

> **I don't know about you, but God has had to do some crazy things in my life to get my attention. And many of us—when God asks us to do something—offer back all these excuses about why we're not the right choice. Even Moses did. There are a few characteristics that seem common to these holy calls from God.**

Activity

Listening for the real instructions

Before your group meets, hide a dollar bill—or if you can afford it a $5 or a $10—where no one will find it. Then write out a list of various instructions for finding the money. You'll want to have only one true direction with lots of bogus ones thrown in.

For example, if you hid the money in the hallway just outside the door, you might want to give directions like—

- Look under the third chair in the second row.

- Check in Steve's back pocket.

- Look in the hallway just outside the door.

- Peek in Laura's purse (clear this with Laura ahead of time!)

- Look behind the picture on the wall with the window.

- Check inside the youth director's mouth.

When you begin your talk, ask for a few volunteers—maybe a guy and a girl or one student from each grade—to compete to find the money first. (Having a bigger bill hidden really ups the tension and excitement!) Tell them you're going to read a list of instructions really fast. Students will have to discern which of the directions leads to the money. The other directions will be there just to confuse them. If they can figure out which instruction to listen to first, they'll get the money. Read the list of instructions quickly, allowing them to start looking only when you've finished reading.

Don't allow other students in the room to help the participants or remind them of the instructions. If you have time (and money!) you can play two or three rounds—with new instructions.

After the activity ask—

- **How was this like trying to listen to God's will?**

- **Do you ever feel that you don't have a good way to know what God's asking you to do? How do you respond to that?**

Getting my attention

Tell two personal stories. First tell about a time when another person tried to get your attention and had a difficult time. (Or the other way around—that you were trying unsuccessfully to get someone else's attention!) It would be great if this were a funny story.

Then tell another story of a time when God tried to get your attention and you weren't listening. Describe what God did to wake you up.

heart of the talk

The Main Event

1   God likes to give us jobs that feel impossible.

- 📣 God spoke to Moses in an unusual way, and his request was something Moses wasn't expecting.

- 📣 **Scripture** *Exodus 3:1-7* ("There the angel of the Lord appeared to him in flames of fire from within the bush.").

- 📣 **Movie clip** *The Prince of Egypt* (see sidebar)

- 📣 Most of us don't hear God's voice speak to us out loud like Moses did— but that doesn't mean God isn't calling us to do wild and outrageous things for him!

- 📣 **Personal illustration** *My Undeniable Call* (see sidebar)

The Prince of Egypt

Start 42:30 Moses walks among his sheep with his staff on his shoulder.

Stop 47:30 "I shall be with you, Moses."

This DreamWorks version of the biblical story uses animation to recreate what Moses might have seen and heard when God showed up in the burning bush.

My undeniable call

Tell a story about a time when you were sure God was asking you to do something that seemed a bit crazy, difficult, or simply out of your comfort zone. If you tried reasoning with God to get out of his request, be sure to include that information. It's not essential that you did what God asked you to do for this story, just that it was clear God was asking you. In fact, a story where God asked you to do something and you wimped out could have more impact on your kids.

2   When God asks, we have to trust him.

🔊 After hearing what God had in mind, Moses did his best to talk his way out of doing what God wanted. He felt totally inadequate to do what God wanted.

🔊 **Discussion** *If I Were Mo* (see sidebar)

🔊 Moses tosses out excuse after excuse, but they're all a variation on the first one.

🔊 **Scripture** *Exodus 3:11-12* ("Who am I that I should go to Pharaoh and bring the Israelites out of Egypt?")

🔊 Moses felt totally inadequate to do what God asked, just as we often do. Moses was basically asking, "Why me?"

🔊 **Illustration** *How Have You Heard God's Voice?* (see sidebar)

🔊 For some of us God whispers. For others he shouts. And some of us don't think we've ever heard God.

🔊 Ask the students how God's given them direction in life. Did they hear him?

Discussion

If I were Mo

Ask students to put themselves in Moses' sandals. Lead a discussion on how your students would have responded to the voice from the burning bush—especially to God's idea of using you to save an entire group of people from slavery.

Illustration

How have you heard God's voice?

Using a stereo, play 10 seconds of a favorite Christian song as loud as you can stand it. Then play another 10 seconds of the song as quiet as you can while still being able to hear it.

Ask students which is more like God's call. Which way was like the way God called Moses?

Interestingly, God seems to speak most often these days in a whisper—a whisper in our hearts—and that's how the scene is portrayed in *The Prince of Egypt*. But the passage in Scripture actually has an exclamation point when God calls to Moses—Moses! Moses! And this would tend to lead you to believe God yelled to Mo.

3   **When we do what God asks, the results in our lives are unbelievable.**

🔊 When Moses gave in and followed God, he was able to do what God wanted. No longer was Moses a shepherd; he was the mouthpiece of God and the rescuer of a nation of people!

🔊 When we ignore God, we're missing a chance for God to change the world or change the world around us. And we're missing the chance to be used by God.

🔊 **Scripture** *Exodus 12:31-36* ("The Egyptians urged the people to hurry and leave the country.")

🔊 **Explanation** *What Happened Next* (see sidebar)

🔊 What might God be asking you to do?

Explanation

What happened next

Some of your students may be able to tell the rest of Mo's story better than you! But it's increasingly likely some of your kids don't know what happens after this burning bush scene. So explain how Moses gave in and did what God asked.

- Moses confronted Pharaoh—the king of Egypt—more than once.

- God brought about all the plagues.

- Pharaoh gave in, and, after 400 years of slavery, Moses led the Israelites to freedom.

- God led them through the miraculously parted Red Sea.

- Moses met with God on a mountain top a couple times, talked with God, saw God from the back (wow!), and got the Ten Commandments—twice!

closing

The Grand Finale

🔊 God's desire to use people didn't end with Moses.

God is calling you to do wild and outrageous—and wonderful and small—things for him.

🔊 God leaves us with one choice—to follow his commands. Stop making excuses!

🔊 **Reflection** *I Hear You, God!* (see sidebar)

🔊 **Further reflection** *Pairs* (see sidebar)

Reflection

I hear you, God!

Give each student a sheet of paper and a pen or pencil. Read the following list to students and have them choose the one they think God might be asking them to do. Or they can identify an item of their own choosing.

- Be nice to a loner kid.
- Talk to the elderly neighbor who's lonely.
- Be cool to your little bro or sis.
- Obey your parents when you don't feel like it.
- Pull out of the gossip chain.
- Invite someone to youth group.
- Open your mouth and share the hope you have in Jesus Christ.
- Sell some of your stuff and give the money to help a good cause.
- Serve someone.
- Show mercy and forgiveness to someone who doesn't deserve it.

After choosing, have students write down two or three specific steps they could take this week to respond to God in this area.

Further reflection

Pairs

Consider having students get in pairs and share what they just wrote. Encourage students to be as open as they can. After they've shared, have students spend time praying for each other. As you notice students finishing their prayers, call students to the center of the meeting room. Close the talk with a time where you pray for your students, and their ability to both listen to God and obey what he calls them to do.

discussion

Encore

Get It? — Middle School

- 🔊 God doesn't speak out loud to us very often. So how are we supposed to hear him calling?

- 🔊 What excuses did Moses use when God called him?

- 🔊 What's the big deal with doing what God wants? Why is it so important?

- 🔊 Will God be upset with you if you ignore him? Why or why not?

- 🔊 Can you be a Christian and ignore God? Why or why not?

- 🔊 What should you do if God asks you to do something you don't want to do?

Get It? — High School

- 🔊 How can we hear God? What's that look like?

- 🔊 What happens to you if you choose to ignore God or use excuses like the ones Moses tried?

- 🔊 What should you do if God asks you to do something you feel totally incompetent to do?

- 🔊 Why does God ask some people to do amazing things and others to do things that are way less thrilling?

What If? The Big Picture

📢 What might happen if you listened to God? How might your life change?

📢 What happened to Moses is a great story, but does this type of thing happen today? Does God still talk to people in the way he spoke Moses? Talk about that.

📢 What do you think about this statement: *All the jobs God asks people to do are of equal value*. What are some God-directed tasks that could be perceived as being more important than others? Why do you think so?

📢 Let's say God asked you to take a stand for him at school. What might happen?

📢 Pretend you are out with your non-Christian friends and you meet someone who takes a bold stand for God. How would you respond? What would you say?

So What? It's Your Life

📢 What do you need to change in your life to take an open, public stand for God at school? How would that affect your ability to do what God wants?

📢 If God wants us to do cool things for him, why does he give us the chance to not do them? After all, he wants the world to be changed, so why does he let us ignore him?

📢 What can you do this week to watch for the burning bush in your life? In other words how can you make yourself ready—we're talkin' specific steps—to hear God speak to you?

📢 What's something difficult you think God might be asking you to do? If it's so difficult, how are you supposed to do it?

My Brother's Keeper

Contributed by **Miles McPherson**

Primary theme sin	
Themes submission, sacrifice, selfishness, worship, God's love, judging others	
Scripture Genesis 4:2-16	
Approximate length through The Grand Finale 20-30 minutes	

You'll need

- Pencils and paper for students
- Several large rocks or lots of smaller ones
- Index cards

God calls us to come to him on his terms, but we want to do it our way—I can't do that for you, God, but I'll attend church a couple times a month, okay? Surrendering to God isn't easy—or we'd all do it in a flash. But God's call isn't diminished by the difficulty of his request. He wants us to give him our best, and he wants us to do this selflessly. But he also calls us to go after people who are broken and hurting to help them give their best too—and not judge them for their sin.

intro

The Opening Act

📢 **Defining** *Submission* (see sidebar)

📢 **Discussion** *Prep 'Em* (see sidebar)

📢 Ask for a volunteer to summarize the story of Cain and Abel for the group.

Definitions

Submission

Have students get in pairs or groups and create a definition of submission. Then have them write out what it means to submit to God—in other words, what does submitting to God look like in the everyday life of a teenager? When they're finished, ask them to imagine they have to communicate their definition and explanation to a seven-year-old. Have a few kids present their simplified descriptions.

Discussion

Prep 'em

Get your students prepped for your talk by using these or similar questions. Be very open-ended—don't look for "right" answers, as much as good thinking and discussion.

- **Why does God love us so much?**

- **Why does God care if we submit to him or not?**

- **How should we think about other people with lots of sin in their lives? What if they're really evil—like drug dealers, murderers, and child molesters?**

heart of the talk

The Main Event

1 God's mind-blowing request—give up everything!

◀)) **Scripture** *Genesis 4:2-5* ("Cain brought some fruits of the soil as an offering.")

◀)) **Explanation** *In the Beginning* (see sidebar)

◀)) Cain and Abel both sacrificed. But they each had a different approach to how they offered it to God.

◀)) Ask if anyone wants to take a guess as to what the difference was between the two offerings.

◀)) God desires an offering—the best of what we have—given by faith. And Abel offered that. But Cain just went through the motions. Cain's offering was like tossing three pennies in the tip jar at the coffee shop.

◀)) **Illustration** *The Lousy Gift* (see sidebar)

◀)) You can't treat God like a waiter and give him a three-penny tip. God wants what he deserves—all of you!

◀)) When God says, "I want you—all of you," we have a choice to make. We can give what he asks or not give anything at all. But often we try to get away with giving leftovers and less than the best.

Explanation

In the beginning

If your group isn't super Bible-knowledgeable—or if they're simply not familiar with this particular story—summarize it for them. Adam and Eve had two sons—Cain, who was a farmer, and Abel, who was a shepherd. When it came time to offer sacrifices to God, Cain brought "a gift of his farm produce" while Abel brought "several choice lambs from the best of his flock" Genesis 4:3-4, NLT). In Hebrews 11:4 we see that Abel's sacrifice was offered by faith. That's why God looked favorably on Abel's sacrifice and not on Cain's.

Illustration

The lousy gift

Think of receiving a phone call from a rich uncle who says, "I want to give you a gift. What would you like?" And you answer, "Well, I'd like a new car, thank you." He responds, "Hey, whatever you want!"

But when the gift comes in the mail, it's a fairly small box. Trying to stay calm, you open the card first. It says, "I decided to get you this instead. Hope you enjoy it." You open the box and find a pair of Superman underwear. What a lousy gift! Not what you wanted at all!

2   Selfishness blows our lives apart.

- 🔊 Cain's choice to offer God a sacrifice on his terms left him living a life apart from God.

- 🔊 **Scripture** *Genesis 4:5-8* ("Cain, why are you so angry? Why is your face downcast?")

- 🔊 Our sin erodes our lives and leads us away from God.

- 🔊 Cain's sin with the offering led him to more sin.

- 🔊 **Illustration** *The Chance to Sin* (see sidebar)

- 🔊 **Object lesson** *Hitting a Wall* (see sidebar)

- 🔊 Just as with Cain, God says to us, "As soon as you're ready to turn away from that sin, I'm here waiting for you. I've loved you the whole time. Everything will be fine if you'll come back to me."

Illustration

The chance to sin

The training camp roommate of football great Keith Jackson tells the story of the night both of them became Christians. Keith called up all his many girlfriends. "It's over." "It's over." "It's over." "It's over." Later that night the two roommates turned out the lights and went to bed.

After a few minutes there was a knock on the door. When they answered the door, three women ran in and jumped into Keith Jackson's bed. Keith yelled out to God, "Oh no, God, please!" and the roommate yelled, "Be strong!" And Keith had the courage to tell the women to leave.

The opportunity to sin is always knocking at your door! When you give God less than all, you walk right into the open arms of sin.

Object lesson

Hitting a wall

If you've got the guts to do this—really, if you're crazy enough—run into a wall as hard as you can without hurting yourself. Ham it up and fall down. Then get up and run into the wall again. And maybe a third time! (If you're a 75-year-old youth speaker or a lady in a nice dress, you might want to recruit someone else to do this!)

Follow up your stunt by saying something like—

This is just like us! Choosing sin is like running into a wall because it doesn't get us anything but pain. Yet we do it over and over again. And God says, "Why are you doing that?" just as he said to Cain, "Why are you so downcast?"

3 God calls us to go after blown-up lives.

◀ᵗᵞ **Scripture** *Genesis 4:9* ("Am I my brother's keeper?")

Cain copped an attitude with God. God called him on his sin, and Cain tried to pretend God didn't have a clue.

◀ᵗᵞ **Scripture** *Genesis 4:10-16* (see sidebar)

◀ᵗᵞ Remind students of the question you asked at the very beginning about judging other sinners—even evil ones.

◀ᵗᵞ God marks sinners with grace. Who are we to judge them?

◀ᵗᵞ **Illustration** *Big Theology Word* (see sidebar)

◀ᵗᵞ We should go to our lost friends as fellow sinners and help them put their lives back together.

Scripture

Genesis 4:10-16

God turns things around here. Cain's sin has big consequences. But Cain assumes it means God doesn't even care for him anymore. Instead God says, "No way, Cain, I still love you and will make sure no one hurts you." Then God puts a mark on Cain so people will know not to hurt him.

Illustration

Big theology word

Explain that there's a theology term that fits here: *prevenient grace*. It could be described as God's grace working to get you to say you're sorry and turn back to him. It's not God just waiting for you to come back. It's his grace working on you, every day, drawing you back. *Psst, I love you. Psst, I love you. C'mon back and everything will be all right.*

closing

The Grand Finale

◀))) Cain asked, "Am I my brother's keeper?" The answer is yes. We have a responsibility to go to people who have spent their lives trying to live without God and help them to him.

◀))) **Activity** *Walking Dead* (see sidebar)

◀))) Remind students of the challenges presented by this talk.

- God wants the best gift of all—us!

- When we try to fake out God by cheating him, we move away from him and mess up our own lives.

- God's just waiting for us to return to him—he's even working in our lives to pull us back.

- Because God is working in other's lives to draw them to him also, we shouldn't judge them. We should come alongside and try to help point them to God's love.

◀))) **Object lesson** *The Altar* (see sidebar)

Activity

Walking dead

Have students think of someone they're avoiding because of that person's blown-up life. Ask them to think for a minute about how that person's life got the way it is. Ask them to think about whether they've been judging and condemning that person. And ask them to think about how they can come alongside them and point them to God. Give students about 30 seconds or a minute for each of these questions.

Object lesson

The altar

Place several large rocks—or lots of smaller ones—in a pile on the floor of your meeting room. Explain to students they represent an altar much like Cain and Abel would have had. Ask students to consider if they've got anything they need to surrender to God.

- Things God is asking for that I won't surrender.

- Friends who've walked away from God that I need to help come back.

Give students index cards and have them write their responses. Then have students place their cards on the altar. If you're outside, light the cards on fire. Spend time praying for your students and their commitments.

discussion

Encore

Get It?   Middle School

🔊 What was the difference between Cain's offering and Abel's offering? Why did God care?

🔊 How are we sometimes like Cain?

🔊 Does turning away from God blow your life apart? Explain your answer.

🔊 Why shouldn't we judge other sinners?

Get It?   High School

🔊 What happens when we try to live for God on our terms and not on his terms?

🔊 What are some ways you're trying to be happy without giving God what he wants? How has that hurt your relationship with God?

🔊 How are we changed when we give up what we want for what God wants?

🔊 How does God's forgiveness bring us back to him?

🔊 What's the best way to go after a so-called dead friend?

What If?   The Big Picture

🔊 What keeps you from giving God everything he wants? Why is this so difficult?

🔊 How would your relationship with God be enhanced if you totally surrendered to him?

🔊 What's your response to knowing God has marked you with his grace? Talk about that.

🔊 Do you think God asks too much? After asking for us to give him "things," he also wants to make sure our attitudes are right. Why does he care about our attitudes?

So What?   It's Your Life

🔊 Think of one area in your life where you're giving God a lousy gift—a tiny bit of what he wants. Are you willing to submit to God completely this week in that one area? What will you have to do to remember this?

🔊 What's the best way to deal with the negative emotions we often feel when we think about giving up something for God?

🔊 Name one way you're going to be part of God's grace in the life of another sinner this week.

Wise Guys (and Girls!)

Primary theme wisdom	
Themes trusting God, spiritual growth, discipleship, sin	
Scripture Proverbs 1:7; 3:5-8; 9:10; 15:33	
Approximate length through The Grand Finale 20-25 minutes	

Teenagers are often encouraged to be wise—to make wise decisions, to choose friends wisely. But what is wisdom? By providing a basic definition and working understanding of wisdom, this talk helps kids to understand exactly what we want them to do. We want them to live life Jesus-style. We want them to have the wisdom to choose God and God's ways.

You'll need

- A large candy gumball

- *The Joy of Fearing God* by Jerry Bridges (Waterbrook, 1999, optional)

- Two student volunteers to run an obstacle course—one prepped ahead of time

- Boxes, chairs, tires, and other portable but bulky items to make an obstacle course

Contributed by **Greg Lafferty**

intro

The Opening Act

◀))) **Illustration** *Fitting into Your World* (see sidebar)

◀))) Transition by saying something like—

> **You demonstrated tremendous skill today at fitting into your physical world. But how did you do in your moral world? Your relational world? Your spiritual world? The ability to work with the deeper principles of life—to fit into the moral, relational, and spiritual world as God has made it—is what the Bible calls wisdom. A few of the most famous verses in the entire Bible explain to us what wisdom is.**

Scripture *Proverbs 3:5-8* ("Trust in the Lord with all your heart.")

Illustration

Fitting into your world

Explain how students are already experts at fitting into their physical worlds. You could congratulate everyone on their physical prowess in dealing with everyday obstacles. For instance—

- They navigated stairs expertly by shortening their strides and lowering their feet—and not even holding onto the handrails!

- They respected the rigidity of walls and only attempted to enter rooms by the portals we call doors.

- They recognized—smartly, you might add—that it was best to take a shower with hot water and brush their teeth with cold water.

- They drove on the right side of the road at the posted speed—courteously honoring all signs and traffic signals—so they arrived in one piece…right? (Obviously this point is for high schoolers only.)

Or you might point out their amazing discernment in use of paper.

- Today no one tried to buy lunch with a Post-it note.

- No one loaded Kleenex into a laser printer.

- People didn't blow their noses into a dollar bill.

- No one dried their hands with a newspaper.

heart of the talk

The Main Event

1   Wisdom is relying on God's strength.

- 🔊 **Scripture** reread *Proverbs 3:5* ("Trust in the Lord with all your heart.")

- 🔊 When you trust in someone, you don't just share a few secrets or loan them your favorite CD. You rely on them! Completely. At least that's what the Bible means by trust.

- 🔊 **Illustration** *Boating on the Chesapeake Bay* (see sidebar)

- 🔊 The Old Testament word for *trust* means "to spread out flat upon." It carries the idea of living one's life spread-eagle on God.

- 🔊 Just about everything can be done from the spread-eagle position. A person can take an exam, eat lunch, go on a date, practice the flute—all relying fully on God. The Bible challenges people to exercise full out trust in all our ways (Proverbs 3:6).

Illustration

Boating on the Chesapeake Bay

One family was filled with skilled boaters and water-skiers. They often skied not on nice, glassy lakes but on the huge, choppy Chesapeake Bay. To one preschool nephew, however, the experience was absolutely horrifying. It seemed to him that everyone would be thrown overboard and lost in the abyss as the boat blasted through rough seas, rolled over swells, and drove alongside massive ships. The little toddler did the one sane and wise thing he could think to do—he laid down flat on the floor of the boat and cried for shore! Eventually he calmed down enough to talk with relatives, play with toys, eat his snacks—but all from the floor of the boat. To him it was the only safe spot on the water.

2   Wisdom is rejecting your own wisdom.

- 🔊 **Scripture** reread *Proverbs 3:5-6* ("Lean not on your own understanding.")

- 🔊 **Illustration** *Gumball* (see sidebar)

- 🔊 We all make a mess of things when we lean on our own understanding. And it only gets worse when we don't learn from the messes we create.

- 🔊 All wise people recognize the severe limits of their own natural smarts. So often what seems best to us is the worst to God; what makes sense to us is senseless to him. So we have to trust in God with all our hearts, lying spread-eagle on him, which leaves no remaining weight for leaning on our own understanding.

Illustration

Gumball

Show students an ordinary gumball, explaining that there's an art to fitting into the world—especially a world with gum. We can chew gum, blow bubbles with it, even use it as a sticky adhesive if we're desperate. But unwise people make a mess of gum, like the little girl who stuck it in her hair. At first she tried pulling it out. Then rubbing it out. When that didn't work, she tried shampooing it out. But her best efforts only made matters worse.

By the time she finally told her parents, it looked like a small rodent had built a nest on the side of her head. It took her father an hour—working with a special solvent—to finally rid her of the gum. When it was all over, there was just a little solvent left in the bottle. The little girl exclaimed, "Oh, good! Now we have some left in case it happens again!"

3   Wisdom is respecting God and repenting of evil.

- **Scripture** *Proverbs 3:7-8* (see sidebar)

- According to the Bible wisdom begins with fearing God (Proverbs 1:7; 9:10; 15:33). Fear is a mixture of horror and honor—being afraid and being in awe.

- **Illustration** *Power Lunch* (see sidebar)

- **Illustration** *The Sergeant and the General* (see sidebar)

- God isn't a person to be taken lightly or treated casually. Sure, he loves us. But he's God—the one who created the universe!

- Real respect for God means recognizing he deserves our total commitment. Ignoring his principles brings consequences.

- It also means trusting his way is best and believing he sets boundaries on our behavior for our own joy and happiness.

Scripture

Proverbs 3:7-8

As great as verses five and six are, apparently they aren't enough for thickheads like us. The next two verses drive at the very same theme. They tell us not to be wise in our own eyes, but to fear the Lord and shun evil.

Illustration

Power lunch

Imagine having the opportunity to lunch with your biggest celebrity hero or with a great world leader. You're thrilled and terrified at the same time. You want to know this person better, but you don't want to mess up. This person is important, so it's not time for belching, spilling, tripping, or saying something stupid.

In some ways God deserves this same respect. And he gets it—just look at Bible stories where God reveals his presence with people. People are hitting the dirt, bowing with their faces to the ground.

The Sergeant and the General

Read or retell this excellent parable about fear and awe told by Jerry Bridges.

Following basic training, Butch was assigned to a divisional motor pool. Meanwhile General Collins was promoted to major general and became the commanding officer of Butch's division. Because of his reputation, Butch was eventually selected to be the general's driver. Butch had mixed emotions about this new assignment. He relished the confidence shown in him; on the other hand he remembered those cold, steely eyes on that memorable inspection day back in boot camp. Awe once again gripped him as he reported for duty the first day.

Sergeant McGregor, as Butch was now called, soon discovered that behind those steely blue eyes was a no-nonsense general who was tough but fair. As he listened to the general's conversations with other officers riding in the car, Butch was often amazed at the general's evident wisdom and military skill. He also noted the increased morale and esprit de corps that the general's leadership gave to the entire division. His awe for the general actually increased, though its dominant aspect was no longer fear but respect and admiration.

Of course Butch had always shown respect toward the general. That was absolutely essential to his job. But now he felt respect. He genuinely admired the general for both his personal character and his military leadership. One day he realized he had even begun to like the general, and he was fairly certain the general liked him. Despite this growing personal relationship, though, Butch never lost his sense of awe toward the general. He was always conscious of the vast difference in rank between them. Even in casual conversation he always addressed the general as "Sir."

In the course of time war broke out, and Butch's division was shipped overseas. As the general's driver, Butch was never involved in actual combat, though they often traveled in dangerous territory.

Then one day the car struck a land mine. General Collins was thrown clear of the car, but was seriously hurt when his body slammed to the ground. Butch, meanwhile, remained trapped in the front seat of the burning vehicle. Despite the general's own injuries, and at the risk of his life, he managed to pull Butch out of the car to safety.

Butch remained in the hospital for weeks. Despite the pressures of commanding a division in battle, the general often stopped by to see Butch and check on his progress. Butch was surprised at the general's obvious concern, but what really astounded him was the realization that at the scene of the accident, the general had literally risked his life to save him.

The general's continued visits made him realize the rescue was not simply a spur-of-the-moment heroic act but was prompted by the general's heartfelt concern for him.

Butch often pondered the question, "Why would a two-star general, in command of a Marine division in battle, risk his own life to save a mere sergeant?" He could readily understand one enlisted marine risking his life for his buddy on the battlefield—but a general for a sergeant? He slowly came to the conclusion that, despite their vast difference in rank, the general genuinely loved him.

Now, in addition to his sense of awe, respect, and admiration, Butch began to experience love and gratitude toward the general. He longed for the day he could once again be the general's driver. He determined that he would be the best driver a Marine general ever had. But he also realized that however much he and the general loved each other, they would never be buddies. It would always be a "yes, sir" and "no, sir" relationship.

That's how both General Collins and Sergeant McGregor would want it.

From *The Joy of Fearing God* by Jerry Bridges (Waterbrook, 1999).

closing

The Grand Finale

🔊 **Object lesson** *Obstacle Course* (see sidebar)

🔊 Ask—

Do you find yourself running into moral walls with increasingly painful consequences? Are you driving down the wrong side of the road relationally? Are your relationships with your friends or parents always strained? Have you tripped on the spiritual stairs, failing to go higher in your relationship with God because laziness or a sinful habit keeps pulling you back?

🔊 Review the main points of the talk.

- Wisdom is relying on God's strength.

- Wisdom is rejecting your own wisdom.

- Wisdom is respecting God and repenting of evil.

We need to adjust to reality and fit into the world as God made it. Point out that verses six and eight contain two promises: straight paths (fewer crashes!) and healthier lives (less pain). Who doesn't want that?

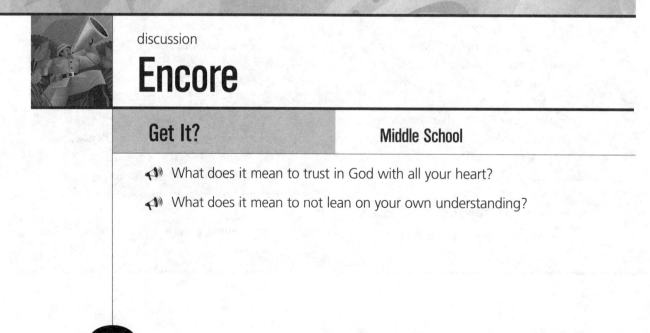

Object lesson

Obstacle course

Set up two parallel obstacle courses so two contestants can run at the same time. Arrange ahead of time for one of the participants to mess up—tripping over obstacles, running into walls, going the wrong way, and so on. Debrief the demonstration by contrasting the wise with the foolish. Wise people adjust to God's moral, spiritual, and relational world; fools run contrary to it.

discussion

Encore

Get It?	Middle School

🔊 What does it mean to trust in God with all your heart?

🔊 What does it mean to not lean on your own understanding?

Get It?　　　　　　　　　　High School

🔊 What does fitting yourself into the moral, relational, and spiritual world mean?

🔊 What were the three main points that help us understand what wisdom is?

🔊 Why do you think we happily adjust ourselves to physical laws but hate having to obey moral or spiritual rules?

What If?　　　　　　　　　　The Big Picture

🔊 In what areas of life do you tend to "get gum in your hair" or run into walls by not fitting yourself into the world?

🔊 What if you started trusting in God with all your heart? Lying spread-eagle on him all the time? How would you do it? How could you eat lunch, hang with friends, date people, or do homework from the spiritual spread-eagle position?

🔊 It's so natural to lean on our own understanding. Give some examples of the kinds of decisions students make using only their own wisdom.

🔊 Students are notorious for paying little attention to the consequences of their actions. But part of fearing God is recognizing that his discipline is nothing to mess around with. What could you do to bring your attitude into alignment with this truth?

🔊 What if we allowed the fear of God to shape our minds? How does fear of God impact the way you live?

🔊 Emphasis on God's love and free grace has diminished our respect for him. Do you agree? Talk about that. How can we balance the experience of God's grace with respect for his discipline and judgment at the same time?

So What?   It's Your Life

🔊 Mentally walk through what your day will be like tomorrow. What are the main things you'll be doing?

🔊 Take those events—one at a time—and figure out exactly how to trust God and acknowledge him as you're living them.

🔊 What are the top two or three areas where you need wisdom right now? Where are your paths crooked and rough, rather than straight and smooth?

🔊 How are you going to get the wisdom you need? Where do you start?

Why, God?

Contributed by **Steve Case**

Primary theme injustice	
Themes anger with God, consequences, evil, fairness, justice, faith	
Scripture 2 Samuel 12:10; Psalms 10; 46:10; 77; Romans 8:28-39; 1 Corinthians 13:12	
Approximate length through The Grand Finale 20-25 minutes	

Sooner or later most people struggle with anger toward God. Some wouldn't even be able to admit it, but for many this anger drives them away from God. How often have you heard, "I just can't believe in a God who would allow _____."

There's plenty in this world to get angry about. There's plenty of pain and evil and injustice to go around. And what's really at the base of it? The theological—but real life—problem of evil. This is a short talk and won't cover the entire subject of evil in the world. But it will offer some answers that may prove be helpful to your kids.

You'll need

- A personal story about being mad at God
- Pencils and paper for each group
- Index cards—one for each student
- A stereo
- "Losing My Religion" from the album *Out of Time* by R.E.M. (Wea/Warner Brothers 1991) or "Dear God" from the album *Skylarking* by XTC (Uni/Geffen, 1986)
- Puzzle pieces—one for each student
- Chocolate-chip cookies for everyone
- Cookie ingredients like flour, butter, salt, and chocolate chips

intro

The Opening Act

🔊 **Personal illustration** *When I Was Ticked!* (see sidebar)

🔊 **Activity** *Group Gripe* (see sidebar)

🔊 **Reflection** *Why I'm Angry* (see sidebar)

🔊 Then say something like—

> **Let's get honest today—we know God loves us; we know God is in control; we know God is aware of what's going on in the world and in our lives. But almost everyone eventually feels like God is distant and uninvolved.**

Personal illustration

When I was ticked!

Share a personal story about a time when you were mad at God. C'mon, 'fess up! Be honest with your students, and don't try to wrap your story with a nice ending—*And then I saw the reason for it all!* Your transparency on this will set up a safety zone for kids to wrestle with questions most of them struggle with. If you can't bring yourself to do this—maybe you've have a blissfully naive and charmed life!—find someone else to do it.

Activity

Group gripe

Divide your students into groups of five to eight—or, if your group is smaller than 15 students, consider doing this as one group. The success of this exercise is dependent on the safe climate you set with your opening illustration. Give a pencil and piece of paper to a scribe for each group, then ask the teams to make a list of all the things in the world that seem unfair.

Explain that these can be global issues—like the thousands of people who die every day of starvation. Or they can be personal issues—like why a teen's parents split up last year. Although the global ideas will be easier for most, there's no self-disclosure involved, so you may have to actively encourage adding personal issues. If you have time, have the groups share their lists.

Reflection

Why I'm angry

Hand out index cards and pencils to your students and have them write their biggest God-gripe. What one thing makes them frustrated or mad at God or makes them doubt him the most? Don't ask them to share this—and let them know they won't be asked to. They can be completely candid with God. Tell your group they can phrase something as a statement ("I'm bugged that…") or as a question ("God, why did you allow this to happen?").

heart of the talk

The Main Event

1   Almost everyone gets mad at God from time to time.

- 🔊 **Song** *"Losing My Religion"* or *"Dear God"* (see sidebar)

- 🔊 **Scripture** *Psalms 10 and 77* (angry psalms!)

- 🔊 **Reading** *Angry Psalms* (see sidebar)

- 🔊 Surprise, surprise—God is big enough to handle your anger! He's not going to send you to hell or zap you with zits for expressing anger at him.

- 🔊 Anger is a normal part of any relationship, although anger is often based on misunderstandings or misinformation. This is almost always the case when we get angry at God.

Song

"Losing My Religion" or "Dear God"

"Losing My Religion"

This R.E.M. song will make your student think. If you have access to the video for this song—don't use it! It's full of bizarre images that will distract from your point. In many ways this song is an angry letter to God. During an interview Michael Stipe said he was trying to write the ultimate unrequited love song—meaning it's about a love that isn't returned.

"Dear God"

An even darker song with more real anger is "Dear God" by XTC. Written as a child's letter to God, this song sums up a lot of the frustrations many people feel about how God works—or doesn't work—in their daily lives. The lead singer and songwriter, Andy Partridge, sings, "I can't believe, I won't believe...in you!" Make sure you debrief these songs—not by countering everything wrong about them, but by checking for understanding and asking if students ever feel this way or know others who do.

Reading

Angry psalms

If you're not too freaked out by this whole discussion—if you are, maybe you shouldn't deliver this talk!—consider having someone read these psalms or portions of them in a dramatic way. Full of anger. It would be cool to divide the verses into a reader's theatre and have two or three dramatic readers. Some of your students will be uncomfortable with this presentation of a Bible passage—which would be great!

2   Why does bad stuff happen?

◀)) First we have to admit—or realize—we don't always get to know the reason.

◀)) Christians have a way of trying to settle on a reason for every bummer. That's not always possible—and forcing a fake reason doesn't do us any good.

◀)) **Object lesson** *Puzzle Piece* (see sidebar)

◀)) **Scripture** *1 Corinthians 13:12* ("Now we see but a poor reflection as in a mirror; then we shall see face to face.")

◀)) **Scripture** *Romans 8:28-39* (see sidebar)

◀)) What's the best response when we don't understand why bad stuff happens?

◀)) **Scripture** *Psalm 46:10* ("Be still, and know that I am God.") God has everything under control. Reminding ourselves of this truth will help us deal with our angry and upset emotions.

Object lesson

Puzzle piece

Pass out one puzzle piece to each student—or if you're really hard pressed, you can just hold one up. Explain that this puzzle piece is a lot like our lives—we get to see some of the picture, some of the colors, but we don't get to see how it all fits together (at least not always). Sure, we can look at the picture on the front of the puzzle box—which in this case would be the Word of God and all God's revealed truth. And we can get enough info to understand what the basic subject of the puzzle is. But we usually don't get to see the whole picture. Allow students to take the puzzle pieces home as a reminder of the main points of this talk.

Scripture

Romans 8:28-39

Point out this Scripture doesn't say, "God causes bad stuff to happen." It does say God takes all things—bad and good—and uses them for good in our lives. Unfortunately it doesn't say we get to know all the details of the plan!

3 Bad things happen because actions have consequences.

📢 This is tough because sometimes we end up suffering consequences from someone else's evil!

📢 **Scripture** reread *Psalm 10* (that angry psalm again!) The writer of this psalm had obviously suffered evil at the hand of someone else and wasn't pleased about it!

📢 This bugs God too!

📢 But God had two options when he created us.

- He could have made us like robots—pure all the time, quick to worship him, and quick to do what's right. But with no real choices.

- Or he could—and did—decide it was somehow better for him and us to allow us to choose between good and evil.

📢 We make unhealthy decisions, and we have to live with the consequences.

📢 **Explanation** *David* (see sidebar)

📢 **Discussion** *Biblical Consequences* (see sidebar)

Explanation

David

Tell the story of David's sin with Bathsheba. (Get the details from 2 Samuel 11-12, with the consequence in 12:10.) Point out this isn't God being mean and getting back at David. It's not a you-blew-me-off-so-I'm-gonna-mess-up-your-life attitude. This is a cosmic, natural consequence to David's sin.

Discussion

Biblical consequences

Ask your group if they know the consequence these Bible people had to live with as a result of their choices.

- Adam and Eve ate the fruit from the forbidden Tree of Knowledge of Good and Evil. *(They had to leave the garden.)*

- Cain killed his brother Abel. *(He had to wander the land, never to settle down.)*

- Lot's wife looked back as she was fleeing from Sodom. *(She was turned into a pillar of salt.)*

- Judas betrayed Jesus. *(He was branded as a traitor for all time.)*

closing

The Grand Finale

🔊 **Object lesson** *Chocolate Chip Cookies* (see sidebar)

🔊 Review the points one more time.

- Most people get angry with God from time to time. God can handle that!

- We can't always see the reason for bad stuff, because we can't see everything from God's perspective.

- Sometimes bad stuff happens just because there's evil in the world—which God allows and will use for our good.

- Sometimes bad stuff happens to us as a consequence to our own bad choices and sin. But God still wants to turn that into good stuff!

🔊 **Reflection** *Why I'm Angry, Part 2* (see sidebar)

Object lesson

Chocolate chip cookies

This object lesson requires you to prepare a bit—but it's worth it! Display a few of the ingredients in chocolate chip cookies. At least have chocolate chips, butter, flour, and salt.

Now ask it there's anyone who would like to come eat some flour. Or some butter. If you can get some crazy kid to do it—go for it. The gross-out factor will only help your point. Now pass out chocolate chip cookies (homemade would be best—ask some student's mom to make 'em for you) and ask everyone to hold them for minute. Explain no truly normal person would want to consume the ingredients separately—this will be a badge of honor for any kid who took you up on eating ingredients. Say something like—

You might like eating a cup of chocolate chips, but you probably don't want to eat the flour or salt or butter separately. It's the mix of all the flavors together that makes the cookie so good. In the same way God loves to use the sweet things and the bitter things in life to bring about a wonderful result.

Reflection

Why I'm angry, part 2

If you used the *Why I'm Angry* exercise from the introduction, have students pull out those cards and look at them again. Explain that God knows what we feel. He knows if we're angry or sad. We have to trust God wants to use that bad thing for good somehow. If students are willing to trust God on this—willing to try trusting him—ask them to write GOD IS IN CONTROL on top of their earlier writing and take it home as a reminder.

discussion

Encore

| Get It? | Middle School |

🔊 Do you think God ever did something mean to you on purpose? Talk about that.

🔊 Is it okay to be angry with God? Talk about that.

🔊 (If you played the R.E.M. song) The singer sang, "That's me in the spotlight, losing my religion." Why do you think he wrote that?

🔊 (If you played the XTC song) The singer sang, "I can't believe in you!" Why do you think he wrote that?

🔊 So why does bad stuff happen to us?

🔊 People make unhealthy decisions all the time. Who's to blame when bad stuff happens then?

🔊 What's one of the worst things you've seen on the news lately? Did God make it happen?

🔊 Why can't we see how the puzzle fits together?

| Get It? | High School |

🔊 Have you ever yelled at God? Have you ever mumbled in anger at him? How does God respond to that?

🔊 (If you played the R.E.M. song) The singer sang, "That's me in the spotlight, losing my religion." Why do you think he wrote that?

🔊 (If you played the XTC song) The singer sang, "I can't believe in you!" Why do you think he wrote that?

🔊 Do you think God will bless us only when we love him?

🔊 Explain the puzzle thing. How does it work?

🔊 What about the chocolate-chip cookie illustration—how would you explain that concept to a child?

🔊 How can we be sure God is listening to our prayers? Even if our prayers sound like complaints—like that psalm writer—is he listening?

What If? | The Big Picture

- What would you say to someone who doesn't believe in God because she says God's never spoken to her?

- What would you say to a small child who thinks God has taken away a grandparent who just died?

- Why do you suppose God doesn't let us see the whole puzzle?

- How should we respond to bad stuff when we can't see a reason for it?

- Can you think of a time in your life when good came out of bad?

So What? | It's Your Life

- Psalm 46:10 says, "Be still and know I am God." Basically God is saying to chill. How can we just chill about bad stuff at school? How can we chill about tough family issues?

- Many of our problems occur because we forget God can see our puzzle completed and perfect. What are some ways we can tell God we know he's got the situation under control?

- Your best friend says, "Well, God allowed this to happen to me, so I'll never be able to think of him as good or loving." How can you respond to your friend?

- Has one small event ever changed your life in a thousand ways? Do you think God has the puzzle done or is it constantly changing? Talk about that.

- Sometimes we feel like we have absolutely hit the bottom. Then we start to build our way back. Do you think God has ever cleared the puzzle and started over? In what way?

- Have you ever heard the phrase, "Let go and let God." What does it mean?

- "Letting God" involves giving up control. Why is control so hard to give up?

- If you were God, would you make everything perfect for everyone? Do you think people could appreciate a blue sky if they never had rain? Talk about that.

- How can you apply these ideas to your life this week?

- During the closing prayer think of one thing—no matter how small—you can let go of. Allow God to be God and trust he has a plan and will make it turn into something good, somehow.

Worship under Fire

Primary theme worship	
Themes Christian living, tough times, pain, evangelism, God's glory	
Scripture Psalms 16:8-9; 34:1; 90:1-2; Acts 16:12-40; Hebrews 13:5-8; James 1:17	
Approximate length through The Grand Finale 30-35 minutes	

O ur lives aren't always easy, but worship is always necessary. It's one thing to worship God when life is good and easy. But how do we worship God when life stinks? Going beyond simple just-praise-God platitudes, this talk looks at the story of Paul and Silas worshiping God while in jail and uncovers four transferable truths. In that sense, this talk is very practical, since most of your kids would find it difficult to focus on God during hard times.

Contributed by **Louie Giglio**

This outline is saved as GTO_31 on the CD-ROM.

intro

The Opening Act

◀)) Ask students for definitions of worship.

◀)) **Object lesson** *Mirror and Flashlight* (see sidebar)

◀)) Point out that it's one thing to worship God when life is good, but ask how we worship when life is tough. (Silence and thought is a fine response to this question, but if students want to talk about possible answers, allow responses.)

◀)) **Scripture** *Acts 16:12-40* (Paul and Silas in jail, see sidebar)

◀)) Then transition by saying something like—

> **We're going to look at four truths that allowed Paul and Silas to worship God in that hard situation. Your tough times might not be the same as Paul's, but the four truths don't change and will help us be better mirrors to reflect God's goodness and glory back to him in all situations.**

Object lesson

Mirror and flashlight

Use this object lesson to redefine worship for your students.

Hold up a flashlight and explain that many Christians think of worship this way. Then turn on the flashlight and point it at the ceiling. We think of worship as a one-way transaction—us exalting God. But that definition lacks some of the true wonder of worship. Hold up the mirror against your body, facing out—any size mirror will work, from a hand mirror to a full-length dressing mirror—and by extending your arm holding the flashlight, shine the light into the mirror and angle the reflection to the ceiling.

Tell your students they've just seen true worship—reflecting God's glory back to him. We become mirrors of God's glory when we worship.

Acts 16:12-40

This wonderful story of Paul and Silas in jail is the foundation of this whole talk. It's crucial that you familiarize yourself with the story enough that you can jump back and forth between reading portions, paraphrasing portions, and expounding on the story. Here are the story points you should be sure to highlight.

- **Verses 16–18** Paul and Silas are on their way to a prayer spot outside the city and they come across a slave girl with an evil spirit that allows her be the Philippian Psychic Hotline. Her owners are making lots of money off her ability. But the evil spirit can also sense God is with Paul and Silas, and she calls out, "Hey, these guys are servants of the Most High God and are telling you how to get saved!" At first Paul and Silas may have thought, "Oh! Well, thank you. That's very nice!"

  It's not clear why Paul didn't choose to cast that demon out of her right away. But she continues to do this for days! Everywhere they go, this girl walks behind them, announcing that they are servants of God. Paul and Silas get totally annoyed by the whole thing and Paul whips around to say to the spirit, "In the name of Jesus Christ I command you to come out of her!" And the spirit leaves.

- **Verses 19–24** The slave owner isn't pleased! He has Paul and Silas dragged into the town square before the magistrates, stripped of their clothes, and beaten with rods. Their time in Philippi had been going so well. They led a bunch of people to Christ and were staying with them; they had this girl who could see the power of God in them; they had cast out an evil spirit. And all of a sudden they're being falsely accused, stripped, and beaten in front of the whole town—and thrown in jail!

  As the day comes to a close, they find themselves beaten and bruised and stuck in jail with their feet in stocks. Seems like a pretty good time to grumble and complain—or to pull out their Roman citizen ID cards and cash in a get-out-of-jail-free card.

- **Verses 25–40** Paul and Silas sat in their jail cell worshiping God! What's with that? How could they? And how can we?

heart of the talk

The Main Event

1 We can worship God at all times because God is worthy of praise.

🔊 In the midst of our problems, we always have a choice to make.

- We can stay focused on our problems.
- We can focus on God.

🔊 Paul and Silas chose to focus on God.

🔊 God hasn't changed even though your situation has.

🔊 **Scripture** *Hebrews 13:8* ("Jesus Christ is the same yesterday and today and forever.")

🔊 **Scripture** *James 1:17* ("The Father of the heavenly lights, who does not change like shifting shadows.")

🔊 God's worth never changes. That means if he was worthy of praise yesterday—when things seemed good—then he's worthy of praise today when things seem bad.

🔊 God's worth isn't attached to our circumstances.

🔊 **Illustration** *A Cruddy Day* (see sidebar)

🔊 **Illustration** *Way Worse* (see sidebar)

🔊 Here are a few passages you can read as prayers to help you remember God doesn't change and is always worthy of worship.

- **Scripture** *Psalm 90:1-2* ("Lord, you have been our dwelling place throughout all generations…from everlasting to everlasting you are God.")

- **Scripture** *Psalm 34:1* ("I will extol the Lord at all times; his praise will always be on my lips.")

- **Scripture** *Psalm 16:8-9* ("I have set the Lord always before me. Because he is at my right hand, I will not be shaken.")

A cruddy day

Make up a story about an annoyingly bad morning for a teenager. Say something like—

You wake up one morning to find there was a short power outage last night. Your clock is blinking 12:00 and the alarm didn't go off. You're late—which stinks because you've got a major test in your first class, one you were hoping to study a bit more for this morning.

You race to school, sign in at the office since you're late, and run to your locker to get a quick last-minute glance at your notes. But the lock is jammed and your locker won't open. You close your eyes and lean your head against the locker in frustration. When you open your eyes—with your head still facing down—you realize you've worn your Winnie the Pooh slippers to school. Now this is a pretty lousy start to a day! But has it changed who God is at all? Of course not!

Way worse

Suggest that often our problems are much worse than a cruddy morning. Maybe your mom was just diagnosed with cancer and isn't expected to live through the year. [If that's actually true for one of your students, you might wanna change the example.] The solution to this isn't wimpy, easy cheeseball faith that says, "Hey, your Mom's got cancer? I tell ya what. Let's just praise God. Let's just praise the Lord. And if we praise God enough, maybe we can act like that cancer isn't real."

That's not what Paul and Silas are doing. They aren't saying, "Okay don't say the word stocks—'cause if we don't say it, we won't be in 'em. Let's pretend we're at the Ritz Carlton Hotel. We're living large. We're out by the pool. Let's keep thinking about being out by the pool, and let's not act like we're at the bottom of a dungeon."

Instead, before they get their eyes focused on their problems, they start thinking about the worth of an awesome, glorious God who's still in power, who's loving, who's greater than they are, who's more wise than they are, who's got infinite understanding, who's running the whole universe, who works all things according to his will, and who searches out all things and knows all things. They're looking at God first and saying, "You know what? God is worthy today, no matter where we are or what we're doing. He's always worthy because he is God. Our situation might stink, but it doesn't change the fact that God is still God."

2   We can worship God at all times because God is with us.

🔊 What happened when Paul and Silas were worshiping God?

🔊 **Scripture** *Acts 16:26* ("Suddenly there was such a violent earthquake.")

🔊 God was with Paul and Silas in the stockade.

🔊 But this is important—God's promise isn't that you'll never have trials. His promise is you aren't alone.

🔊 **Scripture** *Hebrews 13:5* ("I will never leave you or forsake you.")

🔊 Ask why this knowledge would make a difference in our ability to worship God during tough times.

3   We can worship God at all times because God has freed us.

🔊 **Scripture** *Hebrews 13:6* ("God is my helper, what can man do to me?")

🔊 Paul and Silas understood this. You can put our bodies in prison, but you can't put our hearts in prison.

🔊 **Illustration** *Not on the Inside!* (see sidebar)

🔊 **Explanation** *The Gospel* (optional, see sidebar)

🔊 Ask what God has freed the students from and allow a few to share.

Illustration

Not on the inside!

A mom asked her seven-year-old daughter to clean up her bedroom. The little girl didn't want to clean her room and ignored her mother. An hour later the mother clarified that it wasn't a request, but a directive. "You will clean up your bedroom."

The little girl got risky and said, "No, I don't want to clean my room."

The mother responded, "You will clean your room or there will be a serious consequence young lady."

The girl took a deep breath, slumped her shoulders, scowled at her mother, and said, "I may be cleaning my room on the outside, but I'm not on the inside!"

What's going on inside our hearts and minds is often different than our actions. In this way we can be captive to some difficult situation but still be aware—on the inside—that we're free because of Jesus Christ.

Explanation

The gospel

At this point students who don't know Christ might be a little curious about what it means to be set free. Even though you're not talking specifically about that here, students might wonder about being free from more than a momentary problem. Certainly, it's a tangent from the primary thrust of this talk; but if you've got a a number of non-Christian kids in the room, you might offer a quick explanation of what it means to be set free from sin.

4   We can worship God at all times because God is working.

- Worship God when your life is great and people will ignore you. Worship God when your life is rotten and everyone will listen. The jailer listened. Look what happened to the guys.

- **Scripture** *Acts 16:29-34* ("Sirs, what must I do to be saved?")
    - Make sure you point out verse 25. This is a big deal—the other prisoners were willing to stay awake to listen to these strange guys who were singing to God while bruised and in stocks!

- Our trials are a megaphone for our worship.

- We don't know the result of what happened after this evening. No one knows how the jailer's story affected his friends and their town.

- **Illustration** *Partial Picture* (see sidebar)

- This is how it is with us. We only see a part of the picture God has for our lives.

- God is always working in our lives. Always. But we often don't understand the bigger picture of what's happening in our lives. We see the problem; we don't see why we're stuck in the problem.

Illustration

Partial picture

A certain college pastor had an abstract painting framed and hung on the wall behind his desk. Students would come to his office and unknowingly say, "What's that? It looks like someone threw up on your wall!"

And then he'd have to explain, "My dad painted that. He painted this huge, somewhat dark painting of a magician, and it hung in the stairwell of our home. My mom didn't like it—too dark. One day my dad got a rare brain virus and lost the ability to paint forever. And some time later he compromised with my mom on that painting of the magician. He and I took it outside and cut the bottom of it off and reframed it. Somehow, this made the other part a little softer. So after my dad died, I took this part—the part he signed—and framed it."

Of course this description always made the college students feel awful about calling it puke! The problem was they didn't see the whole picture. Not just the whole painting—but the whole story. And that's what made it special to its owner.

closing

The Grand Finale

📢 You've covered a lot of ground in this talk. Make sure you review the key points.

📢 **Reflection** *Worship!* (see sidebar)

📢 As students are talking write—I'M COMMITTED TO WORSHIPING…EVEN WHEN LIFE IS TOUGH. at the top of a large sheet of paper. Have kids sign their names on it. After students sign, have them stand at the edge of the paper. When everyone's finished, lead students in a prayer asking God for help in praising him when times are tough.

📢 **Take-home item** *Psalms Bookmark* (see sidebar)

Reflection

Worship!

It would be too strange to give this talk and not allow students to respond by worshiping their unchanging God! So spend some time in silence; some time in directed prayer; some time reading Scripture as prayers—use the psalms from the first point—and singing about God's greatness.

Take-home item

Psalms bookmark

Make bookmarks by photocopying **Always on My Lips** (page 285) on cardstock. Trim and add a ribbon. Encourage students to keep these in their Bibles or in their bedrooms and to pray their verses whenever they're having a difficult time focusing on God amid their problems.

discussion

Encore

| **Get It?** | **Middle School** |

🔊 *Worship is singing only God-songs.* Explain why you agree or disagree.

🔊 Why is it so hard to focus on God when life is tough?

🔊 What do people mean when they say God is worthy of worship?

🔊 If God is with us all the time, why doesn't he fix all our problems? And why don't we always feel his presence with us?

🔊 What comes to mind when you hear, "God is with us." What does that sentence mean?

🔊 Why is being set free so important?

| **Get It?** | **High School** |

🔊 Is your definition of worship any different after hearing this talk than it was before it? Explain your answer.

🔊 Pretend you just whacked your thumb with a hammer by mistake. Should you just smile and say, "Praise God! Praise God! I'm happy this happened!" Why or why not? Talk about that.

🔊 How does the fact that God is with you make a difference in what you do or what you think? How should it make a difference?

🔊 How does God set us free? What does he set us free from?

🔊 Some people say our trials are a megaphone for our worship. What does that mean?

🔊 Can you name a time when you were sure—beyond a shadow of a doubt—God was with you? What was that like?

What If?   The Big Picture

🔊 How can you focus on God when you're in the middle of tough times? What if you're ticked or consumed with sadness—should you blow that off? What would Paul and Silas say?

🔊 What if you were to live with the confidence that God's always with you? What difference would it make in everyday life? What difference would it make this week?

🔊 It's great God busted Paul and Silas out of prison. But most of us have never been in prison, and we've never experienced anything like this. How can we know this teaching is for us today?

🔊 Does God set us free from prisons—so to speak—in our lives today? Talk about that.

🔊 How might your life be different if you chose to be a worshiper every day?

So What?   It's Your Life

🔊 What tough experiences are going on in your life right now? What would it take for you to worship God in the middle of that pain? Are you willing to try it?

🔊 How can you be more of a mirror this week, reflecting God's glory back to him?

🔊 How can you be more aware of God working in your life?

🔊 Sometimes God wants to set us free from a personal prison, but we won't let him. We enjoy the suffering more than the risk of being free. Do you do that? What things do you need to let go of, so God can set you free?

Always on my lips

Copy this page onto cardstock. Trim. Punch a hole in one end and add a ribbon.

Lord, you have been our dwelling place throughout all generations. Before the mountains were born or you brought forth the earth and the world, from everlasting to everlasting you are God.

PSALM 90:1-2

I HAVE SET THE LORD ALWAYS BEFORE ME. BECAUSE HE IS AT MY RIGHT HAND, I WILL NOT BE SHAKEN. THEREFORE MY HEART IS GLAD AND MY TONGUE REJOICES; MY BODY ALSO WILL REST SECURE

PSALM 16:8-9

I will extol the Lord at all times; his praise will always be on my lips.

PSALM 34:1

The Godzone

Primary theme kingdom of God	
Themes seeking God, grace, community, God's love, accepting others	
Scripture Matthew 5:1-12; 13; 20:16; Mark 1:14-15; Luke 10:9, 11; 17:20-21	
Approximate length through The Grand Finale 30 minutes	

hen Jesus described the kingdom of God he used a series of stories and parables. This talk takes the same approach to get students thinking about where the kingdom can be found, what it's like, and who's in it. It uses the made-up term Godzone for the kingdom of God. This talk is different from most in this book since it relies on storytelling—again, much like Jesus often taught—rather than on the logical presentation of points.

The storytelling approach may be new to you. It's important to be familiar enough with the illustration that you can tell it like a story, rather than read it. You might find it's also tempting to explain each illustration and its point, but often it's best to tell the story and let people work it out for themselves. "He or she who has ears, let them hear," as someone once said!

One more thought—this talk will be tough for younger teens to grasp. You'll probably want to save it for high school students. If you forge ahead and give this talk to middle schoolers, be sure to choose your words and explanations carefully.

Contributed by **Jonny Baker**

This outline is saved as GTO_32 on the CD-ROM.

intro

The Opening Act

◀)) **Activity** *Brainteasers* (see sidebar)

◀)) Transition by saying something like—

> **Sometimes, we think the same way for so long, it's difficult to see things from a different perspective. That's also often true of our understanding of spiritual truths. Jesus was passionate about helping us understand that the Kingdom of God is different than we might expect! When Jesus started teaching and healing, his explanation for what he was doing in Mark 1:14-15 was that the kingdom of God was near.**
>
> **Instead of the phrase the kingdom of God, I'll use the term Godzone—as in the zone or space inhabited by God. Let's consider three questions about the Godzone.**

Activity

Brainteasers

Begin with these brainteasers. Write on a whiteboard—

OSRIAXLENTGTEERS

Tell your teens that the challenge with this first brainteaser is to cross out six letters and leave a familiar English word. The answer is to literally cross out S, I, X, L, E, T, T, E, R, and S and leave the word *orange*.

For the next brainteaser draw two short vertical lines on the whiteboard like this—

II

Ask if anyone can change this into a three by adding one line. It can become a Roman numeral three by simply adding another straight vertical line to the two already there.

III

Draw a—

V

and ask if it could be changed into a six with one line. Your kids should catch onto this one. Make a Roman numeral six by simply adding a vertical line at the end.
Finally draw something like this—

IX

Ask if it could be turned into a six with one line. This will likely stump your students, but it can easily become a six when you draw a squiggly line in front—a squiggly line otherwise known as an S, which will make it—

SIX

The idea of this series of brainteasers is to get your students thinking in a pattern of Roman numerals so that they find it difficult to see an easy solution to the last question.

heart of the talk

The Main Event

1   Where is the Godzone?

- 🔊 **Illustration** *The Magical City* (see sidebar)
- 🔊 Lots of people are searching. Those who have eyes to see it can find the magical city—the Godzone.
- 🔊 The Godzone isn't anywhere in particular, really. Instead it's everywhere.
- 🔊 As Jesus said, "The kingdom of God is near," *(Luke 10:9, 11)* and it is within us *(Luke 17:20-21)*.
- 🔊 **Activity** *Brainteaser* (see sidebar)
- 🔊 **Movie clip** *The Matrix* (see sidebar)
- 🔊 **Illustration** *Two Men on a Beach* (see sidebar)

Illustration

The magical city

Help your students understand this concept by telling a little tailor-made fairy tale. You may want to use the following script, filling in your own details where indicated.

Once there was a teenager who lived in [insert name of your town or city]. She had lived there all her life and had grown tired and cynical. Life seemed to have lost its magic. She found very little joy. Nothing brought her wonder. So she decided to leave [insert your town or city] and go in search of the perfect magical city where—she had heard—everything was different, new, and rewarding.

After her first day of traveling, she settled down for the night, lit a fire, and had a little bite to eat. Before going to sleep she took off her shoes and carefully pointed them toward her destination. But while she slept, someone came along and—thinking it would be funny—turned the shoes around 180 degrees.

When the teenager awoke she carefully stepped into her shoes and continued on her way to the magical city. After a few days she found it. It looked strangely familiar. She found a familiar street, knocked on a familiar door, met a familiar family inside, and lived happily ever after.

Activity

Brainteaser

Refer back to the introductory brainteasers and point out how obvious the solution is once it's revealed—but how difficult it was to see if you weren't thinking the right way. For example, in the second one you can get so locked into thinking in a pattern of Roman numerals that you can't see differently. The Godzone is the same. When you can't see it, it doesn't make sense. But once you have entered, you can't believe you missed it.

Movie clip

The Matrix

Describe or show this scene from *The Matrix*. Explain for students who haven't seen the movie that the Matrix is a computer-generated, virtual reality world.

Start 2:04:45 Neo stands up again after Trinity's kiss.

Stop 2:06:47 The two evil agents look at each other then run, terrified.

Neo (Keanu Reeves) has been almost beaten by enemy agents but is suddenly revived and able to see the Matrix around him. Once he sees it he can respond and fight the agents with ease. Like the Matrix, the Godzone is all around. Once we see it, it changes our reality.

Illustration

Two men on a beach

Two men were walking along a beach, both focused on their surroundings. Mac saw the deep blue sea, waves lapping on the shore, sunlight reflected off the water, and beautiful shells and pebbles on the sand. Eli saw the glint of oil on the water from the boats further out in the bay, patches of tar where the pebbles were stuck together, and pollution along the tide line.

Suddenly they both exclaimed, "Look what I've found!" Mac bent down to pick up a shell. Eli picked up a hamburger wrapper.

Mac looked at Eli and thought, "With all this beauty around, he's picking up litter."

Eli looked at Mac and thought, "He's picking up shells with all this litter around!"

They both thought in disgust, "How could anyone be so blind?" Same beach—different world.

Wrap up this illustration with a comment like—

So where is the Godzone? Everywhere…if we can see it.

2   What's the Godzone like?

🔊 **Explanation** *Jesus' Life and Teaching* (see sidebar)

🔊 **Scripture** *Matthew 13* (The kingdom parables) Read one or two parables ("The kingdom of heaven is like…"), then ask students if they can think of other parables about the kingdom of God.

🔊 One really helpful idea about the Godzone is that it's upside down—opposite of what you would expect.

🔊 Ask for suggestions of ways in which the Godzone is upside down.

🔊 **Illustration** *The Woman and the Gold Nugget* (see sidebar)

🔊 There are other zones around like—

- Selfzone
- Successzone
- Partyzone

🔊 But in these zones things look very different. Some are closer to the Godzone than others, but, comparatively, the Godzone is definitely upside down. In the Godzone—

- Your worth is based on who you are, not what you do.
- Those who are persecuted are blessed.
- You die to find life.
- It is better to give than to receive.
- You let go to find something.
- The last shall be first.
- You can't earn God's favor.

🔊 **Scripture** *Matthew 5:1-12* (The Beatitudes) Governments have their political manifestos. The Godzone's manifesto was delivered by Jesus and this is it!

🔊 When you live in this upside-down way—surprise, surprise—joy and life are found. It's weird!

🔊 **Movie clip** *Dead Poets Society* (see sidebar)

Explanation

Jesus' life and teaching

In Jesus' life we see what the Godzone looks like. All are welcomed, made whole, and forgiven; the blind see and the deaf hear; good news comes to the poor and justice comes to the wicked; prisoners are released—this is what the Godzone is all about. Jesus also taught about the Godzone in stories—the one about a farmer sowing seed, the one about yeast, and the one about the expensive pearl. It's all quite mysterious. Matthew 13 is a chapter full of stories about the Godzone.

Illustration

The woman and the gold nugget

A certain woman had a vivid dream. In it she saw a man with messy long hair and bare feet sitting on a bench outside the post office. A voice said to her that, if she were to ask this man, he would give her something that would make her rich forever. She woke and shrugged the dream off.

The next day while walking through town she saw the man from her dream sitting on the bench outside the post office. Feeling somewhat foolish she approached the man and explained her dream. He listened and then reached into a bag and produced an enormous gold nugget, saying, "I found this beside the road. Here, it's yours if you want it."

She looked longingly at the nugget. It was huge—huge enough to make her wealthy, but she didn't take it. That night she couldn't sleep. At dawn she set off to find the homeless man, who was sleeping under a tree in the park. She woke him and said, "Give me that wealth that makes it possible for you to give this treasure away."

Movie clip

Dead Poets Society

Start 42:55 "Why do I stand up here?"

Stop 42:40 "Dare to strike out and find new ground!"

John Keating (Robin Williams) has the boys in his class stand on their desks so that they see the world differently. At the time they think he's crazy, but explain to your students that at the end of the film Todd (Ethan Hawke) stands on his desk as a way of thanking Mr. Keating for enabling him to see the world in a different way. This is a similar process to the disciples trying to understand Jesus' upside-down teaching.

3   Who's in and who's out of the Godzone?

- Jesus got into a lot of trouble because there were clearly defined categories of who was in—the righteous—and who was out—the sinners—in that culture.

- Jesus reinvented the categories to suggest that those who were outsiders were especially welcome in the Godzone: the last will be first (Matthew 20:16). He also suggested that those who thought they were in shouldn't be so sure.

- **Illustration** *The Banquet* (see sidebar)

- The invitation is for everybody—especially if you feel like an outsider.

The banquet

In a far off land lived a man who was very religious. He was determined to remain pure until the coming of the kingdom of God. He made it through many hardships, but the day came when his patience ran out. "The kingdom will never come," he said to himself. "I may as well make the most of what I've got." So he withdrew an enormous amount of money and decided to throw a dinner party. He invited all his religious friends and then, for good measure, he invited a lot of other people who lived nearby—people he'd always regarded as sinners.

The preparations for the feast went on for days. Eventually everything was ready and all the people assembled. The religious were very concerned about who they were sitting next to. But gradually the pleasant atmosphere and good food began to soften their hearts.

After the meal there was music and the so-called sinners began to dance. Soon even the religious people were dancing. There was a wonderful atmosphere of laughter and celebration and everyone had a good time. "I haven't had such a good time in years," said one man to the host. "It was almost as if the kingdom of God were already among us."

closing

The Grand Finale

- 🔊 **Activity** *Visualize the Godzone* Have students—individually or in groups—write stories to show something of what the Godzone is like. Or you could have small groups create short dramas along these lines.

- 🔊 **Discussion** *Party in the Godzone* Brainstorm with your group what it would be like to throw a Godzone party. Who would they invite? What would they do? As an application, consider having this party.

discussion

Encore

Get It?	Middle School

- 🔊 What's the Godzone?

- 🔊 Where is the magical city?

- 🔊 What does it mean that the Godzone is upside down?

- 🔊 How do you know if you're in the Godzone?

Get It? — High School

- 📢 Do you know people who seem like they're searching in life? What does that look like? What are they searching for?

- 📢 Why did Jesus tell so many stories? Why did he tell so many stories specifically about the Godzone—the kingdom of God?

- 📢 Talk about the girl who finds the magical city where she began. What was the point of that story?

- 📢 Why did the two men on the beach see it so differently? What did that story have to do with the Godzone?

- 📢 How can sinners be invited to the banquet? What does that story mean?

- 📢 What about those other zones—selfzone, successzone, partyzone? What do those terms mean? What other zones can you think of that people live in?

What If? — The Big Picture

- 📢 How can we learn to see things from the perspective of the Godzone?

- 📢 How much are you prepared to give away to find the magic city—the Godzone?

- 📢 How would life be different if you lived in the Godzone all the time?

- 📢 If Jesus really invites sinners to the party, what does that mean for us? Why do so many people think they have to get all "prettied up" before they come to Jesus? What difference should this make in how we treat people with lots of obvious sin in their lives?

- 📢 Who are the outsiders in your neighborhood? Are they welcome in your youth group? In your church? What might happen if you invited them?

So What? — It's Your Life

- 📢 Have you found the magical city? If not, where do you think it can be found?

- 📢 In what practical ways can you live upside down? List some of those upside-down principles of the Godzone, then brainstorm how you can live them out.

- 📢 What can you do this week to live as a citizen of the Godzone?

Thanks to Mike Riddell for the term *Godzone* and permission to use some of his stories.

Say Grace

Primary theme grace	
Themes faith, mercy, justice, salvation, evangelism	
Scripture Romans 5:8; 10:21; Ephesians 2:8-9; James 1:17	
Approximate length through The Grand Finale 20-30 minutes	

You'll need

 Lyrics for several worship songs projected or on handouts

 A favorite worship song

 A personal story about wooing someone

 Prints or projections of nature photos

 "Nothing to Say" from the album *Carried Along* by Andrew Peterson (Reunion, 2000)

 Another adult willing to share about God's grace in his life

Contributed by **Mark Riddle**

This outline is saved as GTO_33 on the CD-ROM.

Christians—especially those from a nonre-formed background—tend to think of faith as our action or belief. And it's something we can turn on or off completely of our own volition. We often forget grace is the foundation of our faith. Without God's grace, we wouldn't even want to turn to him! Without God's grace, there would be no good reason to turn to him—other than terror! Admittedly grace is a very abstract idea and some of your students—especially your younger, more concrete thinkers—might have a tough time grasping any meaning deeper than "getting what we don't deserve." But this talk takes a swing at a deeper understanding of grace, perhaps the most essential theological concept.

intro

The Opening Act

◀)) **Worship** *Singing* (see sidebar)

◀)) **Worship** *Listening* (see sidebar)

◀)) **Activity** *Grace Skits* (see sidebar)

◀)) Ask several volunteers to take a stab at defining grace.

◀)) Then say something like—

> **Grace is a word we hear all the time. People talk about how graceful basketball players are as they make a difficult play seem easy. Some think of grace as the little prayer said before eating. You might know someone named Grace.**

Worship

Singing

Sing several songs about grace. Here are a few ideas to get you started. Lyrics can often be found online.

- "Amazing Grace"
- "You Are My All in All"
- "Breathe"
- "Come Thou Fount"
- "Every Move I Make"

Worship

Listening

Play a song about grace—perhaps one that's new to your teens. Project or hand out the lyrics so students can follow along. Here are a few suggestions—

- "If You Want to Get Free" recorded by Waterdeep on the album *To Chase Away the Birds* (Hey Ruth, 1999)

- "I'm Afraid I'm Not Supposed to Be Like This" recorded by Waterdeep on the album *Sink or Swim* (Hey Ruth, 1999)

- "I Remember You" recorded by Mac Powell with Gene Eugene on the album *City on a Hill: Songs of Worship and Praise* (Silvertone, 2000)

Grace skits

Gather kids into groups of five or so. Give them five minutes to come up with a one-minute skit that will help the other groups understand grace. Have all the groups perform their skits.

heart of the talk

The Main Event

1   What is grace?

🔊   Basically, grace is God loving us even though we don't deserve it.

🔊   **Illustration** *Nine-Year-Old Neighbor* (see sidebar)

🔊   This is how God deals with us. Instead of death, we not only get life, we get love. Not only does he love us, but he also works in our lives, our families, and our friends because he wants what's best for us.

🔊   **Scripture** *Ephesians 2:8-9* ("For it is by grace you have been saved.")

Nine-year-old neighbor

Imagine you won a contest and got a brand new Corvette. It's your favorite color. You park it in your driveway, and you wash and wax it at least once a week. Your parents occasionally ask if they can borrow it. You let them, after they clean your room.

One day you're out washing your 'Vette and you notice a nine-year-old neighbor from down the street walk out the front door of his house. You're surprised to see him jump in his parents' big ol' boat of a car and start it up. And you're shocked when he backs it into the street and starts racing toward your house. The kid can't drive at all, and he's all over the road, swerving and bumping the curbs. The worst happens. He loses control in front of your house, and that huge car barrels across your front lawn straight into the side of your beautiful Corvette. It gets hit with such force that it slams into your garage and is totaled.

There are three ways you can deal with this little punk. All three are even biblical!

* **Justice**—The first way to deal with the kid is justice. You run to the car. The kid's okay. In fact he's laughing. You grab him by the shirt and tell him how you feel. You drag him in the house and call the police. He gets arrested and now has a record. You call his parents. You make him work until he's paid for a new Corvette, which takes about 16 years! That's what he deserves. Justice means you get everything you deserve.

(continued)

(continued from previous page)

- **Mercy**—The second way to deal with the kid is called mercy. You still grab him by the shirt and tell him how you feel. You still drag him in the house, but you don't call the police. You do however, call his parents. You might even make him pay for some of the damage. Mercy means you don't get some or any of the punishment you deserve.

- **Grace**—The third way to deal with the kid is grace. You make sure the kid's okay. You help him out of the car. You don't get him in trouble with anyone—his parents or the police. You take him out for ice cream, and tell him you'd like to hang out with him more often. Maybe you even figure out a way to replace his parents' car! Grace means you get what you don't deserve—ice cream, a new car, a new friend.

By the way, even though this story deals with owning a car, it still works fine with junior highers. Just add comments about them not being able to drive the car yet.

Adapted from a story by Bill Hybels

2   Grace is even more!

- 🔊 God woos people to himself.

- 🔊 **Personal illustration** *My Crush* (see sidebar)

- 🔊 The ultimate goal of wooing someone is that their feelings will blossom as yours already have and they'll fall in love with you.

- 🔊 God doesn't sit around waiting to give us grace when we turn to him. He's actively wooing us!

- 🔊 **Explanation** *Prevenient Grace* (see sidebar)

- 🔊 **Scripture** *Romans 10:21* ("All day long I have held out my hands to a disobedient and obstinate people.")

- 🔊 Ask how the students imagine God wooing us. What does he do?

Personal illustration

My crush

Tell a story of one of your teenage crushes and what you went through to draw that person to you. For this illustration to work, it's essential there was some serious wooing going on. If you don't have a story from your teen years, use an adult story—even how you wooed your spouse, if you have one. Describe little gifts, notes, glances, the lengths you went to be in the presence of that person.

Explanation

Prevenient grace

The big theological term for God's wooing is *prevenient grace*. It's very much like God is flirting with you, in hopes you'll fall in deeply in love with him. He's actively working in your life, drawing you to himself.

3   God shows us his grace in many ways.

◀))   God shows us his grace in things we see everyday and probably take for granted.

- A beautiful sunset

- A song on the radio that speaks to you

- Your creativity—or seeing someone else's creativity

- The pleasure in life

- Fun with friends and laughing until your drink shoots out your nose!

◀))   **Illustration** *Scenery Pictures* (see sidebar)

◀))   Ask these rhetorical questions—don't get responses.

- What have you done to deserve the beauty of the scenery on a camping trip?

- What have you done to deserve hearing an amazing musician use the abilities God gave her?

- What have you done to deserve the joy of great friends or to deserve the funniest moment of your life?

- What have you done to deserve your next breath?

◀))   These are all gifts from God, and we don't deserve any of them!

◀))   **Song** "Nothing to Say" by Andrew Peterson on *Carried Along* (BMG/Zomba/Reunion, 2000) (see sidebar)

◀))   **Scripture** *James 1:17* ("Every good and perfect gift is from above, coming down from the Father of the heavenly lights, who does not change like shifting shadows.")

◀))   Of course God's ultimate demonstration of grace is Jesus' death in our places.

◀))   **Scripture** *Romans 5:8* ("But God demonstrates his own love for us in this: while we were still sinners Christ died for us.")

◀))   **Explanation** *Grace Initiation* If you're using this talk for evangelistic purposes, explain the important part that grace plays in the salvation that Jesus offers us—in other words, give 'em the gospel.

Illustration

Scenery pictures

Find a collection of beautiful nature pictures to show your group and talk about God's creativity and how it's a gift of grace to us. If your group is large, it would be great to download pictures from the Internet and show them using Microsoft PowerPoint or MediaShout. Or you could print them out and pass them around if you have a smaller group. Show pictures of waterfalls, rivers, trees—anything beautiful in God's creation. Try www.theloughroad.com and www.corbis.com for great nature pictures.

"Nothing to Say"

"Nothing to Say" records Andrew Peterson's experience of seeing the Grand Canyon for the first time. He is drawn to God and called to worship him. He sings, "I'm broken by this majesty ...I don't believe that I believed in you as deeply as today...the mountains sing your glory."

closing

The Grand Finale

- 🔊 **Sharing** *What Grace Means to Me* (see sidebar)
- 🔊 **Sharing** Have students spend a minute or two thinking, then have them share a way they've experienced God's grace this past week.
- 🔊 **Activity** *Grace Hunt* (see sidebar)
- 🔊 Say something like—

> If we're paying attention, we can see evidence of God's grace all over our lives—in our homes, families, schools, health. And just because you've got a hardship in some area of your life doesn't mean God's not dumping grace on you! Literally everything has evidence of God's grace. With sin in our lives we don't deserve anything good, yet God loves us. He woos us to himself and gives us the faith, hope, and love it takes to follow him.

What grace means to me

Invite a student or leader in your group to share a personal testimony of God's grace. Ask her to be specific about how she has seen and experienced grace. It might be impactful to have an older person—much older!—share.

Grace hunt

Give students a small chunk of time to go on a grace hunt. They'll need about five minutes if you're meeting in a church, but much longer if you're in a setting where they can get outside and walk around. Explain they're to walk around by themselves—no talking—and find something that hints or speaks loudly of God's grace. If it's possible, they should bring their items back to the group. If it's not possible, they can describe it. After everyone returns, have as many share as you have time for.

discussion

Encore

Get It?	Middle School

- How would you define grace?
- How is grace different than mercy? Different than justice?
- How does God woo us?
- Do you think God is in love with you? Why or why not? Why is he so interested in you?
- What do sunsets and nature have to do with grace?
- Why is it a sign of God's grace that you get to live another day?

Get It?	High School

- How would you describe grace to a six-year-old?
- What are some ways you've seen evidence of God's grace in your life?
- In what ways have you seen God's grace in difficult or painful experiences in your life?
- If you were to write a definition of grace, reflecting your own experience—what would it be?
- How does God's wooing you show up in your life?
- Can you describe a time when God used nature to draw you closer to him?
- How do good behavior and right living fit into all this talk about grace?

What If?   The Big Picture

- Put yourself in the Corvette story. What would you have done to the neighbor kid? Which option would you have chosen?

- What—if anything—about grace bothers you? What don't you understand about it?

- Is it possible there's nothing we can do to earn salvation? Talk about that.

- What if you lived every day aware of God's grace working in the world around you? What difference would it make?

- If we understand God is such a grace-giver, then why do we have a hard time trusting him?

- What if some area of your life stinks—does that mean God isn't giving you grace? Talk about that.

So What?   It's Your Life

- How can you keep your eyes and heart open for grace sightings this week? What will you do?

- In what ways can you be an instrument of God's grace? Are you willing to do this? What can you do in the next 24 hours?

- Who do you know that can use a grace sighting? What can you do to help that person see and experience God's grace?

- What should your response to God's grace be today? This week? Throughout your life?

Real Power

Primary theme Jesus' power
Themes power, humility, weakness
Scripture Matthew 3:7-10; 14:15-21; 19:13-15; 21:12; 26:63; Mark 15:15-20; Luke 8:22-25; John 11:33-44; 19:8-15; 1 Corinthians 11:1
Approximate length through The Grand Finale 35-45 minutes

Contributed by **Dan Jessup**

This outline is saved as GTO_34 on the CD-ROM.

You'll need

- Pencil and paper for each student
- TV and VCR
- *The Rock*

Who is Jesus? Is he the powerful person who raised Lazarus from the dead? Is he the meek man who refused to fight back? What's the truth?

Well, both, really. Jesus is the perfect picture of power both in strength and restraint. Your students need to know both pictures of Jesus—and how they fit together. They need to understand he calls us to be bold at times and to be meek at other times. As youth workers our greatest desire is to have our kids fall in love with and imitate Jesus. This talk will help them understand more about Jesus and give them an accurate understanding of how Jesus used his power.

intro

The Opening Act

- 📣 **Sharing** *Power People* (see sidebar)

- 📣 **Activity** *Power Defs* Give students paper and pencils and ask them to write out a definition of power. Once they're all finished have several of them share their definitions.

- 📣 Transition by saying something like—

  Power can be a confusing idea. Sometimes it's seen as a strength to be envied. Other times it seems like a tool for abuse or injustice. We're going to look at how Jesus used his limitless power and how we can draw on that same power.

Sharing

Power people

Ask students to share examples of powerful people. These can be examples of any kind of power. Don't screen or discount any of the answers. Make sure they share why that person is perceived as powerful

heart of the talk

The Main Event

1   The *possessor* of power

- 📣 When we look at Jesus in the Bible, we see a wide variety of snapshots.

- 📣 **Movie clip** *The Rock* (see sidebar)

- 📣 How about Jesus? If you look at single scenes from the Gospels, you could come to very different conclusions about what Jesus is like. Have students try to suggest examples of this.

- 📣 After each passage, ask students how they would describe Jesus if this were the only thing they had to go on.

  - **Scripture** *Matthew 21:12* ("Jesus entered the temple area and drove out all who were buying and selling there.")
  - **Scripture** *Matthew 3:7-10* ("You brood of vipers!")
  - **Scripture** *Matthew 19:13-15* ("Let the little children come to me…")
  - **Scripture** *Matthew 26:63* ("But Jesus remained silent.")

- 📣 Jesus was very hard for people to describe. He was always doing things that didn't make sense even to those who knew him best!

- 📣 Jesus is the ultimate possessor of power. But he's totally not what people expected—or are expecting—him to be. He exercises his power in two very distinct ways.

The Rock

Show both of these clips to help students understand how someone can have two very different sides.

Start 28:00 Guards come with chains to remove the prisoner from his cell.

Stop 28:37 Cut away to the airport.

Start 52:00 "I've rehearsed this speech a thousand times…""

Stop 53:20 The daughter walks away.

John Mason (Sean Connery) is the only man to ever escape from Alcatraz—in this fictional tale, anyway. These two scenes show an incredible contrast in his character. In the first he's a wild man, terrifying to look at. But in the second scene everything about him is different, right down to his haircut. As he sits on a park bench with his daughter, he's a different man—gentle and loving.

After showing both scenes ask—

- **What did the main character look like in each of these scenes?**

- **What were some of his characteristics in each?**

- **Is he the type of person you might like to stay as a guest in your home for a week? Explain why.**

- **If you had only seen that first scene, you would think he was a whacked-out crazy man. If you'd only seen the second scene, you might think he was a gentle loving dad. Which do you think he is?**

2 The *act* of power

◁ᵉ))) Jesus used his power to perform miracles and change lives. This use of power was always for someone else's benefit, not his own.

◁ᵉ))) After each of these passages, ask how Jesus was using his power. Ask why he used his power.

Scripture *Luke 8:22-25* (Jesus calms the storm)

Scripture *John 11:33-44* (Jesus raises Lazarus from the dead)

Scripture *Matthew 14:15-21* (The feeding of the 5,000)

3 The *irony* of power

🔊 Here's the weird thing about Jesus' power—he doesn't just use it for miracles. And he never uses it for his own benefit!

🔊 **Scripture** *John 19:8-15* ("Do you refuse to speak to me?")

🔊 Ask why you think Jesus chose not to speak.

🔊 Mention how we're often more comfortable talking about the Jesus who's conquering. But the reality is Jesus used his power to remain silent as often as he used it to do miracles.

🔊 **Scripture** *Mark 15:15-20* ("They put a purple robe on him.")

🔊 Jesus stayed silent again. Why might it take greater power to stay silent and take the abuse than to knock them all around?

🔊 **Illustration** *Two Paths to Greatness* (see sidebar)

🔊 The Jews were expecting the Messiah to show up and be like a powerful king who would take over the earth. But Jesus chose to demonstrate power though service, meekness, and humility.

Illustration

Two paths to greatness

Jesus and Herod were both on the path to greatness. Herod thought of greatness as gaining power though intimidation and making powerful judgments. Jesus practiced power though serving. Take a moment to contrast these two views of gaining and using power.

closing

The Grand Finale

🔊 Jesus wants us to live like him. That means being bold in God's power when we're trying to help people. That also means being meek in God's power when we're persecuted for believing in Christ.

🔊 **Scripture** *1 Corinthians 11:1* ("As I follow the example of Christ")

🔊 **Activity** *Life Outlines* (see sidebar)

Life outlines

Give each student a sheet of paper and pencil. Ask them to outline a typical weekday. Students ought to include what they do to get ready for school, how they spend their day at school, what they do after school, and how they spend their evenings.

Then have students trade their papers with another student. Ask them to look over the outlines and circle different areas where living in power—Christ's idea of power—might change the activity. For example students involved in debate might be challenged to live like Christ in the way they debate. When they're finished, have students look over their own outlines to see what the other person has pointed out.

discussion

Encore

Get It?	Middle School

- Are we supposed to let others abuse us just because we believe in Jesus? Why or why not?
- Why is imitating Jesus so important?
- How is it possible to have the same power as Jesus?
- What's meekness?
- What effect does our meekness have on the world? Doesn't that give people the chance to walk all over us? Talk about that.

Get It?	High School

- What happens when we imitate Jesus' use of power?
- Doesn't meekness give others a chance to treat us like doormats?
- What might be other demonstrations of Jesus' power besides meekness and strength?
- Why did Jesus chose humility over physical power? Why did he allow himself to be beaten?
- If God's power is in us, why can't we do the miracles Jesus did?

What If? — The Big Picture

- What does it take to be like Jesus when it comes to power?

- How does trying to live like him change who we are?

- What would the world be like if Jesus had come as a power-hungry ruler?

- What would happen if every Christian lived like Jesus did?

- What difference does it make to your day-to-day life that you can draw on Jesus' power?

- If we believe Jesus gives us the power to do miracles, what miracles should we do?

So What? — It's Your Life

- How does living meekly like Christ make an impact on the world?

- What would it look like for you to practice more meekness this week?

- Talk about a time in the past month when you should have drawn on Jesus' power to confront injustice. How would you have done that? What might the result have been?

- What areas of your life prevent you from fully living like Christ? What can you do to change these areas?

Whose Kingdom Do You Live In?

Primary theme kingdom of God	
Themes outreach, evangelism, missions, holiness, Lord's prayer	
Scripture Psalm 145:13; Matthew 6:10, 33; Hebrews 12:28	
Approximate length through The Grand Finale 15-20 minutes	

Contributed by **Curt Gibson**

You'll need

🔊 Personal illustration about your toys and your bedroom when you were five

🔊 Small caged animals—like fish, hamsters, or ants

This short little talk is handy for helping students understand God's kingdom—especially students who don't have much knowledge of the Bible, which makes it an effective evangelistic talk. It's built on the simple premise we all live in kingdoms other than the country we reside in. We have kingdoms and so does God. The question is, am I willing to surrender my kingdom to God's? This talk is also a great challenge on a missions trip—to remind students they're workers in God's kingdom.

intro

The Opening Act

📢 **Personal illustration** *My Kiddy Kingdom* Tell a story about the toys that existed in your room at age five and how your bedroom was your own little kingdom. It was safe, warm, and fun. Play it up and have fun with this.

📢 **Object lesson** *Hamster Cage* (see sidebar)

📢 Then make a transition by saying something like—

> **There are kingdoms all over the place! You don't have to be a member of royalty and have a royal lineage to establish a kingdom. A kingdom is wherever your will has an effect.**

Object lesson

Hamster cage

Bring in a hamster cage or a fish bowl or some other small animal in a container—an ant farm would be very cool. Talk about the kingdom this little animal lives in. Ask students to think up some of the laws and values of this kingdom.

heart of the talk

The Main Event

1 You got a kingdom; I got a kingdom.

📢 Every single one of us has a kingdom—or a queendom—that is completely our own, where everything we choose takes place.

📢 **Illustration** *My Kingdom* (see sidebar)

📢 **Discussion** *Lotsa Kingdoms* Have students pair off and describe their kingdoms. Tell them they each have to make at least four descriptive statements about their kingdoms.

My kingdom

Describe your kingdom. Here is one example of how you could do this and things you might want to include.

Let me tell you about the kingdom of Curt. My kingdom is the range of my effective will.

- Curt's rule takes place on a 50 x 150 lot in Pasadena, California.

- Trees are planted where Curt decides.

- Dogs roam the yard in Curt's kingdom.

- Curt's intern—also known as a slave-boy—expands the kingdom from 9 a.m. to 5 p.m. by eliminating items on Curt's to-do list.

- Curt's kingdom shrinks every day as he returns home and carries out the will of his queen, Kathy.

2   God's got a kingdom.

- God's kingdom has existed eternally—long before creation—and will never end. God's kingdom is everywhere his will has an effect—which is everywhere!

- **Scripture** *Psalm 145:13* ("Your kingdom is an everlasting kingdom.")

- God's kingdom has been around—and will be around—forever.

- **Scripture** *Hebrews 12:28* ("Therefore, since we are receiving a kingdom that cannot be shaken…")

- God's kingdom has never been in trouble. It isn't manmade. And we have an invitation to be a part of it. Turning down the invitation only hurts us.

- **Scripture** *Matthew 6:33* ("But seek first his kingdom and his righteousness.")

- The kingdom of God is here and now.

- **Illustration** *Radio Is at Hand* (see sidebar)

- When Jesus taught us to pray the Lord's Prayer in Matthew 6:10, "Thy kingdom come" doesn't mean we're praying for God's kingdom to come into existence. Instead Jesus is teaching us to pray his kingdom will take over every inch of our lives, especially areas where we aren't allowing it to exist now.

Illustration

Radio is at hand

An easy way to explain the kingdom of God existing all around us is to compare it to a radio signal being broadcast. You're not even aware it's there unless you're willing to understand some general information about radio signals and recognize specific things that need to be done in your life to receive them—like buying a radio with an antenna.

3 Surrender your kingdom to God's kingdom.

- God has allowed all of us to have a kingdom of our own that we rule.

- Understand that God's kingdom comes with an invitation—the invitation is for us to surrender our kingdom and allow it to exist as part of God's kingdom.

- The wisest thing we can do in life is to surrender our kingdom and say, "God, your kingdom is in charge."

- This is how we allow the Lord's Prayer to be carried out in our lives, by allowing God's kingdom to come here in our lives "as it is in heaven."

- The kingdom isn't something you wait to experience when you die. Instead the kingdom is alive and present and exists all around you right at this moment.

closing

The Grand Finale

- **Illustration** *Puerto Rico* (see sidebar)

- Simply put, the way one joins the kingdom of God is by surrendering your own kingdom.

- **Explanation** *Surrendering the Kingdom* If you're using this talk for evangelistic purposes, now would be the time to explain the life-giving work of Jesus on the cross. Go for it!

- **Special event** *Missions Application* (see sidebar)

Puerto Rico

Ask the students how the island of Puerto Rico is different than other countries in the Caribbean in how it relates to the United States. The answer is that Puerto Rico is under U.S. governmental jurisdiction.

Explain that Puerto Rico is a commonwealth. It has its own government, laws, customs, and values. Yet it's officially part of the United States, even though it's not a state. And while the leaders of Puerto Rico can use their authority to govern, they're ultimately under the rule of the U.S. president and government, which means the will of the U.S. overrides the will of Puerto Rico.

This is how we can function with God. God expects us to make decisions and exercise our will. But he has final authority over us—which means our choices can't go against his.

Missions application

A great way to adapt this talk to a mission trip setting is to wrap it up by reminding students that as they minister to others they're carrying out God's will. In doing that they are—at that moment—right smack in the middle of the kingdom of God.

discussion

Encore

Get It?	Middle School

📢 How would you describe a kingdom? Describe your kingdom.

📢 How can all of us have our own kingdoms? How does that work?

📢 If we each have our own kingdoms, do they have conflict with each other all the time? Talk about that.

📢 What's God's kingdom?

📢 How can you be a part of God's kingdom?

Get It? — High School

- How would you describe a kingdom to an eight-year-old?
- What's the difference between your kingdom and your parents' kingdom?
- What's the difference between your kingdom and God's kingdom?
- What's it look like to make your kingdom part of God's kingdom?

What If? — The Big Picture

- Why bother surrendering your kingdom to God's?
- What kind of life would you have if you were to rule your own kingdom and never surrender it to God?
- What kind of life would you have if you were to surrender your kingdom to God's?
- In what area of your life is surrender to God most difficult? Why?
- Pretend you've surrendered to God, but you're still controlling the stuff in your life that isn't the way he wants it. What happens?

So What? — It's Your Life

- Historically when one side in a battle surrendered to the other side, they waved a white flag. What's your white flag? How will you communicate to God that you want to surrender to his authority?
- In what areas of your life have you already surrendered to God?
- In what areas of your life do you want to surrender but aren't sure you'll be able to? Why do you think it will be tough? How do you think God can help you?
- In what areas of your life are you not ready to surrender? Why not? What would it take for you to want to surrender these areas to God? What are you afraid he will do if you surrender that area?
- What choice or commitment are you willing to make today? How will it affect your life this week?

Don't Talk with Your Mouth Full

Primary theme power of words	
Themes the heart, spiritual growth, commitment, lordship, speech	
Scripture Luke 6:43-45; Ephesians 4:29; James 3:5-6	
Approximate length through The Grand Finale 30-35 minutes	

This talk helps students think about the words they choose and the impact their words can have on other people. They'll have a chance to consider both destructive words and words that build others up. Ultimately the talk challenges students to think about the status of their own hearts. The true issue isn't words but the attitudes and values those words represent. Destructive words flow from a troubled heart, and positive words flow from a heart centered on Christ.

Contributed by **Darrell Pearson**

This outline is saved as GTD_36 on the CD-ROM.

You'll need

- A metal trash can, kindling, matches, and a fire extinguisher (optional)

- TV and VCR (optional)

- A video clip showing a small fire become a large, blazing fire (optional)

- A personal story about a time you did some damage with your words

- A video camera (optional)

- Volunteers—students, adult leaders, or even strangers—to talk about a time they were encouraged by someone else's words (on video or in person)

- A piece of ripe fruit

- A few cookies or potato chips—anything that will create lots of crumbs (optional)

- Pencils and paper for students (optional)

intro

The Opening Act

🔊 **Illustration** *Funky Pasta* (see sidebar)

🔊 **Illustration** *Imported Product Names* (see sidebar)

🔊 Say something like—

> **More than 600,000—that's how many words the Oxford English Dictionary says are in the English language. If you add in scientific and technical terms, it's well over a million. That's a lot of words! Enough that we should always have the perfect word to say to other people. So why do we seem to choose the wrong word so often? You know, the word that doesn't say what we mean, or the word that stings someone else when we mean to say something nice. Do you ever find yourself choosing the wrong word and wishing you had said something else? The Bible gives us some helpful advice on this!**

Illustration

Funky pasta

Sometimes language is a funny thing. The Italian language has hundreds of words for varieties of pasta! Give your students an oral pop quiz—not to worry, it's multiple choice—asking them to guess the literal meaning of these types of pasta.

Strozzapretti
  a. Stranded pedestrians
  b. Strangled priests *(correct)*
  c. Pretty songs

Vermicelli
  a. Little worms *(correct)*
  b. Old cellos
  c. Rats and other vermin

Muscatel
  a. Muskrats
  b. Musical fellows
  c. Wine with flies in it *(correct)*

Illustration

Imported product names

The following products from other countries were all considered for distribution in English-speaking countries. But they were dropped because their names translated so poorly. Read the product names aloud and have your students guess what they really are.

Product name	Product	Product name	Product
Alu-fanny	French aluminum foil	Mukk	Italian yogurt
Atum Bom	Portuguese tuna	Plopp	Scandinavian chocolate
Bull	French computer company	Pocari Sweat	Japanese soft drink
Crapsy Fruit	French cereal	Zit	German lemonade
Happy End	German toilet paper		

heart of the talk
The Main Event

1   Words easily become instruments of destruction.

- 🔊 Ask the students if they've ever been hurt by someone's words.

- 🔊 Then ask if they've ever seen a fire raging out of control. Allow someone to share a story about a fire they've seen.

- 🔊 **Scripture** *James 3:5-6* ("The tongue is like a fire, able to burn a whole forest from a single spark.")

- 🔊 **Object lesson** *Fire Can* (see sidebar)

- 🔊 **Personal illustration** *The Fire I Started* Tell a story about a time you hurt someone deeply with your words—either intentionally or by mistake.

Object lesson

Fire can

While you talk about James 3:5–6, create a small fire in a metal trash can to demonstrate how quickly a fire grows. Have an extinguisher nearby to put it out. If you'd rather not go there, simply show a video of a fire growing from a small flame to a full blaze. You can find fire footage in many movies about, uh, fire—*Backdraft* being one of them.

2   Words are supposed to build people up, not tear them down.

- 🔊 It's easy to use words to hurt people, but God wants us to use words to help people, to build them up, to meet their needs.

- 🔊 A few encouraging words from one person can be a life-changing experience for someone else.

- 🔊 **Personal illustration** *Build Me Up!* Contrast your previous story about hurting someone with words with a story about a significant time in your life when someone said something encouraging to you.

- 🔊 **Video clip** *Encouraging Stories* (see sidebar)

- 🔊 **Scripture** *Ephesians 4:29* ("That it may benefit those who listen")

Video clip

Encouraging stories

Record a short video ahead of time, asking people to tell stories of positive things others have said to them. You could do this with kids in your group, adults and children in your church, or with random people on the street or at a shopping mall. If you can't do the video, ask a few students in your group to share a story during the talk.

3   Words flow from the heart, not from the mouth.

- Sure, your brain has a lot to do with choosing words. But how we use words is usually a reflection of what's going on in our hearts.

- If your heart is bitter and angry, your words will probably be bitter and angry also. If you're insecure you might tear others down to try to make yourself feel better. But if your heart is full of goodness and godly thoughts, your words will follow suit.

- **Scripture** *Luke 6:43-45* (people are recognized by their fruit)

- **Object lesson** *Ripe Fruit* (see sidebar)

Object lesson
Ripe fruit

Pull a piece of fruit—obviously ripe and ready to eat—out of a bag. Take a few bites in front of your group, savoring the taste and making it overly obvious the fruit is luscious and juicy. Explain how fruit this good must come from a healthy tree—a bad tree can't produce healthy fruit. The Bible says words come in the same way. Fruitful words come from a full and healthy heart.

closing
The Grand Finale

- Ask students about the status of their hearts. Give them about 30 seconds of silence to think about it.

- Remind students that when they were kids, their parents probably told them not to speak with their mouths full. Then ask them what's so bad about it. It's disgusting! If you're speaking to junior highers, it would be great to say this with a mouth full of potato chips or cookies, allowing crumbs and bits to spill out of your mouth while speaking.

- When we talk with our hearts full of junk, it can have a similar effect!

- **Reflection** *My Heart Condition* (optional, see sidebar)

- Don't talk with your mouth full—talk with your heart full of godly things.

- Close in prayer. Ask God to clean up what's inside, so their words will be encouraging and helpful to others.

Reflection
My heart condition

Have students draw a heart on a small piece of paper, then write down single words representing any negative attitudes and feelings in their hearts. For example they might write *bitter, selfish,* or *angry.* After they've had several minutes to think and write, give them another few moments to silently pray for Jesus to heal that part of their heart.

discussion
Encore

Get It?   Middle School

- Is swearing okay? Defend your answer.

- Some people say swearing just the way people talk these days. What makes swearing so negative?

- What does it mean to have a good heart? Why is it more than having a heart that pumps blood?

- Write down a list of words that are hurtful to other people. Then write another list of words that encourage others.

- Think about a time you may have helped grow plants at your house. Did you have plants that didn't do as well as expected? What was the problem? How does this relate to what Jesus said about bad plants and people?

- Are you the type of person who thinks first, then talks? Or do you speak before thinking?

Get It?   High School

- How important do you think words are in an age of visual media? Are images stronger and more memorable than spoken words? Why or why not?

- Can you think of a recent time when you hurt someone else with your words? Is there a way to give this person a positive word now to undo some of the damage? What might you say?

- What other stories from the Bible can you think of that speak about positive and negative words? How did Jesus speak to people? Jesus did use harsh words sometimes—like when he called the Pharisees snakes! Why did he speak that way on occasion?

- When would be an appropriate time for harsh or negative words?

What If? | The Big Picture

🔊 Describe what your school and youth group would be like if everyone spoke positive words instead of destructive words.

🔊 Have you ever found yourself in an environment where everybody seemed to speak encouragingly to one another? Maybe at a retreat, in a student leadership group, on an athletic team, in a musical group, or on a missions trip? What made the group different?

🔊 What happens when you speak positive words, but everyone around you continues to use destructive words? How can you keep using positive words in a difficult situation like that?

So What? | It's Your Life

🔊 Think about the people closest to you—like your friends and family. Who do you have the hardest time talking to without using negative words? Why? How can you talk to them differently in the future?

🔊 Who has influenced your life the most? What words does this person use when they speak to you?

🔊 What words and phrases are the most hurtful to you? Why are those words painful? What stories lie behind those words? How can God heal you from that pain?

🔊 Think of one person in your life you have a difficult time speaking with. What words or phrases can you use to break the ice?

🔊 Are there any destructive words or phrases you use all the time? How can you eliminate them? (If your group is close and transparent, it may be appropriate to allow group members to give each other feedback on this one.)

🔊 What can you do this week that would allow God to change the condition of your heart?

Are You a Vampire?

Contributed by **Mark Oestreicher**

Primary theme salvation	
Themes Halloween, outreach, connecting with God, perception of God	
Scripture John 8:12; Romans 5:6-8; 1 John 3:1	
Approximate length through The Grand Finale 20-25 minutes	

You'll need

- TV and VCR
- *Dracula: Dead and Loving It*
- A hand-held mirror
- A large flashlight
- A large cross
- Mirrors, penlights, and crosses— enough for each student to have one item

his punchy little talk is a great attention grabber for a Halloween event. Kids love scary stuff. And while this talk certainly isn't scary, it taps into common teen experience in a creative and captivating way. It connects first with the play on words—the surprising twist of definitions. But then it grabs onto emotions and real-life experience—*Yeah, I don't like who I am. Yeah, I don't want who I really am to be exposed.* Of course real hope is offered in Jesus Christ, which makes this an evangelistic talk at its core.

This outline is saved as GTO_37 on the CD-ROM.

intro

The Opening Act

📢 Tell an exaggerated version of a time you were frightened

📢 **Movie clip** *Scary Stuff* (see sidebar)

📢 Transition by saying something like—

> **I think some of you are vampires! You might not drink blood— hopefully you don't! But many of you have other vampire-like characteristics. Let's look at three of them.**

Movie clip

Scary stuff

Show one or two scenes from the vampire spoof movie *Dracula: Dead and Loving It*. (Don't watch the whole movie. It's got some pretty tacky scenes.)

Start 8:15 Guest opens door.

Stop 10:55 "And now, if you're not too fatigued from your journey."

A visitor opens the door to Dracula's castle, gets his first sight of Drac, and watches as Drac falls head-over-heels down the stairs.

Start 36:28 "Master, master…"

Stop 37:10 "I was having a daymare."

Dracula has a "daymare" that he's out in the sun during the day enjoying life.

Start 59:19 "Essie, Essie, your eyelids are growin' heavy."

Stop 1:01:09 "Turn out the lights so no one will see me."

Dracula tries to put one woman in a trance and to lead her outside. But signals get crossed and result in a scene reminiscent of the Keystone Cops.

Start 1:12:28 "Mina, may I have this dance?"

Stop 1:15:26 "You are a very wise man."

Dracula dances a wild and hilarious tango in front of a large mirror, not realizing that everyone sees he has no reflection.

heart of the talk

The Main Event

1   Vampires are afraid of mirrors.

- 🔊 **Object lesson** *Mirror* (see sidebar)
- 🔊 **Illustration** *What I Saw in My Mirror* (see sidebar)
- 🔊 Seeing yourself through God's eyes.

  - **Scripture** *1 John 3:1* ("How great is the love the Father has lavished on us, that we should be called children of God.")

  - God loves you and wants to be his child. He either has adopted you or wants to do so.

Object lesson

Mirror

Use a pocket mirror to give a visualization of your point. This will increase attention, memory, and connection with your talk. Explain with something like—

> **Some of you are afraid of mirrors because you don't like what you see when you look into one. It's not that you scream in fear when you see a mirror. It's that you don't like yourself. When you look in a mirror, what do you see? Are you afraid of seeing who you truly are? Weak? Addicted? In desperate need of love? Someone who will do anything to be cool?**

Illustration

What I saw in my mirror

Think back to your teenage years and tell a personal story about your self-image. Maybe you wanted to be considered cool; maybe you thought you were overweight, underweight, too tall, too short—whatever! Don't make it sound like you want sympathy—in fact a small amount of self-effacing humor would be good. But do help your students see you understand what they never admit to anyone else.

2 Vampires are afraid of light.

- **Object lesson** *Flashlight* (see sidebar)
- **Illustration** *The Titanic* Most people have seen the movie and everyone knows the story. Bring out the fact this tragedy wouldn't have happened in the daytime, without fog, when things were clear.
- **Scripture** *John 8:12* ("I am the light of the world.")
  - God's light exposes the truth—and that can be scary!
- The hard reality is it can be scary to live and walk in the light. But it's the only way to experience life.

Object lesson
Flashlight

Hold a flashlight—in the on position—while you talk through this point. Point out that maybe the students are afraid of the light because it exposes the truth. Explain that light has a distinct purpose—it exposes things and makes reality clear.

3 Vampires are afraid of crosses.

- **Object lesson** *Cross* Hold up a large cross of some sort while you give this point, and point out that maybe students are afraid of the cross because they don't understand what it represents.
- **Explanation** *Cross Symbolism* (see sidebar)
- That's the literal symbolism of the cross. But it's a symbol of so much more.
- Many people see the cross as a symbol of demands, rules, and a boring life.
- It's a symbol of love—of Jesus' amazing love for each of us.
- **Scripture** *Romans 5:6-8* ("But God demonstrates his own love for us in this: While we were still sinners, Christ died for us.")

Explanation
Cross symbolism

Of course the cross is a symbol. When we wear crosses around our necks, they're not there to be used as crucifixion devices. Explain in a fun way that people don't grab little bugs and crucify them on a necklace (make little bug shrieking noises!). Explain the cross then was like the electric chair is now. And if Jesus had lived today, we might wear little gold electric chairs around our necks.

closing

The Grand Finale

🔊 Review the responses you want from students.

- **Look in the mirror from God's perspective. See yourself as his beloved child.**

- **Run to the light. Let Jesus expose the truth in your life. Living in truth is always best.**

- **Run to the cross. God, through Jesus, is waiting for you with his arms wide open.**

🔊 If you're using this as an evangelistic talk, now is a great time to explain the work Jesus did on the cross and what it means for you and me. And—depending on your church tradition—give students some way of responding.

🔊 **Take-home item** *Mirrors, Penlights, and Crosses* (optional, see sidebar)

Mirrors, penlights, and crosses

Consider buying a bunch of miniature mirrors, flashlights, and small crosses at a dollar store and a Christian bookstore. Ask students to spend some time thinking about which of these vampire-like attitudes they've fallen into the most. Then invite them to come take one of the three items as a reminder of God's perspective. After each student has an item in hand, have them spend some time in silent prayer, thanking God for his love and acceptance.

discussion

Encore

Get It? | Middle School

🔊 You aren't really vampires, right? But explain how—in a sense—you are a vampire.

🔊 Why would anyone be afraid of a mirror?

🔊 How about light—what's fearful about light?

🔊 And the cross? Why would anyone have a problem with the cross?

Get It? — High School

- To what extent are your peers are afraid to look into the mirror—to see who they really are?

- Students are afraid of having truth exposed. Do you agree or disagree with that statement?

- And the cross—do you think people even think about the symbolism at all? If yes, what do they think? If no, why not?

What If? — The Big Picture

- Most of us try to get people to see us in a certain way. What would happen if you let people know the real you, what you think, and how you struggle?

- What difference does it make that God sees you as his perfect child?

- It's hard to live in the light. Pretend you have two choices: You can hide who you really are—having shallow friendships based on half-truths or you can live in the light—being honest about who you are, but losing a few friends in the process. Which would you choose? Why?

- Do you ever feel like Christianity is just about rules—can'ts and have-tos? How do you handle this?

- Saying the cross is a symbol of love sounds nice—and would make a nice song or poem—but what difference does it actually make?

So What? — It's Your Life

- What would life be like for you if you chose to see yourself as God's perfect child? How would you live differently?

- What would it take to be able to look in the mirror and like who you see?

- How can you live in the light? What would it look like? What would have to be different about your life? And what are the possible results?

- What can you do this week to respond to God's love, symbolized by the cross?

- How can you have a more intimate relationship with God?

- *(If you are using this as an evangelistic talk)* How do you want to respond to what Jesus has done for you? You can blow him off. You can choose to follow him. You can say, "Not yet." What will you do?

Soul Food

Contributed by **Efrem Smith**

Primary theme spiritual hunger	
Themes outreach, evangelism, Jesus' power, needs, connecting with God, communion	
Scripture Ezekiel 3:1-3; John 4:13-14; 6:5-14; 6:32-35	
Approximate length through The Grand Finale 30-40 minutes	

You've got to eat. So do your kids. And we all know the difference between fast food and a home-cooked meal. This talk uses hunger for physical food as a metaphor for dealing with the deeper hunger of the soul. Just as we hunger to eat, we also hunger for attention, love, purpose, or identity. The talk ends by challenging students to bring their needs to Jesus and dine with him—as only Jesus can meet the deepest longings of our souls.

This is a tough talk for young teens to grasp due to the abstract food metaphor used. If you're speaking to young teens, you'll need to explain carefully so they understand what you're talking about.

You'll need

- TV and VCR
- *Indiana Jones and the Temple of Doom*
- A personal story about your favorite food
- Messy food like ice cream or pies for an eating contest
- Several student volunteers to compete in the eating contest
- Paper towels and drinking water for after the contest—the contestants will thank you
- Unleavened bread and grape juice or whatever elements your church uses for communion (optional)

intro
The Opening Act

🔊 **Movie clip** *Indiana Jones and the Temple of Doom* (see sidebar)

🔊 **Personal illustration** *The Best Food* (see sidebar)

🔊 **Activity** *Food Eating Contest* (see sidebar)

Movie clip

Indiana Jones and the Temple of Doom

Start 41:32 "Captain Blumburtt was just telling me something of the interesting history."

Stop 46:13 Willie passes out.

On their way to tracking down a mysterious cult, Indiana Jones (Harrison Ford) and his two sidekicks Willie (Kate Capshaw) and Short Round (Ke Huy Quan) are guests at a special feast with extremely weird food—to put it mildly.

Show the entire scene then ask the students what they would have done if they were Indiana or Willie. What food grosses them out? What are their favorite foods? Why do you like those foods?

Personal illustration

The best food

Share a story about your favorite food—a time when you were craving it, and how thrilled you were to gorge yourself on this item. It would be best if the food item you chose wasn't something as common as pizza, but was something more unique—like a certain cookie your mother makes or an ethnic food.

Activity

Food eating contest

If your meeting time is a casual youth group meeting (as opposed to Sunday school) or an outreach event, consider beginning with a messy food eating contest.

Of course pie-eating—with hands behind backs—is always a winner in the mess category. Ice-cream sundaes work well for this effect also. For either of these allow two minutes, and see which contestant can eat the most. If you use some other food item—like pizza or burgers—give each contestant a preset amount (four slices of pizza for example) and see who can finish first. You don't want to have some kid eat 23 slices of pizza and then have 12 of the slices revisit the girl in the front row, if you know what I mean.

Award prizes relating to food, such as gift certificates for frozen yogurt or burgers.

heart of the talk
The Main Event

1   Your body needs food.

📢 Say something like—

We all get hungry. It's something we all share in common. Regardless of where you live, your age, your ethnicity, your gender—we can all find common ground around the issue of hunger. How do you know when you're hungry?

📢 **Group discussion** *The Best Place to Eat* (see sidebar)

📢 When you're hungry you have a few options.

- *Fast food*—This is a very easy way to address our hunger, but usually not the most nutritious.

- *Microwave dinner*—Another quick and easy option. It might be quick to satisfy hunger, but it doesn't taste great.

- *Home-cooked meal*—You get the full flavor and taste of the meal, you get the pleasure of smelling this great meal as it's being prepared, and you don't have to worry about not getting enough to eat! It's not the quickest solution, but the satisfaction goes a long way!

📢 There's nothing wrong with being hungry. But we've got to make choices about how we address our hunger.

Group discussion

The best place to eat

Have kids get in groups of four or so. Ask each group to decide on one place they can all agree on as the best place to eat. When the groups are finished, have each group—or a few groups, if you have lots of them—present its conclusion. Allow students to vote with cheers or groans on whether they agree.

2   Your soul needs food.

🔊 Your soul is the spiritual center of who you are—kinda like your spiritual heart. Your soul is the eternal part of you.

🔊 Your soul gets hungry like your body.

🔊 What are the signs of soul hunger?

🔊 **Illustration** *Soul Hunger in Wal-Mart* (see sidebar)

🔊 Ask students what they feed their soul when it's hungry.

🔊 When your soul is hungry, you have a few options.

- *Fast food*—Grab something quick. Anything that will satisfy fast. Things like drugs, alcohol, sex, popularity, money, and even adrenaline rushes can give you a quick fix.

- *Microwave dinner*—A little church here, a little good deed there. It's Christianity lite! Tastes great, less filling. And none of that messy intimacy with Christ stuff.

- *Home-cooked meal*—Let's call this the Jesus Meal. This is a slow meal—a long-term relationship that satisfies your soul hunger. Spending time with Jesus is no quick fix—but it sure won't leave you hungry.

🔊 **Scripture** *John 6:32-35* ("I am the Bread of Life...")

🔊 **Scripture** *John 4:13-14* ("But whoever drinks the water I give him will never thirst.")

🔊 Ask how Jesus fills up our souls.

🔊 People try all kinds of things to fill the hunger of their souls. But only Jesus can fill us up and satisfy our eternal hunger.

Illustration

Soul hunger in Wal-Mart

Wal-Mart has changed over the last several years. Sure, they've got McDonalds in them. Somebody there realized that while shopping, people often get physically hungry. And a quick run over to McD's allows you to keep shopping longer.

But there's another hunger response at Wal-Mart. It's in the book section. Sure, there are lots of cookbooks. But now there are tons of books for people trying to satisfy soul hunger: *Chocolate for a Teen's Soul, Chicken Soup for the Teenage Soul,* and *Hot Chocolate for the Mystical Teenage Soul,* all kinds of Bibles, and books from other religions. People are buying these books by the millions. Just like McDonald's—millions and millions served.

3 Your soul has a favorite food.

🔊 Ask students what the Bible says about feeding your soul.

🔊 **Scripture** *Ezekiel 3:1-3* ("So I ate it, and it tasted as sweet as honey in my mouth.")

🔊 This is a weird verse! It means God can fill our soul hunger when we draw close to him in the Bible.

🔊 Ask how and where else we could pull up a chair at God's diner and fill our souls. Possible answers are through worship, silence, art, music, nature, and being with God's people.

🔊 **Application** *Dining Tips* (see sidebar)

Application

Dining tips

Share these soul food dining tips in your own words. Work the analogy of physical food, using personal illustrations where appropriate.

- **Eat early.** Make a daily breakfast date with Jesus. The earlier you eat, the better. Start your soul out with a Jesus Meal. Don't put off Jesus until lunch or dinner. Begin by reading his word and praying.

- **Don't eat too fast.** When you eat fast, food can get caught in your throat and never get to the place where it's digested. If we rush through a meal with Jesus, the food can get caught in our heads and never get to our hearts. Take your time. Let him speak to you. Rest in his presence.

- **Don't eat too much of the same thing**. Get a well-balanced meal of prayer, praise, worship, and Bible study. Get all the essential vitamins and minerals for the soul.

closing

The Grand Finale

🔊 **Scripture** *John 6:5-14* (The feeding of the 5,000) Read this amazing story or—if you have time—have students create a little drama and act it out.

🔊 **Discussion** *How'd He Do That?* (see sidebar)

🔊 **Activity** *Communion* This is a great talk to lead into a communion service. Talk about how Jesus fills our soul hunger as you remember his act of love for each of us on the cross.

🔊 Close by challenging students to have a meal with Jesus.

🔊 Ask students to sit quietly and consider what they feed their souls. Then lead them in a prayer of confession and commitment to feast on the spiritual food Jesus offers.

🔊 **Future event** *Meal Preparation* (see sidebar)

Discussion

How'd he do that?

After reading the story of Jesus feeding the 5,000, talk about how this miracle is an example of Jesus meeting both physical and spiritual hunger. Ask questions like—

- **How did Jesus meet the people's physical hunger?**
- **How did he meet their spiritual hunger?**
- **How did Jesus meet the spiritual hunger of the disciples?**

Future activity

Meal preparation

Plan to have your group prepare a meal together—either in advance so you can refer back to it during the talk or in the near future as a follow-up. If your group is large, do this in small groups at people's homes so everyone can be involved in the preparation.

discussion

Encore

Get It?	Middle School

🔊 What's your favorite meal and why?

🔊 How is a home-cooked meal different than fast food?

🔊 What's a soul?

🔊 What's soul hunger?

🔊 How do you know when your soul is hungry?

🔊 Why is eating the right soul food important?

🔊 What happens when we feed our souls the wrong type of food?

Get It?   High School

🔊 Why did we talk about food and hunger?

🔊 What's your soul?

🔊 What does it look like to have a hungry soul?

🔊 How do you see people your age trying to satisfy hungry souls?

🔊 How do you know when your soul is hungry?

🔊 What is the food your soul craves?

What If?   The Big Picture

🔊 Have you ever thought spending time with God was the same as sitting down for a good meal? Talk about that. Why is this a good word picture? Are there any ways in which this word picture doesn't work?

🔊 Imagine God fixing you a meal. What would God prepare for your soul?

🔊 What difference does it make if you don't fill up your soul on junk food, but instead fill up on Jesus?

🔊 What would it take for you to let Jesus meet your spiritual hunger? How can you do this?

So What?   It's Your Life

🔊 How have you been addressing your soul hunger lately?

🔊 Who or what feeds your soul right now? Think of at least three ways your soul gets fed.

🔊 What other soul-food dining tips can you think of? How can you apply them to your life this week?

🔊 What new thing are you willing to try this week to satisfy your soul hunger?

Question *Numero Uno*

Contributed by **Kara Powell**

Primary theme salvation	
Themes commitment, lordship, sacrifice, Jesus our Savior, evangelism	
Scripture Luke 9:18-27; John 14:6	
Approximate length through The Grand Finale 20-25 minutes	

This talk is challenging, both for you and your students. For your part, you have the challenge of explaining the entire gospel story in just a handful of minutes. Students will be invited to give—meaning *give*—their lives over to Christ. Because of this talk's dual focus on asking Jesus to be Savior and Lord, it's appropriate for a wide range of audiences—ranging from kids at an evangelistic event to a group made up of Christians.

You'll need

- ◀)) Several student volunteers for a game
- ◀)) Trivia-type questions, a board game, or a computer game
- ◀)) A TV and VCR
- ◀)) A video clip from a TV game show
- ◀)) Several students or leaders to act out the process of salvation
- ◀)) A student to give his testimony
- ◀)) An index card and pencil for each student
- ◀)) Several leaders or trained students available for those who need one-on-one counsel after the talk

intro

The Opening Act

- 🔊 **Activity** *Game Show* (see sidebar)
- 🔊 **Video clip** *Under Pressure* (see sidebar)
- 🔊 **Activity** *Opinion Poll* (see sidebar)
- 🔊 Explain that you'll be looking at the biggest question of all time, one that will give the students more than just a wad of money or a trip to the Bahamas.
- 🔊 **Scripture** *Luke 9:18-27* (see sidebar)

Activity

Game show

Make up your own game show by modifying one familiar to your students—use one based on answering questions, like "Who Wants to Be a Millionaire" or "Family Feud." (The simplest way to do this is to buy a computer game or board game.) Play a few quick rounds, making sure a contestant's ability to answer questions determines whether they'll win—not luck or a fluke.

Video clip

Under pressure

Show a funny or tense clip from a television game show that revolves around giving the right answers to questions. Pause the video before contestants give their answers and have your students guess whether or not they'll answer correctly.

Opinion poll

Do an opinion poll of your students, having them either move to one side of the room or simply stand up, depending on what they agree with. Ask some questions like—

- If you had an extra 30 dollars would you be more likely to spend it on clothes or computer games?

- Would you rather wear the same clothes for five days or not shower for 10 days?

- Would you rather be the richest student in school or the most popular?

- Would you rather have your own TV in your room or your own computer in the family room?

- Would you rather drink curdled milk or clean up your little brother's projectile vomit?

- Which would be harder—waiting until you turn 22 to get your driver's license? Or waiting until you're 22 before you date someone?

- Would you prefer being the only child in your family or one of four kids?

- If you could be the country's most famous music star or its most famous actor, which would you prefer?

- Would you rather go to a new school where you don't know anyone or stay at your own school but lose your five best school friends?

Luke 9:18-27

Jesus commonly used questions when he taught, but instead of letting the disciples stay at the general, less committed level of "Who do the crowds say I am?" Jesus goes right for the jugular. He asks, "Who do you say I am?" Explain to your students that their answer to this question—the most important question of all time—carries eternal significance.

heart of the talk

The Main Event

1 Jesus was either liar, lunatic, or Lord.

- We have a choice to make. We know from our history books Jesus was a real live person, but now we face the biggest question of all. The question numero uno: Who was Jesus?

- **Scripture** *John 14:6* ("I am the way, the truth, and the life. No one comes to the Father except through me.")

- The first possible answer is Jesus was a liar. He came and told a bunch of fibs about himself and God. He pretty much made up what he said.

- The second possible answer is Jesus was a lunatic. What John 14:6 shows us is that he was so crazy, he believed he was the way to life.

- The third possible answer is Jesus is the Lord and what he said in John 14:6 is true. He's the Son of God—there's no other way to heaven but through him. All other paths are dead ends.

2 If he's Lord, what does it mean?

- It means God loves you. When he thinks of you, he smiles.

- But a problem developed. That problem is called sin, which separates us from God.

- Because God wanted to remedy the problem, he sent his son Jesus to be born in a manger and die on a cross 33 years later.

- **Acting out** *Salvation Demo* (see sidebar)

Acting out

Salvation demo

This four-step demonstration of God's love, our sin, God's solution, and our choice is all the more powerful if you work ahead of time for a few minutes with some adult or student volunteers. You'll want them to act it out as you're talking. You'll want someone to play God, someone to play Jesus, a few people to play humans, and someone to play sin.

Their demonstration should follow this basic outline.

- God is surrounded by the humans.

- Sin blocks the humans from God.

- Jesus comes and holds back sin.

- Humans can return to a relationship with God.

3   If you say Jesus is Lord, then your life will be different.

◄ッ **Sharing** *Testify* (see sidebar)

◄ッ As Jesus warned in Luke 9:23-24, you'll lose your life.

◄ッ **Explanation** *The Cross* (see sidebar)

◄ッ Challenge your students to "lose their lives" by turning their words over to Jesus. Making him Lord means asking him to help them—

- Stop swearing

- Stop making fun of people

- Stop gossiping

- Stop telling crude jokes

- Stop talking back to parents

◄ッ Challenge your students to "lose their lives" by turning over their actions to Jesus, making it clear he is their Lord when they're with friends—even if it isn't popular to do so.

◄ッ Challenge your students to "lose their lives" by taking on a new attitude, asking God to help them say yes to him no matter what he asks.

◄ッ The daily decisions of making Jesus Lord are the hardest ones. Ask your students if they're ready to face those decisions.

Sharing

Testify

Because peer-to-peer ministry is so effective, ahead of time ask one of your students to share about how deciding Jesus is Lord of his life has changed him. Work with him to make sure the student shares about specific attitudes or behaviors Jesus has transformed. Make sure he doesn't make vague statements like, "My life is way better now. It's hard to explain. It just is."

Explanation

The cross

When Jesus said the disciples were to take up their crosses daily, they didn't take his words lightly. In that day the cross meant death—a humiliating, ghastly death. It's as if Jesus was saying, "If anyone wants to follow me, he has to deny himself and put his head on a chopping block." Peter—the one who boldly answered that Jesus was the Christ—ended up knowing what it meant to take up a cross. According to church history he died by being crucified upside down.

closing

The Grand Finale

📢 Invite people to answer question numero uno by saying he is Lord for the first time—in other words, invite them to become Christians.

📢 Invite those who have previously answered that Jesus is Lord to give him specific pockets of their lives—words, actions, attitudes—where they aren't letting Jesus rule.

📢 Invite people who are intrigued—but don't quite understand everything you said—to hang out afterward and talk with an adult or student who can answer questions.

📢 **Activity** *Prayer Triplets* (see sidebar)

Activity

Prayer triplets

Distribute index cards and ask students to write down the names of one to three friends or family members who haven't yet declared Jesus is Lord in their lives. Have students gather in groups of three to pray for these people—possibly even exchanging index cards so they're praying for other people's friends and family all week.

discussion

Encore

Get It?	Middle School

📢 So what was the most important question in the world? Do you agree that's the biggie? Why or why not?

📢 What are the three possible explanations for Jesus' true identity? (Hint: They all start with the letter *L*.) Pretend you were alive when Jesus was walking around making huge statements about being God's son. Which of those three L-words would you believe?

📢 How would you explain to a six-year-old what Jesus did for all humankind?

Get It?   High School

🔊   Tonight we talked about the fact that Jesus was either liar, lunatic, or Lord. Can you think of any other options? What would most people at your school say?

🔊   What does it means to lose your life?

🔊   Does Jesus still expect us to die for him? Explain your answer.

What If?   The Big Picture

🔊   Some people think people are more interested in spiritual things and more interested in these questions about Jesus now than a decade or two ago. Sure, you were barely alive then, but do you think people today are interested in figuring out who Jesus is? Why or why not?

🔊   If Jesus is the only path to God, what happens to people who are sincere as they pursue God through other religions or other paths? How does your answer make you feel?

🔊   Is it harder to say Jesus is Lord with someone pointing a gun at your face and threatening you or to say Jesus is Lord with your daily actions and decisions? Explain your answer.

🔊   Today we tend to think of a cross as a nice gold symbol people wear around their necks. If you were to put the Luke 9:23 phrase "take up your cross" into today's language, what might you say?

So What?   It's Your Life

🔊   Which of the following best describes how you felt about Jesus when you woke up this morning—liar, lunatic, or Lord?

🔊   How—if at all—has that changed since hearing this talk?

🔊   If something is keeping you from believing Jesus is Lord, what is it?

🔊   If you have already asked Jesus to be your Lord before today, what differences—if any—has that made in your life?

🔊   What areas of your life are the hardest to turn over to him—your words, your actions, or your attitude?

🔊   How would your life be different if you were to say yes to God, no matter what he asks? What would your parents think? Your friends? Other people at school?

God on the Inside

Primary theme Holy Spirit	
Themes sin, spiritual growth, power, courage, Christian living, Jesus our Savior	
Scripture John 14:6; 16:7-15; Romans 6:4; 12:1-2; Galatians 2:20; Ephesians 2:6	
Approximate length through The Grand Finale 25-30 minutes	

You'll need

- A personal story about one of your marginal talents
- TV and VCR
- *The Mask*

Contributed by **Greg Lafferty**

To most people the Holy Spirit is the most mysterious and least understood person of the Godhead. We comprehend the Father. We understand the Son. But we're clueless about the Spirit. Practically speaking, many of us only rely on two-thirds of the Trinity and we're much weaker because of it. Understanding the Spirit's work is part of the transformation of the mind that renews our entire lives (Romans 12:1-2). And as students grasp what the Holy Spirit wants to do through them, they can better cooperate with the process. This talk gives an overview of the Spirit's role in our lives.

intro

The Opening Act

🔊 **Personal illustration** *My Marginal Talent* (see sidebar)

🔊 Transition with something like—

> **Do you ever feel that way about your spiritual life? You know just enough of the Bible to know how much you don't know. You're enough of a Christian to know the rules, but not good enough to know the joy of living them. You're enough of a Christian to make yourself miserable.**
>
> **God doesn't want you to settle for that! He has provided something—actually someone—to take you to the next level, where the real thrill of knowing him is. And it's not Jesus. It's his Holy Spirit.**

Personal illustration

My marginal talent

Pick one of your marginal talents and build an illustration around it, *marginal* meaning something that you can do but you're not all that good at. Maybe you're a less-than-mediocre guitarist. Or maybe you love playing basketball but can't sink a shot for your life. Be a little self-effacing and humorously expose your inadequacies in this particular area.

Summarize by pointing out that you're just good enough at this talent to know how bad you truly are.

the heart of the talk

The Main Event

1   The Holy Spirit strengthens your life.

🔊 **Scripture** *John 16:7* ("Unless I go away, the Counselor will not come to you.")

🔊 **Explanation** *It's Better without Jesus?* (see sidebar)

🔊 Jesus sends his Holy Spirit, who's called the Counselor. The Spirit is one who comes alongside to strengthen and stand up for believers. He's got your back.

🔊 John 14:16 says he is "another Counselor," which means another of the same kind. In character the Holy Spirit is identical to Christ.

🔊 **Explanation** *The Comforter* (see sidebar)

🔊 Jesus' death on the cross offers us a restored relationship with God, but the Holy Spirit takes it from there—walking with us through the rest of life.

It's better without Jesus?

Explain how it's better for a disciple to not have Jesus around. The idea is simple—the Holy Spirit brings God right inside our hearts, to change and empower us. While Jesus was here on earth he was physically and spiritually separate from the disciples, but the Holy Spirit is a uniquely powerful spiritual presence who offered the disciples strength from within—just as he offers us that strength today.

The comforter

Some versions of the Bible call the Holy Spirit the Comforter rather than Counselor. That's a great translation, because comforter comes from *com-forte* or "with strength." He comes not so much to wrap you in a big hug, but to fit you with a big plug—a big megawatt hookup to his supernatural power.

There's an old McDonald's commercial where a boxer collapses onto his stool at the end of a brutal beating. He looks completely beat. He might not even be able to answer the bell for the next round. Then a manager steps into the ring with strength. Pointing to the opponent, the manager says, "Remember your seventh birthday, when someone stole your french fries and you never found out who? It was him!"

Suddenly reenergized, the boxer leaps to his feet and deals some damage. That's something like what the Holy Spirit does for us. He strengthens us to meet all challenges, overcome the enemy, and successfully achieve all God has for us to do.

2 The Holy Spirit sensitizes your life.

🔊 If you're speaking to young teens, you might need to take the extra step of making sure they know what it means to sensitize something. You could explain this by having them recall a time when their teeth seemed especially sensitive to hot or cold.

🔊 **Scripture** *John 16:8-11* ("When he comes, he will convict.") One of the most important functions of the Spirit is to soften our hearts to often neglected issues like sin, righteousness, and judgment.

🔊 **Explanation** *Sin* Many of us don't feel guilty about serious sin. We assume if we're not killers or child molesters we're not that bad. But sin and guilt are serious matters, even for the cleanest of us.

🔊 **Illustration** *Microbes* (see sidebar)

🔊 **Explanation** *Righteousness* No one can stand in the presence of God on her own merits the way Jesus can. For people to go to the Father as Jesus is going to him in verse 10, they need his righteousness as a gift.

🔊 **Explanation** *Judgment* The result of sin and unrighteousness is judgment. Satan—the prince of this world, according to verse 11—stands condemned and so does everyone else who doesn't have God on the inside.

🔊 We won't understand the critical nature of sin, righteousness, and judgment unless the Holy Spirit sensitizes our hearts to it.

Illustration

Microbes

We don't always feel sinful, even when we're godless to the core. Use this illustration to explain the difference between our perception of our purity and our actual state of purity. Say something like—

Most people feel about as sinful as they feel dirty. And chances are you're not all that dirty right now. Look at your skin. You're pretty clean right? Well, if you could look a little closer, you would find on every square inch of your apparently clean skin there are up to 20 million microbes—microscopic germ animals crawling all over you. That's the truth about us. And spiritually the truth is we have sin crawling all over us! We're sinful to the core.

3 The Holy Spirit supernaturalizes your life.

🔊 **Illustration** *Flatlining* (see sidebar)

🔊 The Spirit's mission is to help you apply everything Jesus did and to unite you to Christ in such a deep way that his life becomes your life.

🔊 **Scripture** *Galatians 2:20; Romans 6:4; and Ephesians 2:6* (see sidebar)

🔊 Jesus said, "All that belongs to the Father is mine" (John 16:15). The Spirit takes "all that" and gives it to us!

🔊 List some of what is included in "all that."

hope	grace	kindness
love	forgiveness	joy
power	truth	faithfulness
purpose	strength	peace

The list goes on and on! The Spirit supernaturalizes our lives with all heaven has to offer!

🔊 **Movie clip** *The Mask* (see sidebar)

Illustration

Flatlining

Ask if students have seen *ER* or another TV or movie where someone wore a heart monitor. What happened when the person's heart stopped? The person flatlined. Without the Spirit we flatline spiritually. With the Spirit, our spiritual hearts are shocked back into action, because he takes the life of Jesus and puts it in our souls.

Scripture

Galatians 2:20; Romans 6:4; and Ephesians 2:6

It's hard to comprehend how closely our lives are tied up in the life of Christ. But the Bible gives us some handles to hold on to it.

- "I have been crucified with Christ, and I no longer live, but Christ lives in me" *(Galatians 2:20).*

- "We are buried with [Christ] in baptism...and raised with him to live a new life" *(Romans 6:4).*

- "We are seated with [Christ] in the heavenly realms" *(Ephesians 2:6).*

In other words whatever Christ does, we also do in him. We participate in his life, death, resurrection, and glorification. We've been united with his past work on the cross. And we continue to be united with his present life. His heart beats in our chests. His character and purpose ooze out in our actions.

Movie clip

The Mask

Start 16:20 "What? You want me to throw that?"

Stop 18:10 "Why? Because I gotta!"

Show a clip from this comedy, where a mask turns an average guy—Stanley Ipkiss (Jim Carrey)—into a smokin' cool dude.

Summarize the relevance of the clip with something like—

Of course the mask only changed Stanley's personality—the Holy Spirit works on your character. The mask made Stanley a more intense Stanley— the Holy Spirit makes you more like Christ. The mask drew out what was already in Stanley—the Holy Spirit gives you resources you don't have in yourself.

closing

The Grand Finale

◄ঈ **Scripture** reread *John 16:7-15* (see sidebar)

◄ঈ **Discussion** *Case Studies* (see sidebar)

Scripture

John 16:7-15

In this passage Jesus tells his disciples about the Holy Spirit. Read the verses and then say something like—

Jesus spoke these words to the disciples on the day before he was crucified. They were saddened and confused by his upcoming departure. They didn't understand why things were about to happen as they were. They had just enough of Jesus to make them miserable. But when the Spirit came, these sad, sorry guys were radically transformed into a joyful army of kamikaze disciples who lived on a whole new level by the power of the Spirit. Their story can be your story too, if you'll respond to what the Spirit wants to do in your life.

Case studies

Toss out some situations and talk together—or in small groups—about what difference the Holy Spirit's supernaturalizing impact would make. You may want to pull from some of the following—

- Your best friend's mom has just been diagnosed with cancer. Your friend is on the phone with you and she's hysterical.

- The lunchtime crowd suddenly turns on you as you describe the awesome outreach event your church is hosting. They want to know what's with you and this church fixation of yours.

- You can't break a bad habit you know is dragging you down. You determine to stop and you're successful for a few days—but then you give in again.

- On Friday night your friends all decide to go to a movie you suspect is inappropriate for you to see. You have to make a snap decision about what to do.

- You're reading some stuff in your Bible you don't get, so you're tempted to just forget it.

discussion

Encore

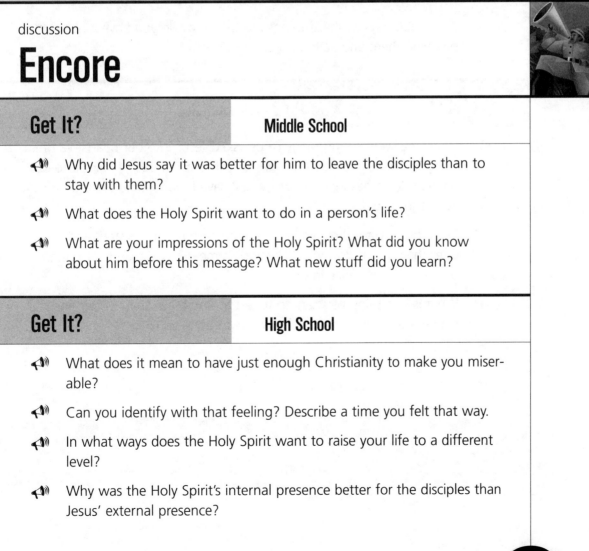

Get It?	Middle School

🔊 Why did Jesus say it was better for him to leave the disciples than to stay with them?

🔊 What does the Holy Spirit want to do in a person's life?

🔊 What are your impressions of the Holy Spirit? What did you know about him before this message? What new stuff did you learn?

Get It?	High School

🔊 What does it mean to have just enough Christianity to make you miserable?

🔊 Can you identify with that feeling? Describe a time you felt that way.

🔊 In what ways does the Holy Spirit want to raise your life to a different level?

🔊 Why was the Holy Spirit's internal presence better for the disciples than Jesus' external presence?

What If?   The Big Picture

🔊 If you had the choice to live one tough week either with Jesus at your side or with the Holy Spirit on your inside, which do you think would be better?

🔊 What if you really knew the Holy Spirit as a strengthening presence? How would he change your attitude or your behavior?

🔊 What do you think it would take to become better acquainted with the Holy Spirit?

🔊 Have you felt the Holy Spirit convict you of sin, righteousness, and judgment? How has he helped to shape your perspective on these important issues?

🔊 What if you saw your sin nature as being crucified with Christ? What if you saw your life as the resurrected life of Christ? What if right now you believed you were enthroned with Christ in a position of spiritual authority and security? How would all these change you?

🔊 If the Bible says all these things are true, why do you have a hard time believing them and acting accordingly?

So What?   It's Your Life

🔊 When we were young many of us asked Jesus into our hearts—a great thing to do. But do you think we ought to ask the Holy Spirit into our hearts? He comes in when we're first saved, but should we ask him to live larger in us?

🔊 The Bible also teaches us the Spirit can be grieved, resisted, and quenched. What do these three words mean? What kinds of things diminish his influence in our lives?

🔊 What is one thing you can do to get to know the Spirit better and cooperate more with what he wants to do in you?

Index of Contributors